1995

ADULT EDUCATION THROUGH WORLD COLLABORATION

ADULT EDUCATION THROUGH WORLD COLLABORATION

Edited by
Beverly Benner Cassara

KRIEGER PUBLISHING COMPANY
MALABAR, FLORIDA
1995

Original Edition 1995

Printed and Published by
KRIEGER PUBLISHING COMPANY
KRIEGER DRIVE
MALABAR, FLORIDA 32950

FROM A DECLARATION OF PRINCIPLES JOINTLY ADOPTED BY A COM-
MITTEE OF THE AMERICAN BAR ASSOCIATION AND COMMITTEE OF
PUBLISHERS:

This publication is designed to provide accurate and authoritative information in regard to the subject matter covered. It is sold with the understanding that the publisher
is not engaged in rendering legal, accounting, or other professional service. If legal
advice or other expert assistance is required, the services of a competent professional
person should be sought.

Library of Congress Cataloging-In-Publication Data

Adult education through world collaboration / edited by Beverly Benner
  Cassara. — Original ed.
     p.   cm.
  Includes bibliographical references and index.
  ISBN 0-89464-828-4
  1. Adult education—Developing countries. 2. Educational
assistance. I. Cassara, Beverly Benner.
LC5261.A38 1995
374'.9172'4—dc20   93-49527
                                                                  CIP

10 9 8 7 6 5 4 3 2

CONTENTS

Acknowledgments

This book was funded in part by the W. K. Kellogg Foundation. The editor wishes to express much gratitude to Dr. Roger H. Sublett of the Foundation who has been supportive of my international activities over some years, and to Malcolm Knowles for his advice and counsel. Many thanks go to colleagues at the University of Southern Maine and at the University of the District of Columbia for their interest and support, but also to colleagues in the International Associates of the Coalition of Adult Education Organizations, the International Unit of the American Association for Adult and Continuing Education (AAACE), the Society for Comparative Adult Education, and to everyone past and present at the International Council for Adult Education, especially Dame Nita Barrow, Budd Hall, and Ana Maria Quiroz. All my graduate students have kept me motivated.

I am deeply indebted to my husband, Ernest Cassara, for the expert advice and his long hours of editing. I dedicate this book to him.

Preface

There is a critical need for the education of adults in the world today, in both industrialized and nonindustrialized countries, for the formally educated as well as the unschooled. The rapid rate of economic, political, and social change leaves some adults confused, and others nearly helpless. Adults have a responsibility to guide the earth and its people into a better future. It is not a responsibility which can be left to posterity. Yet the human race scarcely knows how to do it.

New understandings and new methods are required to meet new situations. While, on the one hand, illiteracy is still a problem in most countries, North and South, other developments, such as technology and the need for sustaining the environment, require adults to acquire new knowledge. Beyond that, they also must learn that peace is more than the absence of war, that justice is the basis for democracy, and that every human being needs respect as much as much as food, shelter, and clothing, in order to develop optimally.

In 1976, the General Conference of UNESCO defined adult education as "the entire body of organized educational processes, whatever the content, level and method. . . . " (UNESCO, 1977, p. 2). In 1993, Makoto Yamaguchi, a professor at Ryutsu Keizai University in Japan, defined it

> as learning designated to promote knowledge, skills and ability among the people to enable them to participate in the process of political, social, economic and cultural development aiming at a democratic society which secures sovereignty of the people, fundamental freedoms and human rights . . . (Yamaguchi, p. 222).

While adult education in some form has existed since the beginning of history, the movement as we know it today has developed since World

ix

War II, and, since the 1960s, has been gaining much momentum. For instance, while there were only a handful of adult education graduate programs in the universities of the United States and Canada in the sixties, today there are approximately one hundred. This is a vital aspect of growth, underscoring the recognition of the needs of the field—more research, new theories of knowledge and practice.

In the Northern industrialized countries, adult education opportunities are provided by many agencies and organizations—schools, universities, governments, business and industry, prisons, churches, and volunteer organizations of all kinds—as a fringe benefit of the workplace, or at fairly minimal charge. Insofar as these countries provide compulsory childhood education, and some provide free university education, adult education is seen as a responsibility of the individual. Certain exceptions exist, as exemplified by some government-supported programs for the less privileged in society. Nevertheless, the need for expanded adult education opportunities continues, for even in the North, adult education is not a high budget priority.

While the Southern nonindustrialized countries also provide similar services, the need is so much greater that neither their private agencies nor national budgets can meet it. In the South the cost for adult education would be prohibitive without assistance from abroad. Where there is compulsory schooling, it often consists of only a few years, and does not include all individuals. This is why the illiteracy problem is so hard to overcome. Those who leave school at a tender age may very well revert to illiteracy if there is no further education available to them later. Many adults, brought up in colonial times, and often since, may have had no schooling. They may have wisdom derived from traditional values of their communities, but today they also need the skills and opportunity to interact with the larger community.

During the past quarter century, many organizations have tried to step in to help newly independent countries jump-start their adult education programs. Aid has been provided by United Nations organizations, bilateral government efforts, the World Bank, church organizations, and any number of other nongovernmental organizations.

Many experimental and innovative programs and methods have been tried, not always with success. However, the need for help still exists, but the philosophy of giving aid has changed. To put it simply, the change comes in the fact that developing countries no longer want to be told what to do. They want to decide what their needs are and how they want to meet them. They want to have the responsibility of carrying out their own adult education projects. People in many countries would agree with Talvi Märja of Estonia when she says,

> We are ready to study any new ideas offered by the good and willing people far and near, but we cannot copy any positive experience from abroad directly. All the innovational changes must be well prepared, taking our local conditions, our cultural background, the ways our people live and think into considertion (1992).

In the past, donor agencies had established guidelines and had trained their staffs and sent them out to carry out the programs. They were charged to oversee the expenditure of funds and to be accountable for evaluation. After all, sources of money could dry up if governing boards were not convinced that their donations were being well used. However, as more people in the recipient countries are becoming educated and know how to care for the education of their own adults, this paternal kind of generosity from the North is being questioned. Yet, financial aid is still needed.

Also the concept of "aid" for adult education in developing countries is anathema in the South. Now, both North and South are beginning to realize that "collaboration" is a better idea. How does collaboration work? What are some of the social, cultural, and political considerations? What has been learned from previous experience? These are important questions which need to be answered.

Where "aid" has been given in a spirit of true collaboration in the development of ideas, methods, solutions to problems, etc., all parties have learned from each other to the benefit of education for adults in the North and the South.

Those who would engage in global collaboration in adult education need current information about what is happening in the field. This book brings together in one volume information about the philosophies and the work of the major donors in the cause of adult education in developing countries, past and present; the changing attitudes of the recipient countries; the collaborative work of the International Council for Adult Education (ICAE).

It is hoped that policy makers, agency administrators, faculty members, and students will find the book a useful resource. Until now, such information has been available, for the most part, in ephemeral literature which is hard to locate, such as reports, newsletters, and speeches of various and sundry organizations. This information, understandably, is not comprehensive enough to be used by adult educators and students, who would have to undertake a major search in order cull it out.

Part One is devoted to the work of multinational organizations, both governmental and nongovernmental. Over the past five decades, the United Nations, the World Bank, and nongovernmental agencies have contributed much to the education of adults in developing countries— each with its own philosophy of education, its own methods, with varying amounts of support and control. This section sheds light on these multitudinous efforts.

Probably it is fair to say that UNESCO (the United Nations Educational, Scientific, and Cultural Organization) has played the major global role in the field of adult education. However, other UN agencies, such as the World Health Organization (WHO), the International Labor Organization (ILO), UNICEF (originally, but no longer, called the Children's Fund), and the Food and Agriculture Organization (FAO), could not accomplish their missions without a heavy component of adult education. Chapter 1 shows how the UN's involvement in adult education has evolved, in light of the fact that donor organizations are facing up to the reality that they now must cooperate with each other to avoid redundancy and to carry out their work more efficiently. It is becoming clear that recipients must now be invited into the process at every level.

Although the World Bank is definitely engaged in the education of adults, the words "adult education" do not appear in its lexicon. It supports projects in literacy, human relations development, teacher training, distance education and vocational training, to name a few. Since there is no "adult education" category, these appear as incidental to other projects. Nevertheless, the Bank is moving toward more comprehensive adult education provisions, with its developing interest in human resource development. However, in addition to the Bank's other educational categories, the authors of this chapter believe a separate category of "adult education" could facilitate research and understanding of the work of the Bank at this level, and, therefore, accord status to a sector of education serving a great need in today's world.

Reference has been made above to the role that has been played by the nongovernmental organizations—and an important role it has been—even though the scene is changing. Two chapters give a clear overview of nongovernmental organizations and how they work. Together, they deliver a strong message from the recipient countries, leaving no doubt that if donor organizations cannot abandon paternalism and undertake collaborative efforts, their future is uncertain. The reader may find the challenge to NGO's very outspoken. However, it must be taken seriously.

Part Two of this book explores bilateral aid (that from one country to another). Six countries have been chosen as examples to demonstrate the variety of philosophies, activities, and results of this work: Canada, Germany, Japan, the Netherlands, Sweden, and the United States. Since little comprehensive research has previously been carried out on the part adult education has played in bilateral funding packages, the authors engage in a ground breaking effort here.

It is interesting to note the differences among the subject countries. For instance, Sweden has taken the position that it has a moral responsibility to fund adult education projects in the developing countries that are comparable to what has been provided at home. Where Sweden has included adult education as a prime aspect of its international aid, the United States has done much international adult education work over the years, in agricultural extension, for instance, and certainly in literacy, but it has had no overriding commitment to adult education per se.

While some governments, such as Japan, have agencies that fund adult education projects directly, others, such as the Netherlands, fund through private institutions, such as nongovernmental organizations (NGO).

While some countries have worked on several continents, as Germany has done, others have concentrated their efforts on particular countries. There are economic, political, and social reasons for the differences, as will become clear.

The role Canada has played in international adult education work is very significant to this book, in that it has provided the principle support for the International Council for Adult Education, among its many other efforts.

Part Three of the book is devoted to the work of the International Council for Adult Education (ICAE), a nongovernmental worldwide organization. While it is not a "donor" organization like those mentioned above, it is a collaborator of great importance, and it is recognized as an official NGO in some United Nations organizations.

A distinction should be made between the ICAE and the various national adult education organizations, which are organized for the purpose of serving their own people. Many such organizations, in over one hundred countries, are national members of the ICAE, or are represented through its seven regional divisions, and therefore play a part in international work. This chapter provides a summary history of the founding, the evolution, the philosophy, and the work of the Council to date.

Over the years, its work has included many endeavors. To make any significant impact on the needs for adult education in many sectors of life in many countries, the ICAE employed the strategy of establishing networks, which targeted needs articulated at the grass-roots levels. However, the catalog of needs multiplied to the point that the Council had to take an arbitrary action of choosing four priority areas of work for a given period. Some former priorities, such as the Participatory Research Network, were so well established that they could continue more or less on their own. While most regions are actively taking part in this work, the Participatory Research Network has been working in many Asian countries, especially in India, where, for instance, women have found it a very useful tool in development projects.

Participatory research is a combination of education, research, and action, organized by people themselves to solve social problems. Those in the field take the position that the three components cannot be treated separately or serially because in all phases of the work interaction is key to success.

Other networks of the ICAE are continuing their evolutionary stages, though they are not current priorities. These include, among others, networks dedicated to the education of older adults, criminal justice, the history of adult education, special learning needs, and participatory formation (training). Some areas, such as health education, have been relinquished to larger well-funded organizations, such as the UN, which has a strong adult education program in this sector.

Currently, the four priority networks are (1) Women's Education, (2) Peace and Human Rights Education, (3) Environmental Education, and (4) Literacy. Adult education alone cannot by itself meet all these challenges, but one thing is more than clear: there can be no solutions without adult education.

This section of the book provides information about the ways in which adult educators as individuals, and various adult education organizations, can tie in with the work of the ICAE to lend strength to the international adult education movement.

Adult educators are becoming ever more engaged with their colleagues in other countries—North/North, North/South, and South/South. Much information must be shared among them. Administrators of donor organizations, and especially policy makers at various levels must also accept the value of shared learning, of collaboration. The North and the South have much to learn from each other in developing a better quality of life for all.

BIBLIOGRAPHY

Märja, Talvi (1992). Adult education in Estonia. *Adult Education and Development, 39*. Bonn, Germany: DVV/German Adult Education Association.

UNESCO (1977). The General Conference adopts a recommendation on adult education. *Adult Education Information Notes, 1*. Paris: UNESCO.

Yamaguchi, Makoto (1992). Deepening democracy in Japan: Adult education. *Adult Education and Development, 39*. Bonn, Germany: DVV/German Adult Education Association.

Beverly Benner Cassara

Introduction: Adult Education and Democracy

FRANCISCO VIO GROSSI

As part of the democratization process in the Eastern countries, Muscovites will be able to eat the same hamburger that is eaten all over the world, in the same size, taste and sauce.[1]

It is almost a commonplace to affirm that globalization is advancing rapidly. Changes, such as the collapse of state socialism and the technological revolution in communication, lead, as never before in history, to unexpected opportunities in the socialization of knowledge. Nevertheless, this process that could suggest the opening of opportunities for equality on a world scale, takes place within the frame of world unipolarism, with no economic, political, or military counterweights. Thus, we are witnessing an expansion of the application of the neoliberal economic model, with democracy as a political system. However, these processes are, by nature, contradictory and limited.

This chapter introduces an analysis of how these processes influence adult education, and conversely, how adult education is facing new challenges to continue trying—as it always has—to exert influence for the benefit of the most deprived. More specifically, analysis will center on the relationship between the deepening of the democratization processes and adult education, as part of other more comprehensive efforts to reverse tendencies in the concentration of power and knowledge.

Geography is a powerful factor in destiny. According to the United Nations, inequality between the rich and the poor (between countries

xvii

and within them) is increasing. In 1989, 20% of world population held 82.7% of the revenue, 81.2% of world trade, 80.6% of international savings, and 80.5% of investment. In addition, they consumed 70% of world energy, 75% of metals, 85% of wood, and 60% of the food. According to the United Nations Development Program, the sustainability of such a development model requires maintaining this extreme degree of inequality. Otherwise, resources would not be sufficient (UNDP, 1992). According to Gorostiaga (1992), inequality is not a deformation of the system; it is the system's need for growth and permanence. Inequality does not enhance democracy.

There is a madness in geography. The commemoration of the five-hundredth anniversary of the so-called "discovery" of America has served to emphasize our limitations in observing reality. We have all watched the same celebration and drawn different conclusions, depending on our physical and cultural standpoint. For some, it is a celebration of civilization. For others, what reached America (or Abya Yala, as some of its inhabitants called it) was barbarity. And while the Spanish believed they had reached India, they discovered that they were not in the East, but in the West.

It seems that geography has again gone mad. The North and the South move, mix, and intermingle. The South exists in the North in the form of increasing unemployment, poverty, and homelessness. The South has its North, with its transnationalized oligarchies controlling cheap labor. The East wants to journey toward the North, but there is a premonition that they will lose course and end up in the South. Africa seems to have disappeared, and Latin America suddenly emerges as a continent in accelerated modernization. In any case, the poor are increasingly less important. The past culture of the South, the "strength of our backwardness," as Garcia Marquez calls it, is diluted under the "magic" wand of neoliberalism and the market.

REVALUING DEMOCRACY

"Democracy" is a concept that is neither clear nor univocal.[2] There are very few terms so largely used by human beings throughout history as the word "democracy." Its capacity to summon humanity's dreams is only comparable to the discredit in which it has fallen due to concrete political experiences.

Today, it is possible to observe almost everywhere a process of revaluing democracy as a political system respectful of popular sovereignty, division of powers, political pluralism, and civic and political rights. However, as in other periods of history, practice shows that in most cases the operation of those principles and rights is constantly restricted or denied for structurally political reasons.

The democracy that most people know is "representative" democracy, i.e., characterized by the concentration of decision-making in the so-called "political class." Most citizens are mere spectators to decisions that are made in their name elsewhere. In this democracy, economically, socially, and culturally dominant sectors use expedient channels to influence the political class. Conversely, excluded or marginalized sectors encounter enormous difficulties in defending their interests. Adult education has a role to play in reversing this tendency, and in strengthening real democracy at the base.

Democracy is not so much an accomplishment as it is a naturally unstable situation, which often does not correspond to its promise and always demands further improvement. In other words, democracy, by its own existence, demands processes leading to more democracy. Institutions that vouch for the rights and duties of citizens are an important development and a necessary condition for fuller democracy, in economic and social terms.[3] It is not possible to aspire to substantive democracy without formally consolidating the advances already achieved in the democratic field. Nonetheless, formal democracy becomes insufficient if it is not a pathway to advance toward more democracy.

The contradiction between direct democracy and representative democracy is also present. The very emphasis in the election of representatives leads to disinterest in what those representatives decide and do between elections. The ideological adhesion accepted by representatives (indispensable in fairly complicated societies) should be complemented with a much more active and direct practice in aspects related to daily living. Since the beginning of modern times, liberal sectors have understood democracy as the institutional system that assures the conditions for the dissemination of free individual initiatives, and not just a democracy that solely defends the free initiative of those who control power. The latter is the base of a flat and drab society that assures basic consumption for all, but in which only initiatives that conform to the official line are accepted and the others are disqualified as "dissident." Every society will tend to uphold one of these two outlooks, but active democracy will have to be careful to react against unilateral emphasis. Active democracy is the purpose of adult education.

ADULT EDUCATION IN SERVICE TO DEMOCRACY

The founding fathers of the present educational systems were immersed in modern rationalism and proposed a positive and direct relationship, in which the extension of education would strengthen the integration of citizens and would result in more democracy. Marxist theorists, on the other hand (Althusser, Bourdieu and Passeron), viewed education as an efficient reproductive mechanism of the unequally divided system, in which, they concluded, the more education, the less democracy.

Both premises, opposed as they are, coincide in applying a direct relationship between educational action and its effects on democracy. In fact, owing to the existence of various connections between the two ideas, we can understand that education by nature bears more than one possible dynamic. Education itself is open to accept the political direction that is imposed on it and, in practice, it will always be possible to find examples to support either of the two premises: the democratic and the anti-democratic one. In some cases, education has contributed to a process of greater freedom and equality, and in some cases the effects have been exactly the opposite.

Thus, in the midst of such a tangle of participating variables, education cannot propose or promise stable and full democracy. Its desirable commitment has to be found in its action and is more modest. For instance, adult education for democracy has to establish itself as one where participants will be active, capable, and responsible individuals. Education may strengthen aptitudes, abilities, and values to persuade persons to encourage more democracy in their different environments, from the family to the local community to the relations and operation of society as a whole.

Thus, education for democracy does not merely seek to increase enrollment or to assure the retention of the educational system. These efforts contribute to democratization only if they contribute to forming individuals in charge of their own destiny.

Until recently everyone seemed to know what education meant. Educational systems had been developed and consolidated as of the mid-nineteenth century as a modernization and social integration apparatus for conveying culture and enhancing abilities that enabled participants to produce, distribute, and coexist in society.

There have been voices that criticized the content and methods of that education. Renowned names, such as Pestalozzi, Dewey, Freinet, Freire, and Illich, were allowed expression of their different ideas without radically changing the system that we identify as education. The strongest dissatisfactions forthcoming from other quarters, however, have been related to quantitative concerns, such as student-teacher ratio, retention of students, number of courses, etc. Thus, educational reforms almost always pointed to the need for greater extension of the same activity. In recent years, the crisis of rationalism and the acceleration of technological and cultural changes have shattered the confidence in the content and methods of an education that tends to be increasingly judged as "traditional." The voices of the critics are multiplying daily.[4]

From the author's experience accumulated in years of practice in nonformal adult education, democratic education is an activity that intends to guide participants' theoretical-practical capacities to comprehend and operate in the most immediate context (everyday), as well as in the most extensive one (societal). The educational action is based on the personal, community, or political needs and tasks of the participants. Content and methods always intertwine and at the same time transmit values and attitudes. Therefore, adults need to learn to take the responsibility of judging and evaluating the progress and direction of their learning. Additionally, values and attitudes permeate all of learning, so that subjects like human rights, peace, and democracy lend themselves better to practice throughout all learning, than to being treated as separate content courses. Furthermore, it would follow that making a categorical distinction between education and training is fallacious.

The strengthening of democracy has to begin with democratic ideals on the part of the people in their daily lives. Toward this end the following four dimensions should be viewed as a system.

In the first place, democratization depends on the people's capacity to drive it. If democracy is to be established, visionary and capable constructors of that desired order become essential, helping individuals through education that is theoretical-practical (not theoretical and practical). Educational contents should relate directly to a competent and intentional practice based on the challenges arising in the environment and linking the experience to the construction of the entire society.

Secondly, education should teach sharing. Only the very powerful can aspire to act unilaterally. Most human beings are excluded from major decisions; accordingly, to be effective, they can only act collectively.

Today in most countries, education does not train for cooperative action. Students are permanently forced to compete, to oppose one another. An education that does not teach sharing, or working collectively in groups, will not be an education that contributes to the construction of democratic individuals.

In the third place, the whole must not absorb or dilute its parts; the collective should not swallow the particular. The concept of community would become flat, drab, and boring, if it opposed the different contributions that make up a community.

Democratization recognizes differences. For example, women cannot be incorporated into democracy if they are not recognized as different from men, and indigenous peoples will not be full citizens if the contribution of their distinct history and culture is not recognized and respected. The same is true of young people, who are not strange but different (T. Todorov, The Conquest of America, 1987, cited by Gorostiaga). To the extent that Western democracies fail in this regard, they are only partial democracies.

Education is improved by stressing the importance of acknowledging others in common practice. Participants should be encouraged to overcome egoism and to realize that the only way to grow and flourish is to appreciate individual differences.

Finally, neither groups nor democracy are ends in themselves; they are means. People are ends. Groups are important only because they are vehicles that allow individuals to become democratic agents. They are important in helping individuals recognize the reality of their life situations and learn how to confront them. This is especially important today when no one knows what tomorrow's reality is going to be. It is no longer possible to propose an education to provide the students with all they are going to need to know during their entire lives. Education for democracy must allow participants to learn to investigate circumstances and discover solutions, concentrating more than ever before on learning how to learn. Research should not be a liturgy of positivism, but an attitude and a procedure permeating all learning processes.

McDonald's hamburgers may be seen as a part of the "democratization process" by some, and Muscovites should eat them if they wish, but democracy is greater than that. Individuals and peoples must be free to decide what the important challenges in the new era offer them, and, being consistent with their own historical legacies, build more democracy for all.

NOTES

1. World President of the McDonald Company, upon inaugurating their first restaurant in Moscow.

2. On "democracy" the author has followed some ideas presented in Macpherson (1977) and Sartori (1988).

3. This is what Hannah Arendt has called "the right to have a right."

4. For example, Latin American Ministers of Education, assembled in Quito in 1991, recognized the depletions of this concept of education. "This crisis [of economy that has cutback fiscal spending on education] has also revealed the existence of another crisis, a deeper one, in the field of education: the loss of dynamism, and the depletion of a concept and style of educational development that has not been able to reconcile quantitative growth with satisfactory levels of quality and equity. . . . The countries in the region are facing the challenge of defining a concept and a new style of educational development to satisfy not only the unfulfilled goals of the past, but also the demands of the future." Recommendations of the Proyecto Mayor de Educación de América Latina y el Caribe de UNESCO (PROMELAC) IV Meeting, Quito, April 1991.

BIBLIOGRAPHY

Colbert, V. and J. Arboleda (1990). *Universalization of primary education in Columbia: The new school programme*. Paris: UNESCO-UNICEF.

Gorostiaga, X. (1992). "¿Está la respuesta en los paises del Sur?" *Envio*. Managua, Nicaragua.

Macpherson, C. B. (1977). *The life and times of liberal democracy*. Oxford, U.K.: Oxford University Press.

Sartori, Giovanni (1991). *Teoría de la democracia*. 2 vols. Buenos Aires: Editorial Rai [1988, Madrid: Alianza Editorial].

Schiefelbein, E. (1991). *In search of the school of the XXI century. Is the Colombian "Escuela Nueva" the right pathfinder?* Santiago, Chile: UNESCO-OREALC (Oficine Regional de Educación para América Latina y el Caribe)-UNICEF.

UNDP (1992). *Desarrollo humano: Informe 1992*. Santa Fé de Bogotá, Colombia: Editorial Tercer Mundo.

UNESCO (1992). Economic Commission for Latin America and the Caribbean (ECLAC-UNESCO) *Education and knowledge: The axis of productive transformation with equity*. Santiago, Chile.

Vio Grossi, F. (1993). "¿Donde está el Norte?" *El Canelo* 7 (38) Santiago, Chile.

Contributors

Daniel C. Andreae is currently the president of the Ontario Association of Professional Social Workers, and, in 1993, was a recipient of the Governor General Commemorative Medal, recognizing significant contributions to Canadian community and society. He holds a master's degree in social work and is a doctoral student in adult education at the Ontario Institute for Studies in Education, Toronto. He has appeared in the media, commenting on a variety of social issues affecting adult learning and development.

Paul Bélanger is the director of the UNESCO Institute for Education, Hamburg, Germany. After study at Manchester University in the United Kingdom, he earned his Ph.D. at the Sorbonne in Paris. He has served as general director of the Canadian Institute for Adult Education, Montreal; as president of the College Evaluation Commission, College Council, Government of Quebec; and as general director of the Institut de recherche appliquée sur le travail (IRAT), Montreal.

Beverly Benner Cassara, a visiting professor at the University of Southern Maine, was for twenty years a professor of adult education at the University of the District of Columbia, where she also served for thirteen years as dean of the graduate school. She was awarded the Ed.D. by Boston University. With her prime interests in multicultural and international adult education, and the education of women, her work has taken her to many countries. Her books include *American Women: The Changing Image* (Beacon Press, 1962) and *Adult Education in a Multicultural Society* (Routledge, 1990).

Darlene E. Clover was programme assistant to the secretary-general of the International Council for Adult Education from 1987 to 1992. She has been the editor of the *International Literacy Year Newsletter*, the *ICAE News*, and *Pachamama* (newsletter of the environmental education program). At the Earth Summit in Rio de Janeiro, she coordinated the "International Journey for Environmental Education" for the ICAE. She is completing a degree program in Environmental Studies at the University of Toronto.

John P. Comings is a vice president of World Education. He has more than twenty years of experience in adult education in Asia, Africa, the Caribbean, and North America. He has served as a consultant in program design to USAID, the World Bank, the United Nations Development Program, and the Peace Corps. He holds an Ed.D. from the University of Massachusetts at Amherst.

Lawrence S. Cumming is a consultant in international development and voluntary action policy, and has extensive experience in adult education and in international work, as teacher, consultant, administrative officer, and board member. He earned the M.A. degree at St. Francis Xavier University. He has taken a leadership role in international conferences in several countries, and has served African Emergency Aid, OXFAM, Broadcasting for International Understanding, the Canadian Civil Liberties Association, and the Canadian Council for International Cooperation.

James R. Dorland is dean emeritus of the School of Liberal Arts at the State University of New York at Morrisville. He was awarded the Ed.D. by George Washington University and served for many years as executive director of the National Association for Public Continuing and Adult Education. He directs the Dorland Network, a consulting group, located in Montgomery Village, Maryland.

Patricia Ellis is managing director of the Pat Ellis Associates, Management and Development Consultants. She holds a doctorate in adult education from the University of Southampton, England. She is a member of the Barbados Adult Education Association, the Caribbean Regional Council for Adult Education, and a member of the Executive Committee of the International Council for Adult Education. She has written extensively on Caribbean women and adult education, and is currently doing research on "Community Development in the Caribbean," and writing resource and training material for community development workers.

Kees P. Epskamp is in charge of documentation and is editor of publications at the Centre for the Study of Education in Developing Countries in The Hague, Netherlands. He has conducted evaluation studies of media-supported educational projects in South America and Africa. He is the Coordinator of the CESO inter-university course on "Education in Developing Countries." His special interest is reflected in the title of his Ph.D. dissertation at the University of Amsterdam, *Theatre in Search of Social Change*, published in 1989.

Budd L. Hall is professor of critical global and community issues in the Department of Adult Education, Ontario Institute for Studies in Education, in Toronto. He earned the Ph.D. at the University of California at Los Angeles. He worked with the International Council for Adult Education, 1975–1991, serving as its secretary-general for eleven of those years. His publications are on topics in participatory research, environmental adult education, global networking, critical adult education theory, and the role of poetry in social change. He is currently the president of the Canadian Association for the Study of Adult Education and also of the Doris Marshall Institute, a Toronto-based popular education organization involved in antiracist education.

Heribert Hinzen is director of the Institute for International Cooperation of the Deutscher Volkshochschul-Verband e.V. (DVV/the German Adult Education Association). He received the Ph.D. from the University of Heidelberg, where he specialized in comparative adult education. He is the editor of the journal, *Adult Education and Development*, of the DVV.

Yasumasa Hirasawa is an associate professor on the Faculty of Human Sciences, Osaka University, Japan. He was a Fulbright scholarship student at Harvard Graduate School of Education, 1981–1983, and returned to take his Ed.D. at Harvard in 1989. A professional conference interpreter, he has also published books and articles on literacy, multicultural education, and human rights education.

John B. Holden is an internationally recognized leader in the World Federalist movement, and has traveled extensively on behalf of peace education. He earned the Ph.D. at Ohio University. He is director emeritus of the graduate school of the U.S. Department of Agriculture, Washington, D.C., and has served in many positions with adult education associations locally, and as president of the Adult Education Association of the U.S.A.

Helena Kekkonen, Lic. Eng. and Ph.D. Ed. h.c., received the UNESCO Prize for Peace Education in 1981. She is the former secretary-general of the Association of Finnish Adult Education Organisations (1974–1985) and of the Peace Education Institute (1985–1990). She is currently the vice-chairperson of the Institute and the Chairperson of the Green Namibia Community Project. Her film, *A Window onto the Future*, features her philosophy on peace education.

Jack D. McNie for many years was chairman of the Management Committee of the International Council for Adult Education, participating in Council activities in many countries. He received his M.Ed. from the Ontario Institute for Studies in Education, University of Toronto. He has been president and chairman of the R. T. Kelly Inc., a national advertising agency in Canada. He has served as chairman of the Co-ordinating Committee of the Hamilton Place Arts Centre; as Ontario Minister of Colleges, Universities and Culture; and as a member of the Board of Governors of McMaster University.

Ken Motoki is a professor on the Faculty of Human Sciences at Osaka University, Japan. He holds an Ed.M. degree from Tokyo University. His published works include *Methodology of Technical Education* (1963), *Human Rights and Education* (1989), and *Technology and Human Formation* (1990).

Ana Maria Quiroz is a former secretary-general of the International Council for Adult Education, Toronto. She studied at the Pedagogic Institute of the University of Chile and did graduate work at the University of British Columbia, Vancouver. She taught Latin American literature and Spanish language at Simon Fraser University, Dalhousie University, and Acadia University. She worked as a popular educator with shantytown women organizations around Santiago, and for the Latin American Council for Adult Education (CEAAL), in charge of international cooperation.

Patricia Rodney, Ph.D. (University of Toronto) has worked with the International Council for Adult Education in several capacities, holding the position of international coordinator of the International Task Force on

Literacy (1989–1991) and of the International Literacy Support Service until mid-1992. Prior to her emigration to Canada, she worked with the Women and Development Unit of the University of the West Indies. She is presently a research analyst for the Canadian Advisory Council on the Status of Women in Ottawa. She is serving as a board member of the Resources for Feminist Research at the Ontario Institute for Studies in Education, where she is one of the editors of the publication, *Colonialism, Imperialism and Gender.*

Gunnar Rydström is a writer, translator, and editor. He received his M.A. at Stockholm University. He has been involved in a variety of adult education efforts in several countries, including Tanzania, where he edited study material for the Institute of Adult Education. He was rapporteur for the ICAE international conference in Kungälv, Sweden, in 1986. He has been involved in social movements against apartheid and nuclear power. He has written five novels, plays, and books on India and East Africa, in addition to many articles, short stories, and historical works.

Francisco Vio Grossi is past president of the International Council for Adult Education, and director of the Centro El Canelo de Nos, an education center located on a farm 25 km south of Santiago, Chile. The main interest of the center is endogenous development, using organic agriculture, peasant technologies, horizontal communications, and popular education. With his Ph.D from the University of Sussex, England, he has been a professor at Simon Rodríguez University in Venezuela, Catholic University in Chile, Sussex University, and the Ontario Institute for Studies in Development, Toronto. He has also been consultant for several United Nations organizations. His main interest is rural adult education and alternative development.

Paul Wangoola is secretary general of the African Association for Literacy and Adult Education (AALAE), Nairobi, Kenya. He studied at Makerere University, Uganda, where he then served as resident tutor in the Extra Mural Department of the Centre for Continuing Education. He also studied adult education at the University of Southampton (U.K.). In Uganda he served as a member of Parliament and chaired the Parliamentary Standing Committee on Public Administration and Public Appointments. His writings include "The Political Economy of Illiteracy: A Global Analysis of Myth and Reality about its Eradication," in *Education and Production Journal* (1984).

PART ONE

Multinational Donors—Governmental and Nongovernmental

CHAPTER 1

Adult Education and the Changing Role of UNESCO and of the UN Organizations

PAUL BÉLANGER

The reality of adult education in 1993 is very different from what it was in 1946, when UNESCO was founded, or in 1949, at the time of the first World Conference on Adult Education. We need to look back at the functions of UNESCO and the other UN Agencies during the period 1946–1990, in order to appreciate their historical contributions; but also in order to contrast the past and the present contexts.

Indeed, at the beginning of the fifth decade of its existence, the expected and actual role of UNESCO is evolving. All organizations, including the UN agencies, now have to cope with an overall explosion of the social demand for education among the adult population; but at the same time they are confronted with very severe constraints when they attempt to increase and renew the required learning opportunities. This contradiction between the rising expectations of adults and the limited and problematical institutional responses constitutes the new context in which UNESCO and the UN agencies must presently operate.

The question I would like to address in this chapter is clear and simple: how far has UNESCO, together with the other UN organizations, been able to make a difference in the prevailing existing political economy of adult education in the past, and how likely is it to do so in the future?

THE HISTORICAL ROLES OF UNESCO

Since the inception of UNESCO, and in almost every General Conference until now, references have been made to the educational rights of the adult population and to the need to foster international cooperation in adult education. The name of UNESCO is in fact closely associated with the history of adult education that has taken place in most countries since 1946.

The promotion of adult education which was the main contribution of UNESCO took many forms: awareness-raising activities, facilitation of international exchanges, adoption and dissemination of normative instruments, and technical services.[1]

THE HISTORICAL ROLES OF UNESCO AND OF THE UN FAMILY

Awareness Raising

The most manifest initiatives taken by UNESCO for the promotion of adult education were the four world conferences held in 1949, 1960, 1972, and 1985, each one bringing together more participants from more countries and organizations.

Already in the first five years of its existence, UNESCO decided to convene a world conference dealing exclusively with adult education, at a time when this new field of education was still a marginal reality in most countries as well as at the international level. At this first conference, held at Elsinore, Denmark, the major concern was the contribution of adult education to a lasting peace, to the stimulation of a genuine spirit of tolerance, and to international understanding. Inspired by the Danish Folk High Schools' ideology, the participants asked UNESCO and the member states to promote "an enlightenment sense of belonging to a world community" (UNESCO, 1949). Seminars were organized to develop this initiative, the first of which took place in 1951 in Hamburg at the UNESCO Institute for Education, which had been created just one year earlier.

The Second World Conference, held in Canada in 1960, brought together representatives from fifty-one countries, including a majority of delegates from the South and from Eastern Europe. This Montreal Conference will be remembered for its insistence on the necessity that

UNESCO and the national authorities recognize adult education "as a necessary part of the educational provision of every country," and that the governments provide public support for the education of adults (UNESCO, 1960).

Twelve years later, in 1972, a Third International Conference took place in Tokyo. Attended by more than four hundred delegates from eighty-two countries, it confirmed "the new weight being attached to adult education" (Lowe, 1985), be it to literacy, greater access to formal education, or distance education. The main theme of the Tokyo Conference was the limited access to adult education in almost all countries. The delegates underlined, and criticized, the prevailing tendency to provide further education for those who are already educated. "Adult education," wrote the rapporteur of the Conference, "is no exception to the rule, for those who most need education have been largely neglected. . . . Thus the major task of adult education . . . is to seek out and serve these forgotten people" (UNESCO, 1972). It was at this conference that the concept of lifelong learning appeared in the public discourse of UNESCO as part of the Organization's attempt to encompass initial and adult education in a comprehensive and integrative perspective.

A Fourth International Conference was held twelve years later in Paris at UNESCO headquarters. It was attended by nearly nine hundred delegates from 122 countries, plus participants from more than fifty NGOs, thus attesting to the fast development that had taken place in adult education during the seventies and the early eighties. However, the circumstances this time were very different: it was no longer a marginal reality, yet the current economic crisis had started to have a profound impact on the provision of adult education. UNESCO, itself, was going through a huge crisis, following the departure of the United States[2] and the threat of a similar decision by the United Kingdom.[3]

At the 1985 Conference, the contradiction mentioned at the very beginning of this chapter, between a rising social demand and a decreasing capacity to develop or even sustain public adult education services, became very obvious, thus indicating a trend that would become critical in the years to follow. Many delegates acknowledged that the adult education budgets were decreasing or frozen. Yet, they also acknowledged that their countries were getting increasingly involved in diverse educational activities for adults, organized under various names and through different institutional arrangements: manpower training and retraining, agricultural extension, public health education, etc.

Concluding too rapidly that the decrease in the traditional provision

6 ADULT EDUCATION THROUGH WORLD COLLABORATION

indicates a loss of momentum, if not a decline of adult education, the multilateral agencies would take more than five years to grasp the meaning of this critical semantic and policy shift and to reorient their programs accordingly to the diverse needs mentioned above. We shall deal with this issue later in the second part of this chapter. It was also at this Paris Conference that the declaration on "The Right to Learn" was adopted. This "manifesto" was subsequently translated into many international, national, and local languages and widely disseminated by the adult education movements.

However, within the domain of adult education and its promotion, it is on the issue of adult literacy that UNESCO has intervened with the most vigor and continuity. Since its first General Conference in 1946, UNESCO has never stopped reminding international public opinion that "illiteracy is one of the great social problems of our time." One should remember that it was at the 1960 Montreal Conference that the proposal to launch a vast campaign for the eradication of illiteracy was made, a recommendation that would lead to the launching of the well-known Experimental World Literacy Program (EWLP) four years later in Teheran. It was also in the sixties that UNESCO created two institutions that became important awareness-raising instruments: the International Literacy Day, which was first celebrated on the 8th of September 1966, and the International Literacy Prizes, among which the International Reading Association Prize (U.S.A.), donated in 1979, the Noma Prize, given in 1980 by a Japanese publisher, and the King Sejong Literacy Prize, awarded since 1990 by the Government of the Republic of Korea, still remain in 1993. Other prizes, the M. R. Pahlevi, the N. K. Krupskaya, and the Iraq Literacy prizes, created respectively in 1967, 1979, and 1981, have unfortunately been discontinued.

The last two major initiatives of UNESCO to raise public awareness of the basic learning needs and rights of millions of adults and to mobilize financial resources were the 1990 International Literacy Year (ILY), proclaimed by the United Nations with UNESCO as lead organization, and the World Conference on Education for All (WCEFA), also held in 1990 in Jomtien. It is significant that, in these two recent events, and even more in the second one, UNESCO did not intervene alone, but within a larger cooperation framework directly involving other UN agencies. It should also be underlined that in both initiatives an important shift in the meaning given to basic education and literacy in the discourse of UNESCO and the UN Agencies occurred: literacy was no longer defined negatively and identified as a disease to be eradicated. A more developmental and inclusive view was proposed of adults who already have learning experiences and other abilities, but feel that they need to improve their communication and numeracy skills, in order to ameliorate their quality of life. In so doing, the role of awareness-raising is of course becoming more difficult; it does not rely anymore on the publication of a single dramatic number stigmatizing a percentage of individuals as illiterate and reducing them to this unidimensional pathological characterization. Such a short-term tactic may be useful in attracting first-page coverage and getting good headlines, but may also have a deterrent effect on the organization of literacy education activities which take into account the existing modes of communication of people, the local culture, and which rely on the experiential positive assets which adults can draw on to develop further their skills.

This is precisely one of the issues raised by the many practitioners and researchers whom UNESCO has regularly brought together in its many initiatives for the promotion of intellectual cooperation.

Promotion of Intellectual Cooperation

Thousands of small, medium, and large meetings held every year at UNESCO headquarters, its three institutes,[4] and regional offices, and the dissemination of these exchanges[5] in a variety of publications and periodicals—including the more numerous seminars and conferences organized by public institutions or NGOs and for which UNESCO has only played a facilitating role—constitute a critical mass of interlearning activities whose impact is low profile and long term, but nonetheless very real.

This role of UNESCO has not been implemented without contradictions and controversy: criticism has been made as to the appropriateness of investing so many resources in travel and exchanges, rather than in field work; reproaches have been voiced regarding the high costs of some of these meetings and the limited dissemination of results (Hancock, 1991). Though ways must be, and, in some places, are beginning to be found in the UN organizations to lower these costs and counter the effect of budgetary restraints, one should recognize that it is in such seminars and conferences that many critical issues have been revealed, analyzed, and brought to the attention of decision makers: the phenomenon of cumulation of privileges being furthered and reproduced through education, including adult education; the specific and complementary contributions of initial and adult education within the overall perspective of lifelong learning; the different levels of literacy skills among the adult population in industrialized areas; the links between literacy and postliteracy, the intergenerational dimension of any global literacy development; and the correlation between adult learning and the sustainability of any development program.

Through its international cooperation activities, UNESCO has contributed, on a significant number of occasions, to the reversal of the prevailing trend towards limiting travel and international meetings. Otherwise, exchanges are only available to those individuals, institutions, and countries who can afford them, thus thwarting the tendency toward unilateral intellectual cooperation between regions, cultures, and scientific disciplines.

The Normative Role

In order to realize actual improvement in the delivery of adult education services, most UN organizations have worked with their member states to establish guidelines requiring accountability. UNESCO was founded a year after the adoption of the Universal Declaration of Human Rights, which includes the 26th article recognizing explicitly the fundamental right to education. In the first article of UNESCO's constitution (paragraph 2b), a direct reference was made to adult education, asking member nations to "give fresh impulse to popular education[6] and to the spread of culture. . . . "

However, it was not until thirty years later that the first normative texts dealing directly with adult education would be adopted: the "Declaration of Persepolis" in 1975 and the Recommendation on the Development of Adult Education in 1976.

While the Declaration is a general statement urging a more encompassing vision of adult literacy, the Recommendation adopted by the 19th General Conference constitutes a detailed and major reference for the development of policy and legislation in the overall field of adult education.

After proposing a broad definition[7] of adult education, the Recommendation sets forth general objectives for adult education and recognizes that priority be given to "educationally underprivileged groups." Two chapters are devoted to the specific and flexible approaches and structures which are required in adult education. Indications are given regarding the relation between initial and adult education, and the links between adult education and work. The member states are also asked to recognize the role played by adult educators and literacy workers, and to give them the status and conditions needed for an efficient implementation of their task. A last chapter suggests orientations for international cooperation and technical assistance.

In 1985, sixty countries provided reports on the development of adult education, in light of the propositions enunciated in 1976.[8] They reported progress in the institutionalization of adult education through new legislation and policy development, but underlined serious financial difficulties and inadequate recognition of the specificity of the field, and stressed the priority to be given to adult literacy, particularly in rural areas.

In 1992, after UNESCO sent a questionnaire to all member states asking them again to report on the action taken to implement the Recommendation, only fifty-nine member states, i.e., 36 percent, responded to the request.

The statements indicated the following trends:

— the recognition of the place and of the specificity of adult education within the overall system of education, with some reported attempts of greater harmonization,
— the growing involvement of the private sector and of NGOs in a difficult economic context that limits the financial contribution of the state,
— the increasing demand for adult vocational training programs and the broadening of such programs to include general education,
— a diversification of content: literacy education, general education, vocational training, cultural emancipation, agricultural extension, environment education, women's participation, family planning, health and hygiene education, civic education, consumer education, foreign languages, etc.,
— the variety and flexibility of organizational structures, and the heterogeneity of public and private providers,
— the predominant priorities being programs for women, young adults, and rural populations,
— the emergence of intersectorial coordinating mechanisms.

Yet, the most significant positive trends to be found in these reports concerned legislation. Since 1976, fifty-one out of the fifty-nine reporting countries had adopted specific legislation on adult education. It is to be noted also that, though literacy and its corollary postliteracy remain the priority goal in developing countries, a majority of countries referred to the overall contribution of adult education to development.

These trends, mentioned in the study made for the 1993 Executive Board (UNESCO, 1993), give interesting indications regarding the changing role of UNESCO, in particular, movement toward a diversification of institutional arrangements and curricula to meet adult education needs more comprehensively.

The text of the declaration of "The Right to Learn," adopted in 1985 at the Fourth International Conference on Adult Education, states:

> Recognition of the right to learn is now more than ever a major challenge for humanity. The right to learn is: the right to read and write; the right to question and analyze; the right to imagine and create, the right to read about one's own world and to write history; the right to have access to educational resources; the right to develop individual and collective skills. ... The act of learning, lying as it does at the heart of all educational activity, changes human beings from objects at the mercy of events to subjects creating their own history.

This text has become a widely used instrument to help people assert their right to learn and to define it in comprehensive ("integral") terms.

Two other normative instruments, indirectly related to adult education, were adopted by UNESCO during the same period: the 1974 "Recommendation Concerning Education for International Understanding, Cooperation and Peace, and Education Relating to Human Rights and Fundamental Freedoms," which will be revised in at the 1994 International Conference of Education, and the 1976 "Recommendation on Participation by the People at Large in Cultural Life and Their Contribution to It," which gives a renewed vision of lifelong learning in relation to cultural life.

A review of UNESCO's normative role in adult education cannot leave aside such instruments as those on museums, on libraries, on the use of media, and on the democratization of science, but this goes beyond the scope for this chapter.

It is difficult to assess the effectiveness of the different legal instruments that the United Nations organizations have adopted in recognizing and legitimizing minimal standards and in insuring that they are respected. It is evident that the standards set by the UN system are only considered and honored when the political will exists for a minimal number of countries to raise questions in reference to such conventions or recommendations, or when NGOs take the responsibility or the initiative to monitor their application and report publicly. The trade unions have done this in the domain of paid educational leave, or women's groups for fair access to jobs and education, and the adult movements in expanding the concept of literacy and of vocational adult education. Then, but only then, does the normative function of the UN organizations and the obligation of the member states to report on the application of the standard-setting tools become really efficient.

Technical Cooperation

A fourth contribution of UNESCO to the development of adult education is the concrete technical cooperation that occurred in the field through expert missions, complementary financial support, studies, action research, pilot projects, planning of nonformal education programs, assistance for the development of national statistics on literacy, and for the monitoring of nonformal education, training of trainers, etc.

Within the domain of adult education, literacy has been a high priority in UNESCO technical assistance programs. One needs to refer, for example, to the Experimental World Literacy Program and the role played by UNESCO in the preparation, and, later, in the critical assessment of actions like mass campaigns or functional programs (Jones, 1988). Precisely because such a role requires major resources, the financial crisis with which UNESCO has been confronted since 1985 has reduced and significantly transformed this last function of educational assistance, into which other UN agencies are becoming increasingly involved.

THE ROLES OF OTHER UN AGENCIES

Two UN organizations have played important roles in promoting and supporting nonformal and adult education: the International Labor Organization (ILO) and UNICEF.

The International Labor Organization (ILO)

Since the ILO's establishment in 1919, the adoption of international labor standards has been a prime consideration of the Geneva-based organization. The ILO Conventions and Recommendations deal, of course, with the working conditions and the regulation of various aspects of labor relations (ILO, 1992). Of particular importance for our purpose are its standards concerning the questions of employment policy; vocational guidance and training; paid leave; introduction of technological changes; working conditions of specific groups, such as women, children, etc.

Many normative ILO instruments have played decisive roles in the development of adult education. The Convention No. 140 on Paid Educational Leave (PEL), adopted in 1974, is well known: It stipulates that workers shall be authorized to take "leaves granted for educational purposes for a specific period during working hours, with financial entitlement," and that the educational activities may be related to work, or may be academic and general, or may even be related to trade union education. Such a convention has proved to be an important factor for those who work in the primary labor market, have permanent jobs, and enjoy fair working conditions negotiated through collective bargaining. The PEL measures seem far less efficient for contractual workers, or those working part-time, or in small firms, without permanent employment status.

A second important ILO text dealing with adult education is the Convention No. 142 on Human Resources Development, adopted in 1975, and completed through the Recommendation No. 150 on the same subject. This requires the member states to ensure that "all have equal access to vocational training" and "have possibilities to re-enter the educational system," in order "to meet the needs for vocational training throughout life both for young persons and for adults in all sectors . . . and at all levels. . . . "

Similarly, Recommendation No. 149 on rural workers states in paragraph 16: "Steps should be taken to . . . promote . . . education and training to which women and men should have equal opportunities of access." The 1985 ILO resolution on equal opportunities for men and women identifies specific measures and emphasizes the importance of special programs for the elimination of occupational segregation in the labor market. This resolution pays particular attention to the situation of rural women and to the difficulties faced by women wishing to re-enter the work force after periods of absence, and requires that the "programmes incorporate measures on education, training, vocational guidance, counselling and placement. . . . "

The same is true of the difficult and still dramatic issue of child labor. The ILO's normative texts for the protection of children, Recommendation No. 146 and Convention No. 138, which were both adopted in 1973, refer explicitly to the right of these out-of-school children to basic education and vocational training. Because child labor was, and still is, found in many countries, a new Resolution Concerning the Improvement of Working Conditions and Environment was adopted in 1984, which reaffirmed the ILO's commitment, and required that "particular attention should be paid to the provision of appropriate education, training and welfare facilities which are needed to foster the future development of children and to establish a basis for effective action for the abolition of child labor."

Since 1980, technical cooperation at ILO has become more important than the normative interventions: training of experts, support of regional and national vocational training programs, special assistance for policy and program development, promotion of positive action for women workers, support for workers' education, advisory services for national action programs, training activities of policy makers, fellowship programs, etc. The ILO also has the Center for Advanced Vocational and Technical Training, a unique international residential center in Turin, Italy, for the training of specialists in adult education programs related to work.

In the field of adult education, ILO and UNESCO have developed a long-standing cooperation, with exchange programs in trade union and cooperative education, literacy programs in the workplace, and in rural areas, and vocational education.

UNICEF

While it has always maintained its intensive health and nutrition programs, UNICEF only started to get really involved in education through a close cooperation with UNESCO in the sixties, fifteen years after it was founded. At its 1972 session, the Executive Board of UNICEF adopted a new policy reinforcing the educational commitment of the agency, but decided from then on to focus its efforts on formal and nonformal *basic* education. The amount of UNICEF's educational aid increased more than six times from 1960 to 1979, a growth rate much higher than for its major programs in health, hygiene, and nutrition. While UNICEF's overall expenditures in education reached a peak in the early eighties, the contribution to nonformal basic education has continued to grow, to attain in 1985 the level of 11.5 million U.S. dollars, or one third of the overall educational commitment of the organization for that year, in comparison to \$3 million, or 12% of the expenditure for education in 1975. The collaboration between UNESCO and UNICEF was ensured through a special cooperation unit situated in Paris.

Because of UNICEF's mandate and focus on children's welfare, the nonformal education programs supported by the agency have always been dealing with out-of-school children and youth, with second chance programs for school drop-outs, with informal meetings and literacy programs for mothers, the development of life skills through education and training of girls and women, and on the consolidation of national nonformal basic education programs, as in Indonesia.

Another important historical contribution of UNICEF to adult education is not included in the above-mentioned figures, namely, the addition of nonformal educational components to its major programs in health, sanitation, and nutrition. Through this, UNICEF is supporting a huge volume of adult educational activities which often used school facilities in out-of-school hours.

The involvement of the UN and other multilateral organizations in the promotion and support of adult education, such as that of UNICEF and ILO, will grow even further during the present decade, thus following a trend that can be observed at the national level, where many different noneducation-related ministries and nongovernmental organizations are also increasingly involved in adult learning activities. In such a context, both UNESCO at the international level and the adult education institutions in countries have to review their role, taking into account the changing political economy of adult education.

THE CHANGING ROLE OF UNESCO

Following the economic crisis of the 1980s, the global socio-economic situation has deteriorated, especially in Africa, Latin America, and Southeast Asia. The economic downturn and the budgetary constraints have eroded the states' possibilities of providing public services. With few exceptions, the Structural Adjustment Program (SAP) of the World Bank and International Monetary Fund (IMF) to redress the economic situation in developing countries and in some Eastern European countries, has had the effect of cutting substantially the support to public health services, to social programs, and to educational provision, especially outside the area of primary school education. UNICEF and

UNESCO have insisted, but with limited results, on the protection of public investments in these three areas.

Two related consequences can be observed, which will have a significant impact on the future role of UNESCO and other UN agencies in adult education. Firstly, the usual provision for adult and nonformal basic education is being frozen, if not decreased, with the effect of returning the overall political economy of adult education to an inertial function of reproduction of educational inequalities. Secondly, the provision of adult learning opportunities is expanding, most of the time in a diffused and a disconnected way, organized outside the recognized adult education domain and developed as integrated components of health, agriculture, industrial, and environmental interventions. In other words, even in the present context, an upsurge in the demand for education is going on, but it tends to bypass the adult education institutions in favor of a diversification of responses outside the recognized public delivery system. Indeed, in spite of the rising demand, adult education, both at national and international levels, is going through an institutional and epistemological crisis.

NEW TRENDS IN THE UN AGENCIES

We are observing, in this respect, an increasing support on the part of many UN agencies to a variety of opportunities for out-of-school learners and adults. Let us again take the cases of UNICEF and ILO, though the same could be said of UNIFEM (United Nations Development Fund for Women), WHO, FAO, the UN Environment Programme, and the other UN agencies.

UNICEF, for example, is increasing its assistance to adult learning activities in the areas of health, nutrition, sanitation, and women's empowerment. It supports an increasing number of nonformal programs of NGOs; literacy projects for women, linked to income-generating activities; and other nonformal basic education programs for youth who have been bypassed by the formal school system. The agency has also promoted new educational delivery systems, such as distance education ("the Third Channel"). Since 1991, UNICEF has even recruited more than sixty regional advisors and program officers to implement its new basic education policy.

Although UNICEF, in contrast with ILO and UNESCO, has focused most of its activities on assistance and technical services in the domains of health and nutrition, and, later, on education, the New York based agency began during the present decade to assume a complementary role of standard setting as well. It has, for example, played a central part in the adoption of the Conventions on the Rights of the Child, in 1990, and has been one of the initiators of the World Conference on Education for All (WCEFA), convened also in 1990, by UNESCO, the United Nations Development Program (UNDP), and the World Bank. In both the Convention and the WCEFA Declaration, goals related to adult learning were set, namely, the expansion of primary education through nonformal approaches, as well as the augmentation of opportunities for adults to learn literacy and life skills.

The "World Declaration on Education for All," adopted by the WCEFA, represents a new consensus and a commitment by the four UN conveners and the participating national delegations, to ensure that "the basic learning needs of all children, youth and adults are met effectively in all countries (Inter-Agency Commission, 1990)." It stipulates that "the basic learning needs of youth and adults are diverse and should be met through a variety of delivery systems." The Framework for Action to meet the Basic Learning Needs, also adopted in Jomtien, stipulates comprehensive policy reviews at regional and global levels in 1995–1996 and in 2000–2001.

While there was a consensus among the conveners on the basic learning needs of children and youth and the urgency to give priority to this social demand, it is worth mentioning that the World Bank and the UNDP seemed more inclined to frame the issue as a choice between child education and adult literacy and to retain primary formal education as the priority, as well as to focus on the "basics" of basic education, whereas UNICEF and UNESCO, which have maintained their close collaboration through a joint mechanism, tended to insist more on the complementarity and the synergy between formal and nonformal basic education, as well as on the need for an integral vision of "fundamental" education.

After a strong involvement in standard setting in the seventies, the International Labor Organization (ILO) has tended since the eighties to focus more of its attention on technical assistance, giving a high priority to vocational training, not only for youth but also for adults; that is, for people at work or in search of work. Indeed, ILO's most important current technical programs are in this area, with special emphasis on displaced and aged workers, on out-of-school youth, on rural areas, and on informal economic sectors. ILO provides financial and technical support to training projects in more than sixty countries. A new program for the development of adult training and retraining programs in Eastern Europe was initiated in 1992 and currently supports projects in eight countries, including the Federation of Russia.

The critical trend towards placing nonformal education and adult learning at the center of their development strategies can be found not only in the UNICEF's programs, in ILO's plans, but also in the new WHO priority on primary health care, in the rural development schemes of FAO, and in the recommendation of the Rio conference on sustainable development. The role of UNESCO in adult education, therefore, needs to evolve.

THE CHANGING ROLE OF UNESCO AMONG THE OTHER UN AGENCIES

Less attention was given to adult education and literacy, and more was given to the benefit of formal schooling during the 1984–1989 Plan (Jones, 1988, pp. 212 ff). However, UNESCO's long-standing commitment to nonformal and adult education was renewed, and can be seen again in the Third Medium Term Plan (1990–1995), as well as in the two biennial programs of 1990–1991 and 1992–1993. In spite of financial constraints, a clear priority was then given to the education of children *and* to adult literacy. This can be seen in the activities coordinated by its Basic Education Division, the Inter-Agency Cooperation Unit, and the Section on Literacy and Adult Education, as well as at the Hamburg Institute and in the regional offices. The four historical functions mentioned in the first part of this chapter have been carried on during the last two biennia and will remain in force, though the fourth one suffers severe constraints and requires an important mobilization of extra-budgetary support.

In UNESCO, adult education is becoming a diversified reality going beyond the circumscribed realm of the adult education and literacy section. In the Third Medium Term Plan of UNESCO for 1990–1995, for example, the main contribution to adult education is to be found in the program of Education for All, and has to do preeminently with adult basic education, and with additional interventions to support adult education institutions. It indicates that adult education is also present in the different educational divisions, as well as in the other major programs on science, culture, and communication. In Chapter 1 of the Plan, explicit references are made to nonformal education for international understanding, retraining, and continuing education, distance education for out-of-school learners, and adult participation in university-level education. Chapter 2 concerns relations between formal and nonformal education and industry-run learning programs, adult environmental education, the promotion of reading, the strengthening of art education in the nonformal sector, and the development of rural libraries. Chapters 3 and 4 emphasize the relation between the media and the uses of literacy, and the promotion of the educational role of the media. Other chapters include population education (under the title "public information"), the analysis of the relation between human resources and development, and peace education. An important new effort will be made to develop adult education statistics. The chapter on "Transverse Theme on Women" pays attention to the interconnection between literacy, vocational training, and access to scientific studies.

The demand for adult learning in the present context requires provisions that often get developed outside the territory of institutionalized adult education. The learning demand leads to responses organized around new terms of reference related to the logic of the different fields of intervention. One of the challenges of UNESCO will be to collaborate in the development of conceptual tools, to support the networks needed to monitor and research this expanding and cross-sectorial educational domain, to reconstruct the whole reality of organized adult learning, to trace it under its various names and its different institutional arrangements. This is important because, through the rapid growth of the various forms of adult education, the general political economy of education is being transformed.

What can be observed at the national level is then also true at the international level. The reality of adult learning is now too expansive and pervasive to be monitored in countries, or at the world level, by a single agency. No more, for example will it be possible for UNESCO to organize the Fifth World Conference on Adult Education in 1997 without the other agencies, as it is no more meaningful to have any national conference on adult education without the participation of the different ministries and the social movements active in the related sectors of interests.

In that context, the proposed Plan for the 1994–1995 Biennium stipulates an increase in the resources allocated to adult education, with a mandate being given to the UNESCO Institute for Education for research and development in adult education, and a mandate given both to UNESCO headquarters in Paris and UIE (UNESCO Institute for Education) in Hamburg to start preparing the 1997 World Conference. One of the roles of the UNESCO Institute for Education will be to find ways and collaborations to reconstruct this critical mass of problem-oriented adult learning activities, in order to understand their significance. It will be necessary to ascertain how this enormous invisible open university helps individual learners.

A second major challenge for UNESCO and the adult education networks has to do with the already mentioned impact of the Structural Adjustment Programs (SAP) of the International Monetary Fund (IMF) and the World Bank. We need to understand the significance of the increase, or reduction, of the learning opportunities given to adults at the work place, in environmental projects, and in health programs. The concern is to analyze the impact of restricting or facilitating investment in human resources, of refusing or giving chances to adults to become more competent and autonomous. There is a contradiction in the SAP programs which require increased citizen participation in development strategies and yet refuse to support the education and training needed by the civil society.

CONCLUSION

Much is expected from UNESCO and, in collaboration with it, from the other multilateral governmental and nongovernmental organizations: the reconstruction of the current diversified phenomenon of adult learning; the monitoring of the whole field, having in mind the issues of relevance and of equality; and the analysis of the changing provision and participation in adult education through different disciplinary perspectives. Other tasks include establishing creative and effective environments for exchange and cooperation, and the formation of an emerging but still invisible and highly fragmented international college of research on adult education. UNESCO must support significant but still unrecognized innovations, effective promotion of the right of adult women and men to learn, and, above all, the capacity of UNESCO itself to listen and raise questions, as well as to give others opportunities to do so.

Though a modest organization—and one hampered by the present weakening of the financial base of the UN system—UNESCO is indeed confronted with a global mandate and rising expectations in all regions. Of course, it cannot but reflect the state of relations between the states; yet, it has also, on the basis of its Charter, and the General Conference, a real capacity for initiative. Both the constraints and the expectations are huge. UNESCO's future role will evolve within these contradictions. In the domain of adult education, what has been reported in this chapter gives reason to hope that it may play a significant role in the future.

NOTES

1. A detailed description of the functions of UNESCO under the title "UNESCO and Adult Education," by the present author, will appear in the Second Edition of the *International Encyclopedia of Education*, to be published by Pergamon Press in 1994.

2. A decision which has not been revoked since then.

3. In the following months, the governments in London and Singapore decided to follow the initiative of Washington, but the movement did not go further.

4. The International Bureau of Education (IBE), the International Institute for Educational Planning (IIEP), and the UNESCO Institute for Education (UIE).

5. Since 1988, UNESCO has also developed an Exchange Network on Literacy and Post-Literacy in Developed and Developing Countries, at the UNESCO Institute for Education (UIE).

6. At that time, adult education was often referred to, in French speaking countries, as popular education.

7. "The term 'adult education' denotes the entire body of organized educational processes, whatever the content, level and method, whether formal or otherwise, whether they prolong or replace initial education in schools, colleges and universities as well as in apprenticeship, whereby persons regarded as adults by the society to which they belong develop their abilities, enrich their knowledge, improve their technical or professional qualifications or turn them in a new direction and bring about changes in their attitudes or behavior in the twofold perspective of full personal development and participation in balanced and independent social, economic and cultural development" (UNESCO, 1976).

8. Cf. UNESCO, 1985, Conf. 210/4.

BIBLIOGRAPHY

This bibliography does not include the archives, unpublished documents, reports of seminars, and the reference books that Ursula Giere, in charge of the UIE library, has gathered and screened to help the author find the relevant data.

Hancock, G. (1991). *Lords of poverty*. London: Macmillan.

Inter-Agency Commission (1990). *World declaration on education for all*, and *Framework for action to meet basic learning needs*. New York: UNICEF House.

International Council for Adult Education (1986). *Making the connection: The adult education movement and the 4th UNESCO conference*. Toronto: ICAE.

International Labour Organization (1992). *International labor conventions and recommendations, 2* (1963–1991). Geneva: ILO.

Jones, P. W. (1988). *International policies for third world education: UNESCO, literacy and development*. London: Routledge.

Lowe, J. (1985). UNESCO World Conferences in Adult Education. *The International Encyclopedia of Education, 9*: 5345–48. Oxford: Pergamon Press.

United Nations International Children's Emergency Fund (1990). *UNICEF in education: A historical perspective*. UNICEF History Series, Monograph IX. New York: UNICEF House.

UNESCO Reports, published in Paris, arranged by date:

(1949) *Report of the First International Conference on Adult Education (ELSINORE)*.

(1960) *Report of the Second World Conference on Adult Education, UNESCO (Montreal)*.

(1972) *Report of the Third International Conference on Adult Education (Tokyo)*.

(1974) *Recommendation concerning education for international understanding, cooperation and peace and education relating to human rights and fundamental freedoms*.

(1975) *The experimental world literacy program: A critical assessment*.

(1976) *Recommendation on the development of adult education*.

(1976) *Recommendation on participation by the people at large in cultural life and their contribution to it*.

(1985) *Report of the Fourth International Conference on Adult Education (Paris)*.

(1989) *Third Medium-term plan 1990–1995*.

(1993) *Report by the director general concerning the implementation of the recommendation on the development of adult education*.

CHAPTER 2

Adult Education
and the World Bank

JOHN B. HOLDEN AND JAMES R. DORLAND

Although the name "World Bank" is well recognized and seems to strike a familiar chord almost everywhere, there is considerable lack of knowledge and some misinformation as to exactly what this institution is and what it is designed to do, i.e., its ultimate purpose. Therefore, it seems logical to provide the following background information, so that the reader may understand this rather complex organization and get a handle on the extent of its present and potential involvement in the education of adults.[1]

What is popularly called the "World Bank" is officially known as the International Bank for Reconstruction and Development (IBRD). It was conceived at the United Nations Monetary and Financial Conference held in the midst of World War II, in July 1944, at Bretton Woods, New Hampshire (U.S.A.). IBRD began its operations on June 25, 1946.

The World Bank, which is how it will generally be referred to in this chapter, was founded on the principle that many countries would not only be short of foreign exchange for reconstruction and development after World War II, but would also be insufficiently credit worthy to meet all their needs by borrowing commercially. Designed as an official multilateral institution, whose share capital was owned by countries in proportion to their economic size, the Bank could serve as an intermediary by borrowing on world markets and lending more cheaply than could commercial banks. It would also be able to exercise judgment about the projects it would help finance.

The goal of the World Bank is to provide loans to developing countries, to help reduce poverty, and to finance investments that contribute to economic growth. It supports the building of roads, power plants, schools, and irrigation networks, as well as activities like agricultural extension services (a prime example of adult education), training for teachers, and nutrition improvement programs for children and pregnant women. Some of its loans finance changes in the structure of countries' economies, to make them more stable, efficient, and market oriented. It also provides "technical assistance," or expert advice, to help governments make specific sectors of their economies more efficient and relevant to national development goals.

The first loans approved by the World Bank helped finance the reconstruction of the war-ravaged economies of Western Europe. Today, more than four decades later, it lends to the developing countries of Africa, Asia, Latin America and the Caribbean, North Africa, the Middle East, and Europe.

The Bank operates under the authority of a Board of Governors, each of its 167 member countries being represented by one person, who is usually a ministerial level government official. The Board of Governors delegates its authority to a smaller group of representatives, known as the Board of Executive Directors, which is based in Washington, D.C. It is the Board which is responsible for decisions on policies affecting the World Bank's operation and for the approval of all loans. Loan decisions are based on economic rather than political criteria. The World Bank's president is the chairman of the Board of Executive Directors. The management and daily operations of the Bank are carried out by about 6,800 staff members, who come from more than one hundred countries around the world.

The World Bank has three affiliated institutions: the International Development Association (IDA), the International Finance Corporation (IFC), and the Multilateral Investment Guarantee Agency (MIGA). The headquarters of the World Bank and its three affiliates are in Washington, D.C. Collectively, these organizations comprise what is known as the World Bank Group. In order to help the reader differentiate among these four entities, descriptions of the World Bank (IBRD) and its three affiliates are as follows:

IBRD (THE INTERNATIONAL BANK FOR RECONSTRUCTION AND DEVELOPMENT)

The interest rate on World Bank loans to developing countries changes every six months and is kept as low as possible in accordance with current conditions. Loans generally have a five-year grace period and must be repaid during periods ranging from 15 to 20 years. In fiscal 1992, which ended on June 30, 1992, the IBRD approved loans totaling $15.2 billion for 112 economic development projects and programs designed to restructure national economies in 43 countries. Some of the money that the IBRD lends to developing countries comes from contributions from the institution's member countries. However, the majority comes from bonds issued in world financial markets.

IDA (THE INTERNATIONAL DEVELOPMENT ASSOCIATION)

Established in 1960, it has 144 member countries. This World Bank affiliate provides "soft," i.e., low-interest, loans to the world's poorest countries. Only those with annual per capita incomes of less than $1,235 can borrow from IDA. However, most of its loans, which are known as "credits," have a ten-year grace period and must be repaid in 35 or 40 years (according to the borrowing country's credit worthiness). In fiscal 1992, IDA approved credits totaling $6.5 billion for 110 development projects and economic restructuring programs in 50 countries. The money that IDA lends comes from contributions from wealthier nations, an occasional contribution from the earnings of the IBRD, and from repayments of IDA credits. Although it is legally separate from the World Bank, IDA shares the World Bank's staff and facilities.

IFC (THE INTERNATIONAL FINANCE CORPORATION)

Established in 1956, it has 147 member countries. It promotes economic growth in developing countries by lending directly to the private sector. Unlike the IBRD, it lends without government guarantees. The IFC may also take equity positions in companies to which it lends, play the role of catalyst to other investors from the private sector, and work to develop capital markets in developing countries. In fiscal 1992, this World Bank affiliate approved financing of $1.8 billion for its own account in 167 projects and other activities carried out by the private sector.

MIGA (THE MULTILATERAL INVESTMENT GUARANTEE AGENCY)

Established in 1988, it had 86 member countries as of August 1992. This World Bank affiliate promotes private investment in developing countries. It provides guarantees on investments to protect investors from noncommercial risks, such as war or nationalization. It also provides advisory services to governments, to help them find ways to attract private investment in their countries. In fiscal 1992, MIGA issued 21 guarantees for projects in eight developing countries having a total cost of $1 billion.

HOW THE WORLD BANK AND THE INTERNATIONAL MONETARY FUND (IMF) DIFFER

The World Bank and the IMF were both established in 1944 at the conference of world leaders in the New Hampshire village of Bretton Woods. The aim of the two "Bretton Woods institutions," as they are sometimes called, was to place the international economy on a sound footing after the end of World War II. One need was to make sure that the misguided, nationalistic monetary policies of the 1930s did not surface again in the postwar period. This goal was assigned to the International Monetary Fund.

As has been previously alluded to, another need was to rebuild the roads, bridges, communications links, power systems, and other basic building blocks of the economies of the war-torn countries of Europe. This job was given to the International Bank for Reconstruction and Development—the World Bank, for short. After help for the countries of Western Europe was provided, in the form of the U.S. Marshall Plan, the World Bank shifted its lending focus to the countries of the developing world—Africa, Asia, Latin America and the Caribbean, North Africa, the Middle East and Europe—an emphasis which continues in the 1990s.

The World Bank and the IMF should never be seen as rivals, but as partners in promoting global economic prosperity. Their structure, size, and country focus are not identical. For instance, both richer and poorer countries are entitled to join the World Bank, but only poorer countries qualify for assistance from that institution. Membership in the IMF is a prerequisite for joining the Bank, and, as of 1992, both organizations had 167 members.

While the World Bank lends only to developing countries, all member countries (rich and poor) can call upon the International Monetary Fund's services and resources. In fact, for the Fund to do its job properly, the vast majority of the world's countries must participate in its work. Since international trade and investment cross borders, nearly every country finds itself buying and selling foreign currencies to finance imports and exports. The IMF monitors such transactions and consults with its members on ways they can contribute to a fluid and stable global monetary system. The IMF also offers technical assistance in macroeconomic management to countries in return for a commitment to economic policy changes.

As of June 30, 1992, the Bank had disbursed over $200 billion in loans for projects and policy changes since it began operations. The Fund had provided over $140 billion in permanent liquidity and short- and medium-term loans to its members, traditionally to help them overcome balance of payments difficulties. The Bank is a much larger institution, which can be illustrated by comparing the size of its staff of 6,800 to the IMF's staff of 2,000.

In its early years, most of the Bank's assistance went to specific development projects, such as installing electric power lines, or building roads, bridges, and railroads. Later, the number of large industrial projects declined, while projects that raised the productivity and living standards of the rural and urban poor gained importance. Of interest to adult educators is the fact that many of the more recent projects—some which are currently being funded—have also included a training component, such as modernizing farms, improving the skills of teachers, or providing business know-how to small entrepreneurs.

While the World Bank makes loans for both policy reforms and projects, the International Monetary Fund concerns itself with policies alone, which is generally not a prime area for funding to adult education practitioners. The IMF tracks its members' monetary and fiscal policies that can have an impact on their ability to finance their imports and exports—their "balance of payments." It makes recommendations during regular consultations with government officials on what changes to make in policy to correct current problems or to head off future ones. It also provides loans to member countries that have a short-term problem meeting their foreign payments requirements. Finally, the Fund seeks to obtain full convertibility among the currencies of its members, under the system of flexible exchange rates in force since 1973. When currencies can be freely exchanged, trade and investment among different countries is greatly eased. As of 1991, seventy countries had agreed to currency convertibility.

Cooperation, not rivalry, between these two important organizations has been the norm over the years. Although the World Bank and the IMF have always been complementary institutions, lending for broad improvements in economic policies has led their staffs to cross the street between their headquarters buildings with increasing frequency in the last ten to fifteen years, in order to step up their cooperation. The World Bank hopes to establish a sounder basis for the success of the specific projects it creates, while the International Monetary Fund is trying to promote greater international monetary stability. For practitioners in the field of adult education who are interested in becoming involved in projects funded through the World Bank, it is crucial to know the difference between the World Bank Group and the International Monetary Fund.

HOW THE WORLD BANK FUNDS PROJECTS

A six-step process governs the World Bank's approach to investment lending. Formally known as the "project cycle," it is the Bank's way of making sure that all projects receiving financial backing meet the same set of rigorous standards. Bank staff work closely with developing country borrowers throughout the project cycle. Adult educators should be interested in knowing that the Bank maintains an independent evaluation department to assess the effectiveness of the projects it supports.

The six stages in the World Bank's project cycle are: Identification, Preparation, Appraisal, Negotiation and Board Presentation, Implementation and Supervision, Evaluation. Some project ideas never make it past the early phase of identification. Others are reworked during the preparation and appraisal phases and end up looking quite different from their original designs. The Bank approves over two hundred projects in the course of a year. Since the funding of projects is what the World Bank is all about, it is important here to quote directly the explanations of the project cycle as provided by the Bank.

Identification — The task of identifying and proposing projects for World Bank financing lies mainly with borrowing governments. On some occasions, a project may be identified as a result of general economic or more specific sector work carried out by the Bank staff. For instance, from an analysis of a country's transportation or agricultural policies might come the idea to build new feeder roads to help farmers reach more markets. A joint United Nations Development Programme-World Bank effort called the Energy Sector Management Assistance Program (ESMAP) identifies priority energy projects.

In this first phase, planners answer questions such as: Who will benefit from the project? Will project benefits be greater than the costs? Are there other options for achieving the same objective? A project must also pass a priorities test: a good industrial project may not go forward because an agricultural project is more urgent. Once a project passes these hurdles, it is incorporated into the Bank's multi-year lending program for a country, to ensure that resources will be available over time to complete all identified projects.

Preparation — Though the Bank will often help, the borrowing country is responsible for examining the technical, economic, social, and environmental aspects of the project. It defines the available options, the feasibility of each, and their costs and benefits. The advantages of a loan to improve a manufacturing industry, for example, must be weighed against any environmental degradation that could occur from increased smokestack pollution. In an agricultural project, the borrower must decide whether oxen or tractors should be used for crop cultivation, while for an urban project the borrower might have to choose between upgrading slum dwellings or building new homes. Such decisions rely on feasibility studies. A project timetable is established during preparation.

Appraisal — Even with all this preparation, the Bank is not yet ready to say "yes" or "no" to financing a project until it has made its own independent assessment of the project—the appraisal. Each on-site appraisal mission takes from three to four weeks. In order to appraise its various projects, the Bank conducts about 150 such missions each year. A team of Bank staff and consultants reviews the studies made by the borrower and undertakes its own analysis of four major areas: technical, institutional, economic, and financial.

Technical questions: Is the dam soundly designed and engineered? Does it meet acceptable standards? Will it displace local people? Will it affect the environment in any adverse way?

Institutional questions: Does the borrower have the organization, the management, the staff, the policies to build a railroad and maintain it? If not, what changes are required to put these into place?

Economic questions: Will the benefits of a water supply system outweigh the costs? What will its impact be on family incomes? Will it provide job opportunities for local people? What is the estimated rate of return on the investment?

Financial questions: Is the borrower's financial plan sound? Is the electrical distribution system financially viable? Is the proposed accounting system adequate?

Negotiation and Board Presentation — The Bank appraisal report summarizing its recommendations for a loan's conditions forms the basis for negotiations with the borrower. The negotiations bring World Bank staff and the borrower together to agree on the measures necessary for a successful project. Through a give-and-take process, the Bank and the borrower review all the issues that have arisen during preparation and appraisal.

One example of negotiation is the case of an electric utility receiving a loan to increase the number of transmission lines. The Bank and the borrower agree that to earn an adequate rate of return on the project and finance a reasonable proportion of its investments, electricity prices to the consumer must be set at a market rate. The details of this understanding and any other obligations of the borrower are set out in loan documents, which are signed by both the Bank and the borrower.

After negotiations, the appraisal report (including any changes made during the negotiation phase), the report of the Bank's president, and the loan documents are presented to the board of executive directors, representing the Bank's 167 member countries, for approval.

Implementation and Supervision — This is the stage when the road or school is built, machinery and equipment are purchased and installed, and people are trained. Since the World Bank is required by its member countries to "ensure that the proceeds of any loan are used only for the purposes for which the loan was granted," about ten staff-weeks a year are spent supervising each project. Bank staff visit the project site to identify problems and help find solutions. Supervision is also an important way for the Bank to provide technical assistance to its borrowers—one of the Bank's primary development roles. [*Authors' note: This is also one of the most appropriate areas for adult educators to become involved in Bank-financed projects.*]

Unlike a commercial bank that approves a loan and hands over the money to the borrower, the World Bank normally does not disburse its funds without evidence that the borrower has spent the money to achieve agreed purposes—bought the trucks needed to build roads or the pumps for the irrigation system. Strict procurement rules ensure that appropriate materials and services are used. These rules usually require the borrower to purchase goods and services through international competitive bidding (ICB), open to firms in all the World Bank's member countries and Taiwan. The ICB process, which involves public advertising, ensures that contracts are awarded in a fair and efficient manner.

Evaluation — An independent department within the World Bank, the Operations Evaluation Department (OED) is responsible for assessing the results of projects. To ensure its impartiality, OED reports directly to the board of executive directors and to the Bank's president. The evaluation compares project costs, benefits, timetable, and efficiency with what had been expected at the time of appraisal. It also suggests how to improve project performance in the future. The annual review of projects, a publication called Evaluation Results, is available to the public. World Bank evaluations over the years have shown that the vast majority of projects are successful in meeting major objectives. (World Bank Information Cycle, 1992)

It should be reassuring for adult educators to realize that the World Bank's six-step project cycle so closely mirrors the principles which are embedded in the training of adult educators and which are essential to the success of any worthwhile adult education enterprise. Furthermore, there is no indication that the need for projects funded through the World Bank is going to decrease. Consequently, for the adult educator astute enough to seek out the action and to practice the flexibility and adaptability so often required for participation in projects in developing countries, the sky is the limit as to the extent of future involvement in the education of adults.

WORLD BANK EXPERIENCE WITH EDUCATIONAL INVESTMENT

It is now widely accepted that education, like other forms of investment in human capital, can contribute to economic development and raise the incomes of the poor just as much as investment in physical capital, such as transportation, communications, power, or irrigation. The World Bank has long recognized the importance of investment in education and has been active in this field since 1962. When the Bank was first established in 1944, however, education was not counted among the productive purposes for which it was authorized to provide investment capital. This attitude prevailed right through the 1950s, when official statements of Bank policy took the view that the Bank should concentrate its lending on projects designed to make a direct contribution to the productive capacity of its members, rather than finance projects such as the construction and equipment of schools, colleges, and universities. Even though such projects were considered essential to the development of a country, the Bank's proper role, as a bank, was said to be confined to providing loans for the more directly productive sectors of the economy. Gradually this attitude changed within the World Bank and in the world.

One of the principal reasons for the shift in thinking was the growing interest during the 1960s in the economic value of education, and eventually World Bank policy reflected this recognition that education is a productive investment in human capital. Today few would dispute that human development contributes to economic growth no less than physical capital. Since 1962, the World Bank has invested more than \$5 billion in more than 260 education projects in more than 90 countries (Psacharopoulos & Woodhall, 1985, pp. 4–5). In the realm of formal education, this investment has helped provide in excess of three million school, college, or university places in more than 20,000 institutions. World Bank experience in the field of educational investment is therefore substantial. Moreover, this investment has been accompanied by assessment and careful analysis of implementation problems and achievements. In addition, the World Bank has commissioned research on the contribution of education to human and economic development, and has cooperated both with other international agencies and with individual countries in carrying out research on the economic value of education and disseminating the results. This is another area where adult educators not only can find a niche, but their research expertise is really needed.

There have been a number of important changes in emphasis in World Bank education projects since 1962. Initially, lending for education could not be for primary education or for liberal arts colleges, but had to be restricted to engineering, technical, managerial, or other vocational education closely allied with other Bank projects which included many adults. Furthermore, investment was confined to bricks and mortar. Today, however, the Bank is investing in primary and basic education (including nonformal education—adult education), as well as in technical and vocational education and teacher training. It is also investing in curricular reform, school textbooks, and other software, as well as school buildings and equipment. Thus, the emphasis now is on both qualitative and quantitative improvements, and there is as much concern with the equity as with the efficiency of educational investment. The World Bank's present strategy in investing in education can be summarized by the following principles:

1. Basic education should be provided for all children and adults as soon as the available resources and conditions permit. In the long term, a comprehensive system of formal and nonformal education should be developed at all levels.

2. To increase productivity and promote social equity, educational opportunities should be provided without distinction of sex, ethnic background, or social and economic status.

3. Education systems should try to achieve maximum internal efficiency in the management, allocation, and use of available resources, so as to increase the quantity and improve the quality of education.

4. Education should be related to work and environment, in order to improve, quantitatively and qualitatively, the knowledge and skills necessary for economic, social, and other development.

5. To satisfy these objectives, developing countries will need to build and maintain their institutional capacities to design, analyze, manage, and evaluate programs for education and training (Psacharopoulos & Woodhall, 1985, pp. 4–5).

Therefore, for those whose principal interest is in the education of adults, it is reassuring to know that education plays such an important role in the projects funded by the World Bank;[2] but, it is also worrisome that adult education per se is so seldom mentioned either in Bank publications or by headquarters personnel. Just as recognition of the importance of investing in education earned its acceptance over time, a full-fledged recognition of the overall importance of adult education has yet to become a reality at the World Bank.

An example of a World Bank development loan is that to a country which has contracted for help from a midwestern university in the United States. While the objective is to focus on policy and operational measures for improving the quality of primary and secondary education, training of adults is necessary. This training serves the needs of teachers, administrators, and staff, and is provided by in-service training rotation, fellowships, and study abroad opportunities.

THE WORLD BANK AND HUMAN RESOURCE DEVELOPMENT

A section of the *1992 Annual Report* of the World Bank, entitled "Human-resource Development," is most relevant to the interests of adult educators. While it is clear that adult education per se, as a category of funding, has not been established by the Bank, various aspects of the field have always been included. Over the past quarter century, it has become progressively more involved in human resource development, which is an important area of concern for adult educators. The Bank itself says:

> The growth in volume and the change in the nature of Bank support for HRD have made the Bank a major partner in HRD efforts. The Bank has also become increasingly active in the analysis and advocacy of HRD. These factors, in conjunction with the Bank's ability to tailor its country-lending programs to its public policy pronouncements on HRD, have given the Bank an important influence on the international HRD agenda.

> Wholesale changes in Bank support for HRD have occurred since the 1987 reorganization of the Bank, which fundamentally transformed this relatively small and fragmented sector. Lending for HRD increased from less than 8 percent of total Bank lending in fiscal 1986 to more than 13 percent in fiscal 1992. These levels of lending are expected to increase further.

> The expansion of HRD lending has meant, foremost, a rise in the Bank's support for basic education and health services, including family planning and nutrition (World Bank Annual Report, 1992, p. 50).

GLOSSARY OF WORLD BANK TERMS RELEVANT TO THE EDUCATORS OF ADULTS

Although the term "adult education" is seldom used by the World Bank, the following definitions, which are contained in the Glossary and Acronyms section of a 1988 World Bank Policy Study, *Education in Sub-*

Saharan Africa, pp. ix–x, are commonly accepted and are found throughout various Bank publications:

Correspondence Education: A type of distance education through which students receive textbooks for individual study in their homes and supplementary mass media broadcasts on the subject matter. Each textbook includes exercises to be completed and mailed to a postal tutor, who grades each exercise and provides an individual evaluation to the student.

Distance Education, or distance teaching: An education delivery system that uses a variety of media and a system of feedback to teach people who are unable to attend traditional schools. Distance education usually combines the use of media broadcasts, printed materials, and some kind of face-to-face study. Distance teaching programs can range from in-school programs, in which broadcasts supplement learning activities in the classroom, to out-of-school programs, such as correspondence lessons in which students may never meet their tutors and may have little or no contact with the regular education system.

Equivalency Program: A teaching program that provides opportunities for education to students who would otherwise be unable to attend formal schools and that emphasizes the acquisition of knowledge rather than the place where the knowledge is acquired. Equivalency programs exist for all levels of schooling.

Nonformal Education: Education and training for out-of-school youths and adults in classes, courses, or activities intended to promote learning but not constituting part of the formal school system and not leading to formal qualifications, such as diplomas or specific trade standards. Nonformal education typically concentrates on short programs of a few months in duration.

Primary or Basic Education: The first level of education, in which students follow a common curriculum. Primary education offers students instruction in primary or elementary schools that are part of the formal education. These schools span grades 1–4, 1–5, 1–7, or 1–8 and teach communication, mathematics, and science. Basic education generally refers to instruction in literacy and numeracy skills for out-of-school youths and adults.

Secondary Education: Secondary education requires at least four years of primary preparation for entry. Students may follow a general academic program that typically leads to admission to a postsecondary institution, or they may study technical and vocational or agricultural curriculums to prepare for direct entry into a trade or occupation. This level may span any subset of grades 5–12.

Technical Education: Training in specialist skills for the higher level skilled worker. Instruction is typically in preemployment training institutions such as polytechnics; administration is commonly the responsibility of ministries of education, labor, or employment, or comes under the authority of specific industries. Courses of study in technical education usually include a component of general education.

Training: Instruction in job-related skills to prepare students for direct entry into a trade or occupation. Such instruction can take place in training centers, through apprenticeships, or at the place of employment (on-the-job training).

Vocational Education: Training in craft or trade skills for the semiskilled worker. Instruction typically occurs in schools and comes under the direction of ministries of education.[2]

THE WORLD BANK FROM THE PERSPECTIVE
OF ADULT EDUCATORS

As authors of this chapter about the World Bank and its role in adult education, and as retired adult educators with only cursory knowledge of the Bank and its operation, we approached our task with open minds and no preconceptions. However, once we got involved in our assignment through collecting and analyzing information and making inquiries from Bank personnel, it became increasingly apparent to the two of us that adult education as an entity or as a commonly-used term is not an integral part of the World Bank's daily operations. This is not a criticism, merely an overall observation.

Both of us have spent most of our careers as adult educators; and, based on our experiences and recent research into the World Bank and its adult education activities, we offer the following additional observations for anyone interested in the education of adults:

1. It is the education (or training) of adults, and not "adult education," on which the World Bank concentrates. Glossaries of World Bank terms are not likely to contain the terms "adult education" or "continuing education." Furthermore, projects are more likely to deal with "nonformal education" or "basic education" and their adult components. The Bank's lending for adult education also includes project-related training in sectors other than education as well as specific education programs in project areas, such as rural development, population, health, and nutrition.

2. Since the World Bank's overarching mission is to alleviate poverty in developing countries, adult educators interested in becoming involved in such efforts must do so through projects funded for that purpose. The key person to contact is a country's official representative on the World Bank's Board of Governors. Bank projects are often "in the pipeline" for quite a while. Specific information about projects is available from: The World Bank, 1818 H Street, N.W., Washington, D.C. 20433. Telephone (202) 473-1793; Fax (202) 676-0578.

3. The World Bank is nearing the end of its fifth decade of existence. Over that period of time its philosophy and practices have changed considerably and have moved more in the direction of investing in human capital, not just in tangible "things." Being able to prove, both qualitatively and quantitatively, the positive results of what the Bank calls "human-resource development" is a formidable challenge, and the outcome will strongly influence the nature of future investments. One of the most challenging roles for adult educators might be to assess the results of some of the World Bank's recent educational efforts.

4. In its six-step Project Cycle, the Bank practices valid principles of adult education methodology. As a result of an enviable record of achievement over the years, its overall image is a positive one. This is a tribute to what appears to be a realistic plan of operations, effective oversight, and sound management.

5. It would be ideal if there were someone near the top of the hierarchy in the World Bank's staff with an understanding of the value of adult education as a discipline and as a separate entity equal in importance to primary, secondary and higher education. Falling short of achieving this utopian dream, adult educators must work within the current structure and involve themselves wherever possible in the activities of the Bank.

38   ADULT EDUCATION THROUGH WORLD COLLABORATION

NOTES

1. Statements concerning the World Bank and adult education in this chapter represent the professional opinions of the authors and are based on their research and on discussions with persons familiar with that institution and its operations.

2. It should be acknowledged that the Bank's lending for adult education also includes project-related training in sectors other than education as well as specific education programs in such project areas as rural development, population, health and nutrition.

BIBLIOGRAPHY

All sources are World Bank publications which are available from the bookstore of the World Bank at 1818 H. Street, N.W., Washington, D.C. 20433, U.S.A.

Specific sources of descriptive material used in the chapter:

Education in Sub-Saharan Africa (1988). A World Bank Policy Study.
Poverty Reduction Handbook (1993).
Psacharopoulos, George, and Maureen Woodhall (1985). *Education for development: An analysis of investment choices*. Published for the World Bank. New York, N.Y.: Oxford University Press.
The World Bank annual report 1992.
The World Bank and the IMF (Series A.02.8-92).
The World Bank information briefs on the World Bank Group (Series A. 01.8-92).
The World Bank information cycle (Series A.04.8-92).

CHAPTER 3

Towards a New North-South Internationalism: Adult Education and the Voluntary Sector

LAWRENCE S. CUMMING

> *"A pen, a song, a play—all can be used to help people exercise their rights and freedom!"*[1]

A useful, if not essential starting point for this discussion is what adult educators and developmentalists—and their enterprises—have in common. Julius K. Nyerere puts it succinctly:

> So development is for Man [sic], by Man and of Man. The same is true of education. Its purpose is the liberation of Man from the restraints and limitations of ignorance and dependency. . . . The ideas imparted by education, or released in the mind through education, should therefore, be liberating ideas; the skills acquired by education should be liberating skills. Nothing else can properly be called education . . . adult education should promote change, at the same time as it assists men to control both the change which they induce, and that which is forced upon them . . . adult education encompasses the whole of life, and must build on what already exists (Nyerere, 1992, pp. 37–38).

Clearly, adult education and development are intimately bound up with and inseparable from each other.

At the outset of this discussion, however, it would be well to note that this chapter will concern itself with that part of the adult education movement which has, historically, emphasized the social development and collective human betterment dimensions of education, and, hence, deserves the title of movement. The chapter makes an implicit assump-

39

tion that the purely individual growth or personal interests stream of adult education, as practiced by some in Europe and North America, has little to offer to the field of international cooperation or development. We are talking, therefore, about a socially engaged adult education.

This chapter concerns itself with those activities which happen in the voluntary sector and other segments of the larger nonprofit sector. It does not consider the activities of the state or of official multilateral institutions, except to the extent that they facilitate or hinder the work of voluntary or nonprofit associations.

Not within the ambit of this chapter are profit-making private sector firms. In the past, private sector businesses tended to be mainly contractors for large economic and infrastructure development projects (public buildings, transportation, power generation and the like). With the shifting of state-private sector boundaries of recent years, however, has come a certain blurring of old distinctions. Just as some voluntary international development organizations (VIDOs) and international development institutions (IDIs) have moved into public service contracting, there are firms which have become involved in social development activities such as adult education—hitherto the preserve of nonprofit agencies. In a few instances, though their corporate structures clearly place them in the business category, firms differ little in their development philosophy and practice from many VIDOs and IDIs.

WHAT IS AN "NGO"?

A nongovernmental organization (NGO) is, by definition, not part of the state or a national or intergovernmental structure. Because the term has been used by official agencies to define that which is *not* of them, it may have something of a second class or marginal connotation. Those who maintain the right to define what or who is not of them, and to consign others to that category, reserve the right to determine what are and are not suitable roles and functions and what are the limits of appropriateness.

The second thing which must be observed is that, in this era of "democratization," the territorial boundaries of the state and of the associations and institutions of civil society are undergoing substantial and far-reaching redefinition and realignment. No longer are NGOs mere fillers of gaps and supplementers of official largesse. It behooves those of the "nongovernmental" sector, therefore, to find self-definitions which are more accurate, precise, and assertive.

This chapter will use two principal terms to define the sectors which constitute its subject matter. The first is "voluntary international development organization" (VIDO). (The term Private Voluntary Organization or PVO is widely used in the United States to describe such agencies.) The word "voluntary," of course, suggests that people choose whether or not to become involved in, or to support, the organization or activity in question. Voluntary organizations are characterized by non-compulsory contribution of time and labor (participation on boards of directors, in public education, in fund raising, and in a variety of other ways) and by donations of financial or in-kind resources on the part of members of the public. The phrase "international development," of course, simply indicates the purpose and nature of the work which the organization does. It does, however, also suggest some degree of mutuality and interchange across national borders.

The second term is "international development institution" (IDI). Such bodies have a less voluntary character than the VIDOs. They may either specialize in international development or, more likely, have taken on an international development role which, though valued and though based on their area of expertise, is but a secondary or tertiary function. Universities or other postsecondary school educational institutions, hospitals as well as professional associations representing nurses, engineers, chartered accountants, and so on, might be cited as examples.

Organizations which straddle these two categories and, depending on particular circumstances, might fall under either the first or second heading, could include trade unions and cooperative societies.

Other terms which will be found in this chapter are "voluntary development organization" (VDO) and "people's organization" or "popular organization" (PO). These terms refer mainly to organizations which exist to do development work within their own societies, countries or regions (whether North or South). VDOs tend to be more formal structures, while POs represent the particular community or sectoral interests of their members.

This chapter also uses the metaphorical shorthand language of "North-South" relations. Though the phrase lacks some precision—"donor countries" such as Australia and New Zealand, for instance, are in the geographic South—this linguistic convenience avoids the difficulties of "developing," "developed," "underdeveloped," "First World," "Third World" (to say nothing of "second world" and "fourth world"), "industrialized," "industrializing," and so on.

As regards sources of financing, there is a wide variety of practice both between and within countries. Some VIDOs receive little or no financial support from organs of government. In some instances, this is by choice of either the government agency or the VIDO concerned. In other cases, they may receive considerable amounts of financial support. As a general rule, the more voluntary an organization is in its purposes, structure and fund raising capabilities, the less it relies on the state. Those of a more institutional character tend to rely for a greater portion of their international development activity income on state contributions. (Needless to say there are a good many exceptions to this rule.) Government funding may come from national governments or multilateral organizations, such as United Nations agencies, the European Economic Community, etc. Broadly speaking, government monies may be either responsive or directive. In the former case, the VIDO or IDI may present a program or a project to the government funding agency for a matching contribution according to whatever cofunding formula obtains in that jurisdiction. (The presenting organization, of course, normally does this on behalf of a partner abroad, hopefully following full consultation and agreement.) In other instances, VIDOs or IDIs may submit bids or proposals to implement programs or projects, often large-scale, initiated by official bilateral (national) or multilateral (international) agencies.

SOUTHERN "NGOs"

Though this chapter is about the role of agencies in the North, it must be emphasized that NGOs exist in the South as well. Indeed their prominence and significance are growing. Such organizations (referred to herein as indigenous VDOs) are increasingly the vehicles through which popular development aspirations, voiced by people's organizations (POs) are realized. In the emerging partnership and division of labor discussed below, the position of Southern VDOs is indispensable.

SOME CATEGORIES OF NORTHERN ORGANIZATIONS IN SUPPORT ROLES

There are several kinds of Northern VIDOs which support adult education activities in the South. For convenience, they might be grouped under three headings.

Adult Education Specialist Agencies

The first category might be termed the specialist VIDOs and IDIs. This might include World Education Inc. (based in Boston), World Literacy Canada (Toronto) and Laubach Literacy International (Syracuse). What these have in common is a focus on adult education. Their histories are rooted in the passionate commitment of their founders to uplifting adult learners, specifically, in these instances, through literacy. In some instances, they have moved into other types of socio-economic development programs, though all the while remaining rooted in and infused with adult education thinking and methodologies.

Professional Associations

There are numerous examples of professional bodies which make significant commitments to adult education in countries in the South. Perhaps the most prominent example is the German Adult Education Association (DVV). On a more modest scale is Adult Education for Development, based at the University of Reading in the U.K., which is "an independent training, research and consultancy organization specializing in the education and training of adults,"[2] providing technical assistance services and acting as a professional North-South exchange network.

Worthy of note as well are professional associations in fields other than adult education. A good example is the Canadian Public Health Association (CPHA). One project for which it is responsible is the Southern African AIDS Training Programme, involving roughly one hundred community initiatives in ten countries of Southern Africa and employing adult education and community development methodologies.

Generalist Agencies

A wide variety of organizations, numbering in the hundreds, might be mentioned under this heading. These are both confessional and non-confessional in their character and bases of support. The former might further be broken down into Roman Catholic and Protestant groupings. The Roman Catholic agencies are mostly grouped under International Co-operation for Social and Economic Development (CIDSE) and include the Netherlands Catholic Organization for Development Co-operation (CEBEMO), the Canadian Catholic Organization for Development and Peace (CCODP, Montreal) and the U.K. Catholic Agency for Overseas Development (CAFOD, London).

Prominent national and international agencies on the Protestant side would include Lutheran World Relief (Geneva) and the Mennonite Central Committee (based primarily in the United States and Canada). Most of the European and North American national denominational churches also have international development and relief wings or offices.

Numerous interchurch bodies are also active, most notably the World Council of Churches (Geneva) and the various national and regional councils of churches around the world affiliated with it. Other interchurch agencies include Christian Aid (British Council of Churches), Church World Service (U.S.A.), the Interchurch Organization for International Co-operation (ICCO, the Netherlands) and the Protestant Association for Co-operation in Development (EZE, Germany). Some of these national councils include the Roman Catholic Church as members or affiliates, and some do not. The World Council, as well as the national and regional councils, typically include various of the Orthodox churches as well.

The other major subcategory of generalist VIDOs is made up of secular or nonconfessional agencies, such as the national members of the OXFAM International family, the major Dutch agencies (NOVIB and HIVOS) and World University Service (Geneva—with national affiliates in a variety of countries). Some VIDOs are purely national and others (the national CARE and OXFAM agencies, for instance) are members of international associations.

The variety of VIDO and IDI forms, structures, shapes, sizes and complexities—to say nothing of basic purposes, orientations, development philosophies and specializations—is well nigh infinite and, undoubtedly, bewildering to the outside observer. Suffice it to say, a full discussion could fill up many chapters, if not books! All, however, can be said to represent some kind and degree of voluntary internationalism—constructive, for the most part, in its intent and often in its outcome as well.

VOLUME OF NORTHERN SUPPORT

It must be candidly noted that hard data which speak to the volume of voluntary development assistance in the field of adult education are difficult to find and educe.

As regards the total value of assistance by and through these channels, the Human Development Report notes that total Northern NGO grants to programs and projects in Southern countries (out of privately generated revenues) amounted to about $5 billion (U.S.), up from $1 billion in 1970. About two thirds of this figure comes from private contributions and about one third from governments, though the proportions vary from about 10% in Austria, Ireland, and the United Kingdom, to more than 80% in Belgium and Italy. Government contributions increased from under $200 million in 1970 to $2.2 billion in 1990. The Report goes on to say that:

> Taking private and government contributions together, the total transferred by and through northern NGOs increased from $1.0 billion in 1970 to $7.2 billion in 1990—in real terms twice the rate of increase for international development assistance (United Nations, 1993, p. 88).

However, this amount remains "still a small proportion of overall flows from North to South, equivalent to 13% of net disbursements of official aid, and only 2.5% of total resource flows to developing countries" (Ibid.).

When it comes to assessing how much of the total volume of voluntary and nonprofit development assistance is devoted to adult education, however, the problem becomes much more complex. There are two reasons why this is so. Since statistics are kept in ways that are not wholly comparable from country to country, reliable estimates are hard to come by. Secondly, programs or projects which would not be categorized under headings such as "adult education" or "literacy" frequently have an adult education component or are infused with adult education methodology. It would be a rare maternal and child health clinic or agricultural extension project, for instance, which would not be, in large measure, about the education of adults. Yet, the project would, in all likelihood, be called a health or an agricultural project for statistical purposes. By the same token, leadership development in cooperatives, trade unions, associations of women, peasant farmers, ethnic or cultural minorities, etc., or the extension of legal assistance to political prisoners and diverse other ventures, might well be called by other names. Yet, they would, in fact, be educational. What can fairly confidently be said is that the portion of the total dedicated to the education of adults, in its broadest sense, would not be insignificant.

SOME TRENDS

It is recognized by all observers of the voluntary development organizations that much evolution of thinking and practice has occurred. One very helpful schema, advanced by David Korten suggests that there are three generations of voluntary development action, followed by a fourth, as yet only tentatively named (Korten, 1990, pp. 113–32; Brown & Korten, 1991, pp. 44–93).

Generation One

Relief and Welfare: based on emergencies or a recognition of shortages, the agency responds in a way which is intended to relieve the distress. The beneficiary is usually an individual or a family, and the benefactor manages the response.

Generation Two

Community Development: the focus is on the mid to longer term and involves some sort of community level organization. The object of the project activity is usually a neighborhood or a village.

Generation Three

Sustainable Systems Development: recognizing that the forces which shape or limit development are larger than the community, and may indeed be global, the focus shifts to changing the system. The agency addresses issues of policy through public education and/or policy interventions with national governments, multilateral institutions, and so on.

These three generations are followed by another, tentatively called "people's movements." These are based on ideas, values, and visions. The global network of activist groups and voluntary development and environmental agencies, which coalesced around the Rio de Janeiro Earth Summit in June 1992, offers a glimpse of what this generation might look like. Korten suggests that:

> Fourth generation strategies look beyond focused initiatives based on changing specific policies and institutional sub-systems. Their goal is to energize a critical mass of independent, decentralized initiative in support of a social vision (Korten, 1990, p. 127).

Within the fourth generation of activity, VIDOs can play a service role, contributing their experience, expertise and contacts. Any voluntary organization may well be engaged in activities from more than one of these generations and, indeed, all four. The International OXFAM family would be a good example. The original member, OXFAM (UK), began during the World War II as a small "first generation" response to the distress resulting from the war (Black, 1992). Though it continues to respond to emergencies internationally (generation one), it is widely known for its support of development projects in the South (generation two). Since the mid 1970s, it has engaged in policy research and advocacy on issues ranging from food aid to pesticides, to the debt problem, and to apartheid as a denial of development, thereby placing itself well within the third generation. That their research, publications and advocacy provide a service to broader international development, social justice, peace, human rights and environmental movements, would presumably entitle the International OXFAM family members to take their place in fourth generation as well.

Many observers of the evolving VIDO scene would agree with the general progression sketched by Korten. Though there are many organizations which find it more comfortable to remain in the familiar first generation cradle, there appears to be a wide measure of agreement that VIDOs and IDIs must address the policy issues which intimately affect their work. Indeed, their observations and experience—to say nothing of their sense of justice—often oblige them to speak out on issues of gender, debt, terms of trade, structural adjustment programs, and other pressing problems. Furthermore, Southern partners frequently expect their Northern partners to play such a role, and official institutions up to and including the World Bank are, increasingly, calling on advice from the NGOs, Southern and Northern alike.

ADULT EDUCATION PROGRAMMING TRENDS

To return to adult education as a special field of activity, most projects would tend to fall under Korten's generation two or three headings. Adult education would not normally be regarded as relief, though emergency response projects often involve education of people in matters such as nutrition, hygiene, human shelter and the like. Notwithstanding the emergency relief character of the response, the educational components would be developmental in their intent.

Northern VIDOs and IDIs have long regarded adult education as a development activity. Within this general recognition, however, different agencies have followed a variety of directions and strategies.

Some of the organizations which, from their beginning, specialized in literacy training still do. Most, however, reflect an evolution of thinking and practice over time. Laubach Literacy International, which traces its origins to the work of its missionary founder, Dr. Frank Laubach, in the Philippines in 1930, is one such agency.

> The mass literacy programs of the 1950s and early 1960s, conducted principally by volunteers from the United States, gave way to nationally run programs in the mid-sixties and early 1970s. Programs that began with the view that illiteracy is the cause of an individual's poverty came face-to-face with the broader social causes of poverty. In the process, the illiterate themselves assumed responsibility for their own educational programs and materials . . . *the programs became more and more immersed in the world of the poor.* The themes are now selected by the people themselves (Griffin-Nolan, 1993, p. 6. Emphasis added).

World Literacy of Canada (WLC) describes three phases in its development, each of which roughly corresponds with a decade of its history. The first decade was characterized by the missionary orientations of its founders and the support it extended to the Literacy House of Lucknow, India, as virtually the only project of its formative years. WLC was deeply influenced by Dr. Welthy Honsiger Fisher, founder of Literacy House and the organization's second honorary president, as well as by Dr. Frank Laubach, its first honorary president. The second decade, one of expansion and diversification, tended to regard literacy as an aspect of economic development. The third decade emphasized human development rather than the more capital intensive projects of the previous ten years. Though the principal focus remained on literacy in its traditional sense, other projects such as popular theater, workers' education, nonformal education, skills training for women, etc., received support as well.

By way of contrast, World Education Inc. of Boston (WEI), which shared common origins with World Literacy Canada, has pursued a somewhat different course. In a discussion of the Tototo Home Industries Project of Kenya, this observation is made:

> Although starting as a literacy agency, WEI gradually came to see that literacy would only make sense to people when they saw the connection between literacy and daily life: money, good health, improvement of community services, etc. As a result, WEI now provides training and technical assistance in non-formal education for adults, with special emphasis on community development, small enterprise promotion, food production, literacy and health education (Leach et al., 1988).

In the same report, the authors underline an issue which is a point of lively debate within adult education circles:

> WEI challenged the conventional wisdom which held that literacy was the necessary precursor to any other development related education. The organization's field experience suggested that people are motivated to learn when they perceive the learning as critical and of immediate importance in their daily lives (Ibid., p. 8).

Nevertheless, group training remains vitally important. As the managing director of this project notes:

> All training is group-based ... at Tototo, we have discovered that those individuals who maintain strong group affiliations are more likely to succeed in their individual micro-enterprise endeavours. . . . Leadership training is just as important as business management training (Mutua, 1993).

This paradox illustrates an old theme of concern to adult educators. Striking the right balance between objectives of individual and collective benefit is an issue with which many have struggled. If WEI's experience is any guide, even so individual an activity as microenterprise credit finds the group and social dimension of the training necessary.

Finally, though beyond the mandate of this chapter, mention needs to be made of the development education efforts of VIDOs and some IDIs within their home societies. From an idea considered somewhat irrelevant prior to the mid-1970s and, in some instances, regarded as an almost immoral way to spend monies contributed by donors, development education has become an essential aspect of the programs of most agencies. Development education, when it addresses church congregations, trade union members, professional associations, VIDO donors, study circles and so on, is adult education.

HAVE THE NORTHERN NGOs MADE A DIFFERENCE?

Any assessment of the cumulative impact of the Northern voluntary organization involvement in adult education in the South—of both the favorable and the unfavorable effects—could fill volumes. Perhaps a couple of examples might be instructive.

Both of these cases involve national literacy campaigns, though their circumstances, origins, content and methodologies differ one from the other. Both proceeded from the assumption that adult education is an essential contribution to development, indeed to a process of human liberation. Furthermore, both attracted a substantial amount of solidarity and financial support of part of the international VIDO community.

Parenthetically, it should be emphasized that the choice of two large projects, one of immense organizational proportions, should not, in any way, suggest a belittling of smaller, more local and modest projects—which are no less significant or valuable to those involved. These particular examples are cited simply because they show what is possible with single-mindedness of purpose, and with concerted national effort and North-South solidarity, and also because so many Northern VIDOs from different countries became involved and lent their support.

Namibia

The first of the two cases is the Namibia Literacy Programme (NLP). It describes itself as a "national service organization" for the purpose of uplifting the socio-economic position of black Namibians and their self-confidence and self-reliance.[3] First established in 1971 as a branch of the Bureau of Literacy and Literature, Johannesburg, it became registered in 1984 as an independent association under its new name and with its own annual general meetings and elected board of directors. From the outset, it was closely associated with the Namibian churches, through the leadership of bishops and pastors at the board level, the use of church buildings for classes, and the supervision of local clergy as monitors, although its membership is individual-based.

Classes in literacy are supplemented by sewing, community health, nutrition, writing, English language, etc. The Programme has also developed post literacy materials on breast feeding, family planning, control of diseases such as malaria and cholera. Thus, literacy was seen as part and parcel of the development process. An orientation to the needs of women is also noteworthy. With the coming of independence, it added voter education to the courses offered in the literacy centers, in this way too demonstrating that adult education is intricately bound up with all aspects of the development of peoples and societies.

The literacy and skill development classes are held in centers throughout the country, although during the war of liberation, especially in the North, with its attendant security threats, travel restrictions, and harassment by the South African military, it became extremely difficult to carry on. Nevertheless, carry on they did!

In one typical year, 1988, the Programme reported that it had trained 151 group leaders and that some 2,609 learners had participated in classes held in seven regions. In the same year, 1,147 students were graduated.

Several Northern VIDOs contributed to the work of the NLP. Among them were Miserior, EZE, and Bread for the World (Germany), two OXFAMs (UK and Canada), Intermedia (U.S.A), Interfund (Geneva) and Christian Aid (United Kingdom).

The NLP is noteworthy, not only for its benefits to individual learners, but also for its contribution to nation building in Namibia. There are two levels of contribution. First and most obvious, there was human resource development of participants and the nation alike. However, the fact that a social organization of this prominence was able to continue functioning during a protracted liberation struggle was, in itself, a significant contribution to that very process of national liberation, as well as to the establishment of a durable institution.

Nicaragua

The second example was the 1980 National Literacy Crusade of Nicaragua. As a national adult education mobilization effort, the Crusade was unprecedented in its scale, its sheer ambitiousness and its outcomes. While numbers alone cannot capture the spirit of the project, they offer a glimpse of its character. As Valerie Miller notes,

> More than half a million people, students and teachers alike, participated directly in the campaign as learners—some 460,000 as students of literacy *and about 95,000 as students of the nation's reality, its problems and its potential* . . . some 406,000 literacy students demonstrated their mastery of elementary reading and writing skills by passing a five-part final examination. From an effective rate of 40 percent, illiteracy was reduced to some 13 percent. Besides reading and writing skills, students also had the opportunity to develop mathematical and analytical skills and to express themselves in public while studying history and the national development program (Miller, 1985. Emphasis added.).

It is estimated that over one fifth of the population participated directly in the campaign as organizers, teachers and learners (Ibid., p. 200). Impressive though the sheer scale and numbers are—and the fact that all this was accomplished in a mere five months—literacy alone was not the only value of the exercise.

Because the programme was conceived of as a mutual process of learning and human development, the teacher corps and support staff were also learners. To varying degrees, these people acquired new depths of understanding about the problems of poverty and the challenge of development (Ibid., p. 199).

Teachers are learners too, and education is development!

For the Crusade's impressive efforts, UNESCO awarded it its 1980 first prize for "distinguished and effective contributions on behalf of literacy."

The heroism and the accomplishments of the Crusade, of course, belong to Nicaraguans—the organizers, the young brigadistas and the learners alike. This was, however, a moment when numerous international VIDOs rose to the occasion. Many had already recognized in Nicaragua a climate favorable to the kind of people-centered development which they wanted to support. Most recognized as well—some intuitively and others more explicitly—the validity of this statement:

> From the beginning, the Nicaraguan experience was intended as a political action with educational implications. In this sense, although literacy was a central objective, this objective was to serve the larger purpose of promoting the growth and development of the learners as full, participating members of the society (Carmen St. John Hunter, Foreword to Miller, 1985, p. xiv).

There was, however, a further political dimension, which participating Northern agencies could not escape. The Sandinista government of Nicaragua was, at the time, under attack by the opposition Contras, aided, armed, and trained by the United States. Other Western governments continued to provide development assistance to the country with varying degrees of enthusiasm and reluctance. At the same time, Northern VIDOs, in the belief that a massive injustice was being done, used their own involvement in the Crusade, and other Nicaraguan development projects, to steer their own governments and public opinion towards greater involvement. This they did through a variety of means: on-the-ground participation (which was the basis of their credibility), coalition-building, research, publications, development education, and policy advocacy.

TOWARDS A CONSTRUCTIVE VOLUNTARY
INTERNATIONALISM

It is obvious to most observers that North-South relations are changing.[4] Korten's first generation activity, while remaining the norm in some
quarters, is manifestly inadequate if the object is well-rooted and sustainable development conceived and directed by indigenous actors within the
South. Mere relief, though necessary in emergencies, is too limiting as an
end in itself. Furthermore, the old missionary style of international assistance is likely to encounter increasing resistance, if not outright rejection,
as Southern VDOs and POs become stronger and better able to assert
their rights, their views and their visions.

Future relations will need to be guided more by the substance, not
only the language, of partnership. In a set of Policy Guidelines for North-
South relations, ICVA asserts, *inter alia*, that,

> Southern and Northern non-governmental organizations (NGOs) should
> collaborate together on the basis of equitable and genuine partnerships
> that grow out of mutual respect and trust; compatible purposes, strategies
> and values; and a two-way exchange of information, ideas and experience
> ... partnership implies *an equality of commitment and involvement* (In-
> ternational Council of Voluntary Action, 1991, p. 111. Emphasis added.).

Partnership implies something fundamentally different from the relationship of donor and supplicant. It suggests a shared view of the world
and a mutual commitment to working internationally and jointly on
problems. No longer, therefore, will it be adequate for northern VIDOs
or development education associations to conduct their public education
efforts from a detached or theoretical standpoint or based on case examples far removed from experience. For reality to prevail, development
education and policy advocacy must grow out of a mutual agenda for
change in the world in which there is an agreed division of labor but also
a shared vision of the world that needs to be built.

Another reality which Northern VIDOs must face is that, sometimes, they may not themselves be the most natural partners for their
Southern counterparts. In some instances, this may mean a mutual agreement to pursue other activities and partnerships. In others, it may mean
that Northern VIDOs need to facilitate linkages with other social movements (thereby entering "generation four" terrain). A European or North
American organization which works locally in energy conservation, co-

operative housing, labor education, or services for abused women, will probably have the potential for more fruitful dialogue and a mutually supportive relationship with Southern counterparts than would a large and successful fund raising organization, important though the transfer of resources may be.

There is evidence, as well, that focus is shifting from the project to a more comprehensive and multifaceted level of organizational or institutional strengthening. If development is, and must be, directed from within and not from outside a society, the position of the national and local VDO and PO is of critical importance. As Northern VIDOs move through the generations, therefore, they must, of necessity, be less and less in a position of delivering services and more and more of enabling and empowering local partners to do the development work.

There are also increasing demands, quite rightly, that development be sustainable in all of its senses, economically, socially, culturally, politically and environmentally. It is difficult to imagine a development form or strategy which is, at once, sustainable and dependent. Sustainability, therefore, requires an independent basis and direction. External assistance, if it is to support and not undermine sustainability, must be of a kind which enables the local VDOs and POs to do what they would otherwise do, based on their own assessment of need, but to do it more effectively or, perhaps, on a somewhat larger scale. It behooves all Northern VIDOs and IDIs to address the question of sustainability squarely and profoundly.

Voluntary development organizations in both the North and the South presently find themselves at the heart of a debate about the proper roles and responsibilities of the state, the profit-making private sector, and the voluntary sector. So that they do not, by default, find themselves in a situation of either dependency on state funding or an assigned role of filling gaps vacated by the state, thereby reinforcing the view that NGOs are defined as *what they are not* by *those whom they are not*, it is vital that they delineate their own mission. A leading international adult educator from Asia, in a timely reminder of where moral authority should lie, calls for a radical rethinking of the hierarchy of social institutions:

> The reformulation of Civil Society-State relationship puts primacy on strengthening Civil Society. NGOs are one set of institutions within Civil Society. They are, therefore, part of the domain of governance by Civil So-

ciety. . . . Conceptually, therefore, NGOs are located in Civil Society which is supreme vis-a-vis the State and the ruling elites (Tandon, 1991, p. 10).

Finally, there appears to be a growing awareness that the truly major problems of the world are not parochial or even national, but, rather, international, if not global. Whether one is thinking about the degradation of the natural environment, the disposal of toxic wastes, the inequities of the trading system, discrimination against minorities, the apparent worldwide increase in social violence, or militarism and the arms trade, these problems are best dealt with cooperatively and internationally by those who share a vision of a just, humane, and sustainable global community.

THREE CLOSING HYPOTHESES

In discerning new forms of international cooperation and division of labor to address international problems, those organizations which specialize in, or place a high value on, adult education as an essential ingredient of development may well be in a better position than others to work constructively in solving those problems. Adult educators have long had a special sensitivity to the experience and the particular needs of adult learners in their unique situations. They recognize that packaged solutions will not suffice. Moreover, adult educators, or at least those who are part of the socially engaged tradition, have always understood the intimate connections between education and social development.

Secondly, historical changes currently unfolding in both the North and the South (democratization, the shifting roles and responsibilities of the state, the private sector, and the institutions of civil society, for instance) are likely to inform the analysis and the endeavors of socially engaged adult educators. In fact, adult educators have a unique role to play since they have long been concerned with such issues as adaptation to change, gaining control over forces which hinder personal and social development, and the balance to be struck between individual and collective values, action, and purposes of adult education.

Finally, as a general proposition, the voluntary development sector, in both the North and the South, remains well suited to addressing challenging issues, to adapting to changing reality, to designing innovations and to continuing to contribute to solutions to a wide range of pressing social, political, economic, and environmental problems.

If these be true, adult educators and development workers alike should not be short of work or of material for fruitful dialogue!

NOTES

1. A literacy slogan (unattributed), quoted in *Wordlit*, as republished in World Literacy Canada, *Three Decades for Literacy and Development, 1955–1985: A History of World Literacy Canada* (Toronto: 1988), 49.
2. Education for Development, prospectus, Reading, United Kingdom.
3. This and other information following was gathered from Annual Reports, Namibia Literacy Programme, 1985–89, and from project files.
4. For a lengthier discussion of the changing situation of VIDOs in the Canadian context, see Lawrence S. Cumming, "Between Recession and Redefinition: A Case Study of Canadian Voluntary International Development Organizations," Voluntary Action Directorate, Department of Multiculturalism and Citizenship Canada, September, 1992.

BIBLIOGRAPHY

Black, Maggie (1992). *A cause for our times: OXFAM, the first fifty years.* Oxford: OXFAM UK and Ireland.

Brown, L. David and David C. Korten (1991). Working more effectively with nongovernmental organizations. *Nongovernmental organizations and the World Bank: Co-operation for development.* Washington, D.C.: The World Bank.

Griffin-Nolan, Ed (1993). *Movement for peaceful change: Laubach literacy in Latin America.* Syracuse, N.Y.: Laubach Literacy International.

International Council of Voluntary Action (1991). Relations between Southern and Northern NGOs: Policy guidelines. *Adult Education and Development,* 36 (March). Bonn, Germany: DVV/German Adult Education Association.

Korten, David (1990). *Getting to the 21st. century: Voluntary action and the global agenda.* West Hartford, Connecticut: Kumarian Press.

Leach, Mark, Jeanne McCormack, and Candace Nelson (1988). The Tototo Home Industries Rural Development Project. Unpublished paper, December. New York: The Synergos Institute.

Mutua, Elvina (1993). Breaking down the barriers for women entrepreneurs. from Banking on the poor: Credit the works. *Reports,* 30 (Spring): 30. Boston, Mass.: World Education Inc.

Miller, Valerie (1985). *Between struggle and hope: The Nicaraguan literacy crusade.* Boulder, Colorado: Westview Press.
Nyerere, Julius Kambarage (1992). Adult education and development. *Adult Education and Development*, 19 (September). Bonn: DVV/German Adult Education Association.
Tandon, Rajesh (1991). Civil society, the state and roles of NGOs. IDR Working Paper No. 9, August. Boston, Mass.: Institute for Development Research.
United Nations (1993). *Human development report 1993.* New York: The United Nations.

CHAPTER 4

The Political Economy of Nongovernment Organizations

PAUL WANGOOLA

Defining NGOs is like defining God in the Hindu tradition. God is defined by what He is not, rather than by what He is. In the case of NGOs, this has two immediate problems. The first is that to define NGOs in relation to government tends to give the impression that government is primary, and has been with us virtually from time immemorial and will be with us for eternity. The second is that an impression is given that NGOs are very different, even qualitatively different, from government.

In reality, government is a recent phenomenon in the long history of humanity. For millennia the human muscle was the basic or a major supply of power. Because mechanically the "human machine" is extremely inefficient, to be able to survive in the face of awesome nature, men and women had to make up for the low technological levels with closely knit and highly disciplined social organization, usually based on blood relationship and kinship. Because the level of technology was such that adequate food and other material needs could not be assured, let alone a reliable surplus realized, every able-bodied person was mobilized into productive action. As a result, each was a producer and a consumer at the same time. Production was only possible in collective production units of families, or groups of families. The demands of survival and the force of social organization, socialization, values, and ethics were such that for members of the production unit (family) the possibility of not engaging in production, so that they consumed without production, could not arise.

For millennia, men, women, and their children survived through collective production and collective consumption. The equalizing power of

59

labor meant that governance was through direct participation: decisions were by consensus—not by the disempowering "representation" and simple majority of today. In this social organization, individual rights and interests were subordinated to the community interests. Indeed, any personal interests and rights could only be enjoyed to the extent that they enhanced the common good. Society was so cohesive that the disabled were a community responsibility and there was no category of the needy. Indeed, among the Imara of Bolivia, for example, there was no word for "poor."

The rise of exploitative socio-economic governmental systems, culminating in feudalism, capitalism, and imperialism made it possible for a section of society to consume without production. Because this was resisted by the people, there were incessant wars for property, territory, and power to extract more of the people's labors. The inevitable disruption which ensued divided the people into rich and poor, powerful, and powerless; and, in addition, increasingly destroyed the capacities of the communities to look after the welfare of everybody. Indeed the communities themselves became a casualty. As the communities were disabled, it became necessary for special organizations to emerge to look after the poor, the disabled, the dispossessed, the wounded, etc. Charitable and relief organizations emerged this way in Europe, as the first NGOs. The first NGOs were mostly church-related or church-sponsored.

By the end of the fifteenth century, Europe had started to globalize her wars for property, trade, annexation, occupation, colonization, and generally disrupted and destroyed cohesive societies, their social forms of organization, philosophies, science, technology, value systems, and knowledge bases. In a word, people's sovereignty was usurped. This process increasingly impaired the capacities of communities the world over to be self-reliant and to care for their communities' welfare. Indeed, whole communities, nations, and empires were subjugated or compromised such that they were polarized between the haves and have nots, with hundreds of millions of uncared-for destitutes, poor, disabled, shelterless, starving, etc. This development spanned several centuries, accelerating especially since the landing of Christopher Columbus in the "New World" in 1492. Since then, the North has employed a succession of forms of militarism, the preference being for force to secure certain political and economic interests, with growing efficiency in the incapacitation of communities to provide for their welfare, including looking after the poor and the weak. The major stages of militarism have included *mercantile militarism*, which involved common cheating and thuggery to perpetuate the exchange of unequal values, and *slave trade militarism*, which involved the greatest and most heinous holocaust in human history. All together, about one hundred million Africans were killed, died on the ships, or arrived in the "New World" to work as beasts of burden. The Africans who survived were brutally "transplanted" to the New World and have never recovered from the bondage of poverty, powerlessness, discrimination, and exploitation—just like their sisters and brothers who remained on the African continent.

Coupled with slave trade militarism was the genocide of whole indigenous peoples in North America, Central and South America, Africa, Australia, New Zealand, etc. The indigenous peoples who survived in North America, for example, have since been consigned to "reservations," as has been done to wild animals. In South Africa, the Africans (27,000,000) have been confined to 13% of the mainly poor land, while about 5,000,000 invaders have occupied or fenced off for themselves 87% of the land, starting with the best of the land.

Slave trade militarism was followed by *colonial militarism*, which involved the forcible occupation of the lands in the South, to directly drive the people to work "in the service of the King and country," and, in the process, to destroy further the viability of the people's political, social, economic, cultural, scientific, technological and other systems and cohesion. The period of colonial militarism also involved the laying of the ideological and institutional foundations for the integration of the colonies' economies (now called Third World) into the imperial, "free market" economy. Colonial militarism was then followed by *neocolonial militarism*, which to date has had two stages: the first stage, under the balance of terror, rivalry, and competition between two super powers, the USSR and the USA; and, the second stage, of neocolonial militarism under the monopoly of military terror by one super-power, the USA.

The period of neocolonial militarism has been a time for the maturity of the Bretton Woods institutions, put in place for the accelerated exploitation and impoverishment of the peoples of the Third World. As a result, for example, Africa's "debt" millstone rose from $139 billion (US) in 1981 to $289 billion in 1992; an increase of 108% over the last decade. Yet, this is not so bad! The corresponding figures for sub-Saharan (black) Africa are $63 billion and $183 billion, an increase of 190%. Put differently, in 1990, for every one dollar which came into Africa as "foreign assistance," investment, etc., at least five dollars were repatriated in debt servicing, repayments, "profit" repatriation, etc. In simple terms, this means Africa's debts are unpayable and uncollectable. If Africa tried to pay its debts (clearly a criminal act), or if it was forced into payment, the African peoples would have to starve to death—or else revolt. As a matter of fact, both of these are happening in the villages of Africa and in the slums of its major cities.[1]

Such is the harvest of neocolonial militarism, under conditions of super-power competition and rivalry, which opens the floodgates to neocolonial militarism under conditions of the unity of the North (against the South) and the monopoly of military terror by a lone super power, the United States. This ushers in a "new world order," which gives the United States (with the subordinate support of a handful of the "big" powers) the "mandate," "legitimacy," "right," and "duty" to bully, invade, occupy, or partition any Third World country, confiscate its assets or resources, or assassinate or kidnap its leaders. This stage also involves low intensity conflict/war as a "total war" at the grassroots level, where the enemy is "more or less omnipresent and unlikely ever to surrender" (Kisembo, 1993). The essence of low intensity conflict/war management is to manufacture, exaggerate and plant contradictions among the people, so as to cause chaos among them, such that they kill each other, while shielding pro-North dictatorial governments and regimes. This total war requires "diplomats, information specialists, agriculturalists, chemists, bankers, economists, hydrologists, criminologists, meteorologists . . . all other scores of professionals" (Ibid.).

It is in this light that we have to view the nongovernmental organizations, NGOs. Some no doubt will plead that not every NGO is motivated by the North's self-interest; which is true! But, then, if one were guided by the exception, sight would be lost of the rule. (Exceptions do not invalidate the rule!)

Further, some will also point to very good, well-intentioned people working for NGOs. Fine! But individual goodness or kindness is not the issue. Even among the American, British, and French pilots who rained bombs on Iraq several times the power of the atomic bomb dropped on Hiroshima in 1945, were hundreds who are humane, humble, and loving. But, then, the impact of their works is not assessed on the basis of their kindness and love, but on the damage inflicted, as designed and intended by the military strategists. What is more, the hard-nosed planners, strategists, and free-market economists do not channel over $5 billion (US) through NGOs for unmeasurable objectives like kindness, love, compassion, etc. Simple business logic demands that a five billion dollar budget does a five billion dollar job. Otherwise, American love would first drive American philanthropy to provide shelter to the 3,000,000

American homeless on their door step, long before they traveled thousands of miles to save the starving Somali. Similarly the British would have long cleared the London streets of over 100,000 street and homeless people, before saving the Kurds from biting winter. Even if there was a particular inclination to help the black people, these are not in short supply in the USA, Britain, or France, either.

THE EMERGENCE OF NGOs

All the major NGOs have, as a rule, emerged out of the debris of political, economic, social, and cultural disasters, especially war, social strife, floods, famine, earthquakes; such occurrences as take away people's social institutions for their internal, endogenous governance, sovereignty, and capacities for self-reliance. In the alternative, establishment NGOs have emerged to forestall or undermine the people's initiatives to assert their sovereignty. It is not by chance that many of today's major NGOs were established in the wake of World War II. Yet another set of NGOs were established on the eve of the independence of the colonies (today's Third World).

For some time, the bulk of the NGO work in the post World War II period was in the North, as part of the Marshall plan to rebuild Europe. In time, northern NGO work was extended to the South. Yet, it must be borne in mind that at this early stage, NGO work, except perhaps in respect of church-related NGOs, was extremely limited in scope and impact. Hopes for social transformation, to enable Third World peoples to reassert their sovereignty, and, in unity, to struggle and gradually achieve democracy, national independence, and social progress, and to enjoy cultural freedom, were blocked by colonial state power. Side by side with colonial state power were what could be described as NGOs, for example trade unions, cooperatives, women and youth organizations, professional organizations, etc. Due to the supremacy of the "modernization development theory," the philosophical, ideological, technological, management and sources of expertise, which informed the bulk of the Third World's development thinking, theory and practice tended to be Eurocentric, either rooted in the capitalist mode of the West or the socialist mode of the East. But, because the West enjoyed a historical and cultural advantage, coupled with the emergence of socio-imperialism in the Soviet Union, Third World postindependence development was in fact a continuation of colonial development, i.e. neocolonialism.

Postcolonial leaders quickly discovered they had inherited the shell of a colonial state without any powers; and, in time, trade unions, youth and women organizations, cooperatives and professional organizations, which had been in the first instance conceived and organized by "experts" from the colonial powers, could not be people's instruments in their search for national unity, democracy, national independence, social progress and cultural freedom. It quickly dawned upon everybody, with growing menace and candidness, that the only thing that the modernization development theory and approach had modernized were the instruments and channels for the net transfer of resources from South to North. For example, according to conservative and formal estimates, between 1982 and 1992, over a period of 108 months, the "debtor" countries of the South transferred to the North a mind boggling $1345 billion (US), or about $12.5 billion per month! During the same period, according to the OECD figures, inevitably conservative and deceptive, the total resource flow to the developing countries amounted to $927 billion, leaving at least $418 billion for the North to pocket (George, 1992).

THE EMASCULATION, DECAY AND WITHERING AWAY OF THE THIRD WORLD STATE

With varying degrees of boldness and forthrightness, the International Bank for Reconstruction and Development (the World Bank) and the International Monetary Fund (IMF) determined the commanding heights of Third World economic and social policies. In the case of East Africa—Kenya, Uganda and Tanzania—in the form of "Mission Reports," the World Bank actually wrote the "development plans" of these countries on the eve of their independence. It was not obvious at the time, because of the public euphoria around "independence," and popular confidence in the African leadership. As it happened, the independence leaders took the World Bank mission reports, made the necessary editorial changes, and presented them at the National Delegates Congresses of the "ruling" parties, which adopted them as their economic and social blueprints. The National Delegates Congress accordingly directed the Central Committee to see to their implementation. The Central Committee, in turn, directed the government of the ruling party to transform party economic and social policy into development action. This was done through five-year development plans.

In all this, the hand of the World Bank/IMF was usually unseen to the untrained eye, because they exercised their influence behind the scenes through "advice" and "guidelines"/instructions on how to implement the policies and programs they had authored. But, on the whole, the new governments were given the time and space to implement the development plans. For a time, it appeared as if Third World governments were in charge. This was helped by the fact that several programs had a "modernizing" effect: for example, free and expanded education, health care, agricultural subsidies, better producer prices, job creation, and general economic growth. However, this development was financed by foreign capital. In time, the loans matured and repayment had to start. This increasingly coincided with the growing profitability crisis of the donor countries. Due to historical and structural advantage, the North was able to pass on the bulk of their crisis to the South through conditionalities such as devaluation, wage freeze, price decontrol, the removal of foreign exchange control, the sale to the North of profitable state businesses, unimpeded repatriation of "profits." All this amounted to the South opening itself up for more unbridled looting, and leaving the countries' economies and resources to the mercy of "free market forces."

Third World countries attained independence on the upsurge of yearnings and aspirations for national unity, national independence, democracy, social progress, and cultural freedom. Each government entered a social contract with its people, by which it had to stand with them in the pursuit of their aspirations. In particular, the government had to provide free or subsidized health care, education, agricultural inputs, and to maintain roads, protect people from profiteering, create jobs, ensure the payment of living wages to workers and farmers, and provide an environment conducive to peace and the pursuit of happiness.

These popular expectations assumed a government that was sovereign, which is incompatible with the doctrine and practice of the "free market economy." The free market economy emasculates Third World governments, renders them impotent and illegitimate before their own people, as the power of making policy and other major decisions is removed from them. The World Bank now no longer operates behind the scenes, but comes to the fore to directly address the people and announce policy decisions. It no longer supplies implementation guidelines to Third World governments, but now formulates policy and directly implements, or supervises, its implementation. This was the logic behind the recent appointment by President Kenneth Kaunda—the choice was actually imposed on him—of an expatriate Canadian as governor of the Zambian Central Bank, twenty-five years after independence; or the requirement in 1989–90 of a World Bank/IMF resident official's signature on all cheques issued by the "sovereign" government of Liberia.

Denied the power to take real decisions or run the country, and incapable of fulfilling the independence social contract, a typical Third World government finds that it does not derive its mandate from the people. In the final analysis, its legitimacy is derived from the IMF/World Bank and big power umbrella protection. But, then, neither the people nor the "international community" (white power) respect Third World leaders; often they are openly despised. Unable to face the people, the "international community," or themselves, and frustrated and frightened about the future, many of these leaders degenerate into the pursuit of personal wealth—an enterprise not particularly difficult, as corruption is an essential ingredient of the "free market economy."

THE DECAY AND WITHERING AWAY OF THE STATE

In the end, the peoples of the Third World increasingly come face to face with the IMF/World Bank and the transnational corporations which are actually sucking them dry. On the other hand, they are abandoned by their "leaders," who join in the loot by lining their pockets with commissions and justifying the pauperization of the people. As the state and its social services are dismantled, of necessity the people have to organize themselves in community and cultural mutual aid and solidarity organizations, in order to cater to their social welfare and assure their survival. In this form of social action, people usually revert to traditional forms of organization as the only humane form of social praxis in their collective survival memory.

On their part, eager to cash in on popular disillusionment with, and opposition and hostility to, the neocolonial state, the IMF/World Bank, the transnational corporations, and big power governments distance themselves from their own creation, the neocolonial state, and accuse and hold it responsible for the deteriorating economic situation. This, the neocolonial state is supposed to have achieved through mismanagement, corruption, and infidelity in the implementation of the policies and programs handed down by them (the World Bank, etc.). Further, they become the self-proclaimed defenders and admirers of grass-roots initiatives, as the real efficient, flexible, popular, and inexpensive alternative to the state. In the meantime, old and established northern NGOs open offices and extend their "services" to the South, while thousands of new ones are founded and funded to extend general and specialized services. Today, billions of dollars are now channeled through these NGOs to do development work, often as an alternative to government.

Northern NGOs, through the use of money, have supported already existing southern NGOs or catalyzed the formation of thousands of new ones to work with as "partners." But, in reality, the southern NGOs are used to legitimize the presence of northern NGOs and personnel ("experts" and "volunteers") in the South. It is the very method which the big powers have used to legitimize their military bases in the South, as this is done "at the invitation of sovereign governments." Experience has quickly demonstrated that, soon after the invitation, northern NGOs want to bypass the southern NGOs, especially in Africa, so as to "directly work with and benefit the grassroots, the poorest of the poor." Consequently, in Africa today there are more white people roaming the continent as "development workers," "experts," "volunteers," "missionaries," etc., than at any other time in its history. They have penetrated nooks and areas which had never been visited by white people before. They carry out some of the simplest tasks, for example, handing out to participants at a village workshop an out-of-pocket allowance of five dollars.

The apparently philanthropic work of northern NGOs in the South has a material base in the harsh conditions faced by the people. That notwithstanding, the systematic manner in which the NGO enterprise has been approached, and big money channeled through this sector, suggests that the driving force is not charity, although this is not to rule out some philanthropic considerations. This is especially the case, since the moneys available to northern NGOs, and through them, or otherwise, to their southern counterparts, are voted by the northern governments. Often the funds are voted through ministries of foreign affairs, strongly suggesting that such "charity" is an instrument of foreign policy. This notwithstanding, northern NGOs are usually not open or forthcoming on their relations with their governments. Moreover, they usually run their affairs in the South without transparency or accountability. Their southern partners are deliberately kept in the dark on the sources of finance, e.g., total budget and allocations, especially the salaries and operating costs of the expatriates. What is more, while the northern NGOs insist on reporting from their southern "partners," they themselves rarely share the reports they compile. While they institute evaluations of their partners every now and then, they rarely allow themselves to be evaluated by their southern "partners."

If there is anything that is clear about NGOs, it is that they are not an alternative to the neocolonial state as vehicles, or instruments, for the people to realize their aspirations for democracy, sovereignty, and social progress. In Zambia and Zimbabwe, for example, it costs about $100,000 a year to maintain one volunteer, in countries with a per capita income of about $300. The NGO initiative, in objective, or effect, is to join in the "total war" against the people, by operating at levels they are "unlikely ever to surrender," but to do so "in order to capture the goodwill of the people."

In the present-day world order, where the line of antagonistic contradiction is no longer between East and West, but between South and North, NGOs are one of the instruments for the continued conquest and occupation of the South. They join in the marginalization of Third World governments and indigenous NGOs and leadership, so as to directly rule the people at the grass roots. This way, the North's latest conquest would be complete: the World Bank/IMF, big powers, and transnationals rule from above, while NGOs govern from below—central authority from above and local government from below.

Needless to say, all of this is usually done in the name of empowering the grass roots. But, how can people who are busy disempowering the leadership of local NGOs be trusted with the empowerment of the marginalized people?

CONCLUSION

NGOs have been the fruit of "modernization" and the disruption/destruction of cohesive societies and their human needs-based economic system, based on collective production and collective consumption for the benefit and welfare of all. In the last five hundred years, NGOs have become a particular necessity in the wake of the globalization of white power and the concomitant destruction and extinction of more humane and environment-friendly societies, and their economic, social, cultural and value systems. More so than before, northern NGOs and their subordinate southern partners are part of the problem, rather than part of the solution. The latter do nothing to assist the people to regain their sovereignty, so as to control resources in their historical eco-regions and take decisions on how to run their lives in participatory, democratic and consensual institutional frameworks. The way forward to people's sovereignty lies in a plurality of economic, political, social, cultural and value systems, without any one of them assuming superiority over, or proselytizing, others. What is needed is a world without the concept of heathens and believers, but where people accept their cultural heritage as second to none but also superior to none: a world where people live within their own material, cultural, and spiritual means.

It would appear that to achieve this, the South and North need to delink. They must learn to live on their own, and to articulate new values, principles, frameworks and institutions, for a new relationship devoid of any form of hegemony.

NOTE

1. For closely argued analysis see *Sustainable Development*, a Fortnightly Bulletin (Sandon NGO Research, 8 Elsworth Avenue, Belgravia, Harare, Zimbabwe), 2 (8).

BIBLIOGRAPHY

George, Susan (1992). *The debt boomerang*. London: Pluto Press.
Kisembo, Paul (1993). *A popular version of Yash Tandon's militarism and peace education in Africa*. Nairobi, Kenya: African Assocation for Literacy and Adult Education.

PART TWO

Bilateral Government Donors

CHAPTER 5

Canada: Official Development Assistance and Human Resource Development

JACK D. McNIE AND DANIEL C. ANDREAE

> "The right to learn is not only an instrument of economic develop-
> ment; it must be recognized as one of the fundamental rights. The
> act of learning, lying as it does at the heart of all education activ-
> ity, changes human beings from objects at the mercy of events to
> subjects who create their own history. The right to learn is an indis-
> pensable tool for survival of humanity."
>
> —UNESCO, Paris, 1985

The purpose of this chapter is to detail Canada's role in, and contributions to, international development from the perspective of human resource development. Human resource development (HRD), as an integral component of international development assistance, will first be
viewed from a historical perspective and then its philosophy, principles
and goals will be outlined. Then, the governmental and nongovernmental organizations responsible for implementing Canada's Official Development Assistance (ODA) will be addressed, together with the impact of
Canada's official aid strategy on adult education and training in the developing world.[1]

Over the years, Canada has adopted and practiced a generous policy
in regard to international development assistance. It currently ranks
eighth among the countries of the Organization for Economic Co-operation and Development (OECD), in terms of budget for Official Develop-

ment Assistance (ODA) as a percentage of GNP. The 1989 comparison shows the Nordic countries, the Netherlands, France, and Belgium ranking higher than Canada, followed by Germany, Australia, Japan, the United Kingdom, and the United States. No measure appears to have been taken of the HRD component in each country's aid program, but Canada is well up front in its overall commitment to economic and social development through education and training.

Historically, Canada has been playing a role in international development since the nineteenth century, when the first missionaries and volunteer educators traveled overseas. However, Canada's Official Development Assistance (ODA) commenced in 1946 following World War II, when planning began for the transfer of technology and funds to developing countries. Countries in Asia, which had supported Britain during the conflict, were seeking independence. Therefore, at that time, Canada began to accept trainees from these formerly British Commonwealth countries.

By 1951 it had become apparent that assistance to developing countries was more of a permanent commitment than had previously been realized and the Department of Trade and Commerce established the International Economic Technical Co-operation Division, which, in addition to comprising a section for trainees and experts, also had a section for capital assistance projects, for example, the building of schools. During the 1950s, most of Canada's foreign aid was targeted to Commonwealth countries in Asia and was primarily composed of food and infrastructure assistance. In 1958, a new central administrative unit, called the Economic and Technical Assistance Branch, was set up within Trade and Commerce. This branch put a greater emphasis on technical assistance and less focus on capital assistance.

In 1960, the External Aid Office (EAO) was formed, consisting of a staff of sixty and a budget of 82 million Canadian dollars. One minister, the secretary of state for external affairs, assumed responsibility for all aid functions. The EAO was headed by a director general, supported by five directors; of these, one was for education, which included academic scholarship programs under which students were brought to Canada, and one was for technical assistance, which involved recruitment of Canadian advisors.

The EAO was responsible for the placement of funded trainees from such agencies as the United Nations Economic, Social and Cultural Organization (UNESCO) and the International Labour Organization (ILO). The year 1960 marked the beginning of the First Development

Decade sponsored by the United Nations. Canadian assistance to francophone Africa began in 1961 and was followed in 1964 with the first Canadian government aid to Latin America. In 1968, the government
declared its intention to seek diplomatic relations with the People's Republic of China.

The name of the External Aid Office was changed in 1968 to Canadian International Development Agency (CIDA), through a policy statement by Prime Minister Trudeau, and was headed by Maurice Strong.
There was a growing realization that human resources development, including education and training, formed an indispensable part of development assistance policy. In 1970, the Liberal government issued a white
paper, entitled "Foreign Policy for Canadians," which set the course for
foreign policy for a decade. The sector paper on international development, which comprised part of the "Foreign Policy for Canadians" series,
stressed the need for balanced development assistance programs that included sufficient technical assistance and education training components
to increase the "absorptive" capacity of developing countries. The paper
also made reference to the need for an International Development Research Centre (IDRC), which was later formed in 1971, which would
help to correct the disproportionate expenditure on research and development being directed at that time to more industrialized countries.

During the 1970s, CIDA increasingly stressed two new areas. An advisor for integrating women into development policy and practice was
appointed in 1976, setting the stage for a new agency policy and plan of
action regarding the integration of women into all developmental capacities. In 1977, the Industrial Corporation Program was established.

At the end of the decade, nongovernmental organizations had yet to
receive significant attention. It is worth noting, for example, that when
the Brandt Commission released its report, "North-South: A Program of
Survival," in 1979, it did not make strong mention of the role of nongovernmental organizations or of the role of adult education in the program
for survival, although it did urge support of UNESCO's efforts to promote literacy and the need for public education.

In keeping with an increasing focus on education and training,
CIDA, in 1984, published "Elements of Canada's Development Policy,"
which emphasized human resource development as one of the three priority sectors, along with energy and agriculture, including forestry and
fisheries.

The section on human resources development (HRD) noted that the
objectives were to increase skilled human resources in developing coun-

tries, to reach target groups which have been bypassed by economic growth, and to meet basic human needs by improving labor productivity.

In 1985, the newly elected Progressive Conservative government submitted a discussion paper in Parliament titled, "Competitiveness and Security . . . Directions for Canada's International Relations." This paper emphasized the need for enhancement of human capital through technical education and training, cooperative education, industry-university collaboration, and development of Centres of Excellence.

A special task force of the Senate and House of Commons, which was set up to report on issues emerging from this discussion paper, reaffirmed that the major goal of Canada's assistance program should be to meet the needs of the poorest countries. The government response argued that Canada's aid program would be placing greater emphasis on human resources in the developing countries. The government paper argued that an aid program that transfers mainly goods and equipment without the skills to manage and maintain them is ultimately doomed to failure.

In 1986, the Standing Committee on External Affairs and International Trade, with members from Canada's three main political parties, began a review focusing exclusively on Canada's official development assistance. Three previous policy papers—"Competitiveness and Security," "Independence and Internationalism," and "Canada's International Relations"—had focused on Canada's foreign policy, with only a brief segment devoted to development assistance. The Committee, chaired by W. Winegard, produced the landmark report in 1987, "For Whose Benefit? Canada's Official Development Assistance Policies and Programs." The primary themes which emerged included:

— Changing emphasis from the building of things to human resources;
— Changing the emphasis from short-term to long-term relationships; and
— Changing the emphasis from Ottawa based decision making to conducting development in the field.

This report highlighted the need for partnerships, indicating that projects defined and implemented without active participation of the people they are intended to benefit, remain the projects of outsiders and are invariably unsupported and unassimilated. According to Rex Nettleford, "Solutions to problems of the developing world will have to be found in the developing world, whatever the help from the outside may be."[2]

The Winegard Report is important because of the priority it places on human resource development. One chapter in the report is devoted entirely to education and training. Human resource development is seen as multifaceted, embracing such sectoral activities as education, health and nutrition, in addition to the learning elements in all development, including technical assistance and personnel training. This report recommended a significant shift in priorities and expenditures in CIDA from large-scale capital projects to human development programs. The report targeted three human resource development areas, including women, primary health care, and education. However, most importantly, it recommended that a basic human needs element be strongly integrated into all bilateral development programs and that it particularly benefit the poor and women.

With regard to education, the Winegard Report indicated that CIDA should substantially increase bilateral assistance for education at the primary level, in particular, for literacy programs. This, it was believed, would, among other things, contribute to lower birth rates and help ameliorate the population problem. Within the educational sector, it was recommended that CIDA should also pay particular attention to institutions providing occupational and technical training. Other specific recommendations include:

- That CIDA establish an additional 1,000 open scholarships for countries over and above the education and training awards currently provided;

- That the government of Canada seek waiver agreements with all provinces that currently apply differential fees to ODA sponsored students;

- That training programs employing Canadian business as a teaching resource be substantially expanded; and

- That the visa and other restrictions that prevent foreign students from gaining work experience in Canada be lifted for ODA sponsored students and trainees.

The Committee also looked at the International Development Research Centre (IDRC), which assists developing countries to build up their research skills and institutions. It was recommended that CIDA and IDRC establish a staff exchange program and that greater efforts be made to use IDRC research in CIDA's human resource development projects, to ensure the practical application of research.

The government's response to the Report by the Standing Committee on External Affairs and International Trade was published in September 1987, entitled, "Canadian International Development Assistance to Benefit a Better World." Of the 115 recommendations of the Winegard Committee, the government fully adopted 98 and partly agreed with another 13.

The government outlined the purposes of development, including:

• To develop human potential;

• To promote social change and improve living standards; and

• To stimulate economic growth and productivity on a sustainable basis.

As well, the government identified six thematic goals for its assistance program that have ramifications for HRD programming. These objectives later became codified as development principles in Canada's Official Development Assistance Charter. These include:

• Poverty alleviation in rural and urban areas, including improved access to education, health, nutrition, employment and decision-making;

• Structural adjustment of economies to cope with debt and reduced export earnings and to improve economic management;

• Increased participation of women in planning and implementing programs and projects, to promote economic growth and solid change;

• Environmentally sound development, which is ecologically sustainable, responsive to human needs and appropriate to the circumstances of the particular developing country or regions, including environmental assessment of all capital projects;

• Food security, including agricultural research, production, extension, post-harvest technology and marketing.

Four major developmental principles for CIDA were outlined in the strategy document, "Sharing Our Future," which was presented in Parliament in 1987. The following paragraphs summarize the principles in Canada's Official Development Assistance Charter:

• Putting Poverty First. The primary purpose of Canadian Official Development Assistance is to help the poorest countries in the world;

• Helping People to Help Themselves. Canadian ODA aims to strengthen the ability of people and institutions in developing countries to solve their own problems, in harmony with the natural environment;

- Development priorities must prevail in setting objectives for the aid programs. As long as these priorities are met, aid objectives may take into account other foreign policy goals;

- Partnership is the key to fostering and strengthening the links between Canada's people and institutions of the Third World.

Canada's Official Development Assistance Charter has placed human resource development, including education and training as a core all-encompassing policy based on the premise that it is crucial if people are to become self-sufficient. According to the 1987 CIDA document, "Sharing Our Future," development is about people. It states that: "People are, in fact, not only the most important resource but the raison d'être of development; both the means and the end. This development of human resources must be a first priority. . . . People must come first if the development process is to make any sense. . . . The new strategy makes human resource development the lens through which all of Canadian development efforts are focused" (CIDA, 1987, p. 30). This is a reaffirmation of the government's response to the earlier Winegard Report, which stated that HRD should be the prism through which all developmental activities will be examined in the context of Country Program Reviews, Projects, and Planning.

According to CIDA, the single most important factor is economic growth and social transformation, and the key to effective systematic and self-reliant development is the capacity which exists within developing countries to manage their own affairs judiciously and effectively. This is corroborated by Serge Wagner in a 1986 report entitled "Adult Education Development and International Aid. Some Issues and Trends." Wagner states:

> Nearly all development projects demand new knowledge and new skills to be acquired. Participation in these projects involves the possibility of responding to such needs. But many evaluations have brought to light the weakness, even the total absence, of educational components inside all projects. What's the use of a development project if the transfer of knowledge and insights is not assured? It has been proven that the impact of many projects has been dependent on the implementation of education activities (Rydström, 1986, p. 17).

Development assistance has the greatest impact when it helps to increase that capacity.

HRD essential elements include:

- Education, formal, informal, and nonformal, which focuses on acquisition of knowledge and general intellectual function;

- Training which focuses on task-oriented skills directly related to employment (including Project Related Training);

- Research which focuses on the generation of new ideas and techniques;

- Institutional development which focuses on the structure and processes for the organization and the management of development.

Government anticipates that these major components will lead to the evolution of values, attitudes, and motivation, and is the organization and mobilization of people in the pursuit of desirable change. Human resource development is intended to cut across all developmental themes and sectors and promote democratization and human rights. It forms the cornerstone for social development, including improved health and nutrition, the ability to regulate family size, to obtain potable water and sanitation, and to provide family and community services which are fundamental to progress and increased opportunities. At the same time, it is recognized that HRD occurs within a broad context, including social and economic institutions that may either impede or facilitate enterprise, affect the constraints of the particular economy, and require increased local infrastructure to implement the economic policies of the identified country. The HRD programs are assigned to address national economic and industrial priorities, strengthen educational systems, improve managerial skills, and improve social delivery systems. Through providing additional resources for training and education in Canada and abroad, it is the government's goal to help develop the knowledge and skills needed for human and technical development.

Consistent with the requirements and job opportunities in developing countries, it is the government's objective to increase resources for high quality and appropriate training and to increase the capacity of institutions in Canada and overseas to meet those needs on a sustained and self-directed basis. To achieve this goal, both nongovernmental organizations (NGOs) and private companies are required to be involved, in order to complement government initiatives in education and training. Also, the government provides support for the development of links among professional associations in Canada and overseas.

CIDA defines the goal of its strategy for education and training programs as strengthening the institutional capacities of developing countries to provide the education and training required for sustainable development. The following objectives tend to address the development issues in this sector, to incorporate the plans and priorities of less developed countries, to reflect CIDA's overall strategy, and to provide more specific directions for pursuing the goal of the strategy. The CIDA goal is:

- To support reform and development of the national and international levels of policies and systems related to education and training;

- To strengthen the quality of the human resource programs and management of education and training systems and institutions;

- To strengthen organizations, improving the quality, relevance and accessibility of education and training, notably for the poor and women;

- To strengthen the capacities of public institutions, NGOs and companies to manage and maintain social and economic progress, technologies and technical capital investments while being responsive to their various communities.

As the federal government agency responsible for official development assistance, CIDA administers 75% of the overall budget. In 1990–91, the official development assistance (ODA) budget amounted to $2.9 billion, of which CIDA's share was $2.1 billion. The remaining 25% of the ODA budget, which is managed by other departments of the Canadian government, is also influenced by the strong continuing HRD focus in ODA's overall strategy and policies. The amount that CIDA receives annually changes in relation to the overall budget. Canada's ODA had reached .5% of the gross national product (GNP) and was maintained at that level until 1991. It is the stated government objective to revise the ODA/GNP ratio by gradual increments that began in 1991–92 to .6% by 1995 and to .7% by the year 2000.

CIDA reports directly to the Ministry of External Affairs and International Development and the Secretary of State for International Affairs. CIDA has 1,250 employees, both in Canada and abroad, with approximately 1,020 at the head office in Hull, Quebec, and 230 overseas. Regional office representatives are stationed in Montreal, Vancouver, Calgary, Winnipeg, and Moncton.

The head of the agency is the president, who holds a position equivalent to a deputy minister and assumes general responsibility for the agency's strategy and activities. The president is supported by the President's Committee, composed of a senior vice president, ten vice presidents and three director generals. Six branches have been established to deal with the internal needs of the agency: Policy, Operational Services, Professional Services, Comptrollers, Personnel and Administration, and Communications which provide services, advice, and specialized support to the agency. Seven other branches have responsibility for implementing development programs. The two program sectors that account for most of the $2.1 billion CIDA budget are the National Initiatives Program and the Partnership Program.

The National Initiatives Program (direct contribution) is the largest, with a budget of $1.28 billion in 1990–91. It includes the important bilateral (government to government) aid, and support for scholarship and other training programs.

The Partnership Program, budgeted at $840 million, supports the efforts of Canadian and international nongovernmental partners. These include universities, colleges, unions, cooperatives, various international service organizations, business groups, and multinational bodies.

The balance of CIDA's budget is accounted for by the agency's Corporate Service Division. Under CIDA's National Initiatives Program, there were a total of 185 bilaterally-funded projects worth approximately $900 million in the four geographic regions and for which CIDA education specialists were assigned as primary resource officers to the project teams.

There were approximately $315 million of active CIDA-funded bilateral education and training projects in Asia, $245 million in francophone Africa, $185 million in anglophone Africa, and $145 million in the Caribbean and Latin America. There were also some 100 projects totaling $1.2 billion in other sectors such as agriculture and energy that have sizable training components and for which CIDA education specialists are assigned as secondary resource officers.

The Partnership Program has several branches. The one most relevant to HRD is the Special Programs Branch, which manages the voluntary sector support projects and the nongovernmental organizations involved in international development work. Their 1990–91 budget was $280 million. Other branches include Business Cooperation, Multilateral Programs, Professional Services, and Personnel and Administration. To varying degrees they are all involved in delivering HRD services to their clients or staff.

A major HRD player in the Special Programs Branch is undoubtedly ICDS, the International and Development Services Program. It was created in 1980 to provide funding for projects which connect Canadian institutions, such as universities, colleges, cooperatives, unions, and professional associations with their counterparts in developing countries. Total funding for ICDS in 1990–91 was $107 million. In that year, there were approximately 190 active CIDA-funded university linkages and 100 active college linkages. Projects are expected to strengthen institutions with regard to local development priorities, and to reflect Canadian strategy for international development, i.e., poverty alleviation, increased participation of women, and sound environmental practices. Complementing this program was a new five-year project to support Canadian universities which wish individually or on a network, collaborative basis, to establish a Centre of Excellence in their area of specialization in international development.

"Elements of Canada's Development Policy" provides, principally through CIDA, considerable opportunity for the education and training of students, trainees, and technical assistance personnel to attend appropriate institutions inside their own country, in Canada, or in a third country, if necessary.

Students are defined by CIDA as individuals from developing countries attending an institution of higher education in a program of at least one academic year, which is leading towards a diploma or degree. Students are classified in terms of level of study, either diploma/certificate, bachelor's, master's, doctorate or postdoctorate. In 1989, there were a total of 4,184 ODA-supported students supported by CIDA, the International Development Research Centre, and other government agencies and crown corporations. Twenty-five percent were female. In 1989, Canadian ODA-supported students were classified as follows: 17% were at the diploma level, 19% at the bachelor's level, 43% at the master's level, 20% at the doctorate level and 1% at the postdoctorate level. Six percent of ODA supported students were studying in their country of origin, 16% in a Third World country, and 78% in Canada. The most popular areas of study for CIDA students were engineering and technology, management and administration, computer science, agriculture, education, economics, and health.

Trainees are defined by CIDA as individuals from developing countries receiving practical training or participating in study and technical tours, or attending short-term courses, seminars or conferences. In 1989, there was a total of 7,868 Canadian supported ODA trainees, of which 33% were female. Sixty-five per cent were in short-term courses, 11% in practical attachments, 10% in study tours, and 14% in conferences. Forty-seven percent were in their country of origin, 18% in Third World countries, and 35% in Canada. The most popular areas of study for CIDA trainees were management and administration, computer science, engineering and technology, agriculture, and education.

Technical assistance personnel are defined by CIDA as personnel who are sent to provide an expert service to developing countries. In 1989, there was a total of 6,347 Canadian ODA-supported technical assistance personnel; of which, 44% had assignments as advisors, 15% as teachers, 14% as trainers, and the balance in assignments such as feasibility consultants, researchers, and evaluators. The most popular sectors of study for them were education, agriculture, health and nutrition.

An extremely important part of the Partnership Program is the Canadian and international nongovernmental sector: the NGOs and IN-GOs, which have been carrying out aid work with counterparts in developing countries at a grass-roots level.

Historically, NGOs are a relatively recent development, at least in their present form. Dr. Hall, former secretary general of the International Council for Adult Education (ICAE), observed in 1986:

> In the age of large and relatively well known governmental and inter-governmental development assistance agencies it may be useful to recall the days not so many years ago when those agencies did not exist. Many of our bilateral agencies are quite young, some ten years old, few twenty years old and very few more than thirty years old. Even the entire United Nations system is a modern project, an institutionalized hope of a better world created after World War II (Rydström, 1986, p. 30).

The literally thousands of NGOs (the Economic and Social Commission of the United Nations has a list of over 20,000), have begun to strengthen links between themselves and other nations, to forge links within sectors such as adult education, to create partnerships between other partners in the South to link up with communities in the north, and, in general, to provide a source of remarkable energy and diversity. Collectively, one could easily assert that the momentum in innovation in either social transformation or economic and social development is provided by this sector.

The 1991 Rio Environmental Conference, for example, demonstrated that NGOs are beginning to represent a third sector different from the state, the corporate sector, and the traditional political parties.

Many INGOs implement education and training projects. In 1990–91, Canadian NGOs with a focus on HRD programs receiving CIDA funding included:

- The Canadian Organizations for Rehabilitation Through Training (ORT), which provides technical training courses for unemployed youth through state and municipal education authorities in Brazil;

- World Literacy of Canada, which focuses on education, particularly adult education and literacy training; and

- The Canadian Organization for Development through Education, which provides paper to organizations producing locally developed educational materials in Third World Countries.

Education and training initiatives are the focus of a number of international nongovernmental organizations (INGOs). In 1990–91, the following NGOs concentrating on human resource development received CIDA support:

- The Inter-American Organization for Higher Education (IAOHE) headquartered in Quebec City;

- The International Council for Adult Education (ICAE) based in Toronto;

- The Foundation for International Training (FIT) based in Toronto.

In Canada, as well as Sweden, Norway, Denmark, the Federal Republic of Germany, and in other western countries, it was the nongovernmental agencies that created the concepts of international cooperation or solidarity. In many countries, committees of citizen organizations, or NGOs, were responsible for channeling development assistance funds from the government before state structures were established. The earliest efforts were often linked to the notion of charity or even religious conversion. But, the history of development assistance draws heavily on efforts from the beginning of this century by media, union movements, the international cooperative movement, the libraries, and other organizations, such as the YMCA.

It was largely as a result of aggressive lobbying by early Canadian adult educators that Canadian governments, during the 1940s and 1950s, undertook unprecedented steps, in concert with the educators, to increase citizen awareness and participation in public policy determination. It was the missionary-like zeal of early popular educators and institutions in Canada that led to the first private, and then public, initiatives to share educational opportunities with the peoples of developing nations. The story of their efforts makes fascinating reading (Welton, 1987).

During the earlier years, CIDA was directly and extensively involved in the organization and implementation of most projects. Today, the implementation is almost entirely contracted out to Canadian executing agencies in the private sector, or by partner institutions in the nongovernment sector. In case of regional programs dealing entirely with training, CIDA may even enter into agreements directly with a partner agency in the developing country. Another CIDA change which has impacted positively on delivery of services is the decentralization of decision making to certain field offices, in cooperation with the Ministry of External Affairs. A number of qualified staff in Canada have been transferred to the field offices, which have authority to approve up to $5 million on their own. Canada maintains control over contributions through binding agreements that determine how the ODA will be expended, usually over a five-year period.

As a result of frequent, independent evaluations in the field, that are an integral part of CIDA programs, changes and modifications will continue to be made. These serve to improve aid delivery and partnership relations, without materially impacting on the overall ODA strategies considered earlier.

However, another kind of evaluation of international aid policy is being performed in all donor nations in these turbulent times, which could have implications for more fundamental changes in policy. In difficult economic times, tax revenues fall, social needs increase, and governments scramble for savings; international aid budgets, often called "soft money," are very vulnerable. How vulnerable depends on many factors: the state of a nation's economy, the leadership and philosophical bent of the government and opposition parties, the influence of special interest groups, the attitude of the media, and, last but not least, the degree of popular support international aid enjoys.

Canada's ODA, unlike some other nations' programs, has been remarkably autonomous and apolitical. Rather than opting for a quick fix to satisfy a domestic political and economic agenda, Canada has sought sustained, indigenous development. Self-reliance, rather than dependence, has been emphasized with human resource development becoming the lens through which all of Canada's development aid efforts are viewed.

Admirable and credible as these long-range approaches may be, international development aid policy understandably lacks the pressing political urgency of a volatile and intensely competitive global scene and of difficult domestic, economic, and social problems.

The Canadian government, recognizing the need for wider public support, has given a high priority in recent years to broadening public awareness and education on development issues and to making its citizens feel they are partners in the program.

However, in the same way that early Canadian educators and institutions played a key role in framing and advancing enlightened international aid in the past, they must now give equally altruistic and spirited leadership if the force and focus of the present HRD strategy is to be sustained and furthered.

NOTES

1. The authors are indebted to many sources. In particular, we recognize the comprehensive February 1991 report by the Canadian International Development agency, entitled "Canadian Official Development Assistance Policies, Programs and Projects for Education and Training," edited by Robin H. Ruggles, Ph.D.
2. In conversation with Rex Nettleford, 1992.

BIBLIOGRAPHY

Beyond North-South: A forum on new forms of international cooperation in adult education (1990). Report on the special international forum held during the Fourth World Assembly on Adult Education for development agencies and nongovernmental organizations to exchange views on the role of international cooperation and adult education, 13–15 January, Bangkok, Thailand. Toronto: International Council for Adult Education.

Jackson, E. T., G. Beaulieu, and I. Pascal (1987). *Expanding the partnership: Report of the evaluation of the International Council for Adult Education.* February. Prepared for the International Council for Adult Education and CIDA. Hull, Quebec: Canadian International Development Agency.

Ruggles, Robin H. (ed.) (1991). *Canadian official development assistance: Policies, programs and projects for education and training.* February. Education and Training Section, CIDA. Hull, Quebec: Canadian International Development Agency.

Rydström, Gunnar (ed.) (1986). *Adult education development and international aid: Some issues and trends.* Final Report of the International Seminar in "The Role of International Aid in Adult Education in Developing Countries," held in Kungälv, Sweden, June. Toronto: International Council for Adult Education.

Welton, Michael (ed.) (1987). *Knowledge for the people: The struggle for adult learning in English-speaking Canada, 1828-1973*. Toronto: Ontario Institute for Studies in Education Press.

The following are publications of the Canadian International Development Corporation, Hull, Quebec, arranged by date.

Canadian international development assistance: To benefit a better world (1987). Response of the government of Canada to the report of the Standing Committee on External Affairs and International Trade.

The first generation: CIDA and international development (1988).

The business of development—CIDA: A guide for the business community (1990). Produced by the Communications Branch, CIDA.

What is CIDA? (1990). Produced by Communications Branch, CIDA.

Canada's aid program in the 1990s and beyond (1992).

CIDA annual report, 1990-91 (1992). Produced by Communications Branch, CIDA.

Executing agencies, Fall/Winter 1992/93 (1992). Coordinated by Consultant and Industry Relations Directorate, CIDA.

Sharing our future: Canadian international development assistance (1987; 1992). Produced by the Communications Branch, CIDA.

CHAPTER 6

Germany: International Cooperation in Adult Education—DVV's Professional Partnership and Solidarity

HERIBERT HINZEN

This chapter outlines the work of the German Adult Education Association's Department [Institute] for International Cooperation (DVV). After reviewing the Department's evolution in the early 1960s, it examines the professional background of its work within the context of aid and solidarity, and presents the guidelines defining its framework, insights, and precepts. It then goes on to describe its partners, programs, and projects, and to discuss matters of organization, management, and financing. Two aspects are given closer attention. The first was chosen to illustrate more clearly, through the example of one of its projects in an African country, an approach taken in cooperation with partners. The other was selected to explain in greater detail the Association's understanding of, and commitment to, the support of literacy.

The scope of this paper is limited in two respects:

(1) There are several other organizations in Germany that also engage in international cooperation in the area of adult education, for example trade unions, political foundations, churches, and development institutions. A separate paper would be necessary to look into the details of their work.

(2) Cooperation with partners in Africa, Asia, and Latin America is a very important feature of DVV's international work. However, the Department for International Cooperation also has an extensive partnership program in Central and Eastern Europe, besides a program to sup-

port professional contacts and activities all over the world. Moreover, there are other DVV institutes and bodies which also maintain international links, in particular with other industrialized countries.

PROFESSIONAL ASSOCIATION

The role played by DVV in adult education in Germany is the backbone of its international work. DVV is the abbreviation for the *Deutscher Volkshochschul-Verband e.V.*, or, as it is called in English, the German Adult Education Association. A more literal translation of the German name would be the German Folk High School Association.

What does DVV do? Every village and town in Germany has a *Volkshochschule* (VHS), or Folk High School, that functions as a center for adult education. In all, there are around 1,070 institutes and 4,230 branches. About six million people are enrolled annually in regular VHS courses and an additional three million attend single-session evening lectures.

The VHS offer programs in foreign language instruction, vocational and secretarial subjects, the liberal arts, as well as in sports and leisure time activities. There are, of course, areas of special concern besides, such as health education, literacy, and social and cultural integration of foreigners.

The VHS are supported and maintained by the local communities, either as voluntary agencies or as part of the respective municipal administrations.

Acting on their own initiative in the early 1950s, the VHS formed eleven regional adult education associations. At that time the Federal Republic of Germany comprised eleven states; now, after unification of West and East, there are sixteen states and the same number of regional associations. The aim was to provide professional services in the form of training, production of materials, consultation and advice, and to represent the joint interests of the *Volkshochschulen* and their participants on a regional level.

In order to represent their local centers and interests at a national level, these regional associations joined in 1953 to form the German Adult Education Association, DVV, which can be described in general as a professional service institution fostering adult education in Germany. It supports organizational and educational work, conducts research and documentation, lobbies for better financing and legislation, and, together with other organizations in the same field, defends adult education on a national level.

In order to meet its many challenges and ever increasing responsibilities, DVV has created three departments or institutes: the Pedagogical Institute in Frankfurt, the Media Institute in Marl, and the Department for International Cooperation in Bonn. In addition, it has established several specialized units and committees. DVV is a nongovernmental organization (NGO), recognized and supported by the German government. Whereas finances for its work in Germany are derived from membership contributions, remuneration for its services, national and state-level funding of specific projects, and its international work in Africa, Asia, and Latin America are fully funded by the German government through the Ministry of Economic Cooperation and Development.

From its professional background it follows that DVV is not an international funding agency, although it readily responds to the call for international solidarity by supporting partners in Africa, Asia, and Latin America.

HISTORICAL ROOTS

The origins of the Department for International Cooperation can be traced back to at least two developments of the 1960s that combined professional work with an aspect of solidarity.

To begin with, adult educators had become more interested in exchanging information and services, and were therefore pursuing international contacts to an ever increasing degree. Already in the 50s there was a growing trend in educational trips and international meetings and conferences for adult educators. This trend reached its culmination in UNESCO's world conferences on adult education. It is clear that the timing of the second world conference in Montreal in 1960 coincided with the rise, particularly in Africa, of anticolonial movements that eventually led to the independence of many new states. There was a notable increase in the number of representatives of governments and adult education institutions from countries in Africa, Asia, and Latin America who participated at the meetings and raised their voices for aid and cooperation in the field of adult education as part of the international development aid programs of bilateral and multilateral organizations.

DVV sent its delegations, too, through whom it was able to generate and strengthen contacts with adult educators throughout the world, initiating the first personal networks of information sharing. Those beginnings were predominantly the work of committed individuals who believed in the importance of international understanding and exchange based on the principle of give and take. It is therefore not surprising that DVV channeled considerable professional input into both the 1960 UNESCO world conference in Montreal and the 1972 conference in Tokyo, and that it followed the invitation to participate in the 1964 founding conference of the Asian-South Pacific Bureau of Adult Education (ASPBAE) in Australia. DVV likewise served as a significant motivating force behind the creation of the European Bureau of Adult Education (EBAE), as well as the International Council for Adult Education (ICAE) in 1973.

However, there is a second factor that led DVV to embark on international cooperation with partners in Africa, Asia, and Latin America. During the late 1950s and early 1960s momentum was accelerating in the international debate and movement to end colonial domination over the people of Africa, Asia, and Latin America. Prompted by growing interest in this area, and in their capacity as local German adult education centers, the VHS began to focus their attention on the countries of the southern continents in their courses, evening lectures, and later even in study tours. They expanded their programs to include such topics as national and international politics of liberation, development aid and international economics, or religions and cultures representing world views different from Europocentric perspectives. During that period, local institutions became important centers for information, discussion, and reflection.

A series of special initiatives paved the way for the expansion and diversification of future work. The first meeting of African and German adult education representatives was held in 1960 at Hirschborn Castle. The first scholarship was awarded to an African colleague in 1961 for further training in the field of adult education in Germany. In autumn 1961 four Cameroonian adult educators participated in a one-year inservice training program at the Volkshochschule in Bremen. During the same year the Cameroonian government invited the director of the residential adult education center Goehrde to implement a training course for adult educators in Cameroon. Then in 1962 an African-German meeting on adult education, with participants from eight African countries, was held at the residential adult education center Falkenstein.

Mention should be made of the important aspect of financial support, without which many of the cited efforts would not have been possible. The independence movements in the colonized parts of the world went hand in hand with the creation of development aid policies, as well as their related institutions, in the industrialized world. In Germany, the Federal Ministry for Economic Cooperation began to take up the challenges and demands issuing from new political and economic realities. It was a fortunate circumstance that contact between the Ministry and DVV was established early on in the process. The people at DVV realized the necessity of securing funds to meet the growing demand for projects of cooperation with a growing number of partners in Africa, Asia, and Latin America. It was clear that the local centers, the regional associations, and other institutions within the adult education movement would be prepared to offer their services and expertise; on the other hand, it was just as clear that their own limited financial resources would not suffice to support the work in partner countries on such a substantial and demanding scale. It soon became evident at the Ministry for Economic Cooperation that confining development aid to financial, economic, and technological aspects would be to neglect important cultural and educational needs and concerns of the people responsible for initiating and carrying on the processes of development. DVV pursued negotiations with the Ministry, and, in 1963, received its first substantial financial support in the field of educational aid.

The two most important projects of the 60s were conducted through the residential adult education centers (VHS) of Goehrde and Rendsburg, where one-year training courses were organized for intermediate level adult educators from Africa and Latin America, respectively. The seminars in Rendsburg for Latin American participants ran from 1965 through 1968, at which point the program was relocated to a DVV supported center in San José, Costa Rica, where it continued to run until 1972. During the program's seven years of existence, it provided training for a total of 250 adult educators from Latin America.

The annual courses in Goehrde for the African adult educators lasted through 1974, for a total of twelve years. Altogether, 277 adult educators from ten countries of Africa participated.

In both courses, the practical matters of teaching and learning, as well as organization and administration, were accentuated, without theoretical foundations being neglected.

In the early 70s, DVV initiated a process of dialogue with representatives from different African countries at the Goehrde seminars for

adult educators, to examine perspectives for developing future cooperation in the field of adult education. It was determined that stronger support should be lent to adult education institutions and projects in selected
countries, in accordance with the interests and needs of the African partners, while taking into consideration the professional experience of DVV
and the availability of funds.

As might be expected, the location of the first bilateral programs of
cooperation was influenced by the institutional and personal ties that had
been formed between DVV and partners from various African countries
who had participated in the one-year residential courses in Germany.
Most of the selected countries had been the setting for courses of several
weeks' duration, designed for adult educators and conducted with
the participation of staff members from the Department for International Cooperation. They included Ethiopia, Sudan, Zaire, Somalia, and
Ghana. The latter was for five years the location of an African Bureau
created in 1975. The regional orientation and the services of this bureau
were subsequently decentralized, and the positive experiences gained
during its existence were passed on to national programs administered
on a bilateral basis.

Although Africa still remained the main focus of the department's
efforts, during the early 1970s extensive programs of cooperation were
launched in Central and Latin America as well. Support went to the In-
stituto Centroamericano de Extension de la Cultura (ICECU) in Costa
Rica, an organization with regional influence, and a project was opened
to help develop the adult education system in Colombia, which even now
is one of the department's major partner countries. Perspectives for new
partnerships were widening, and efforts kept expanding. At the same
time, more and more potential partners from countries in Africa, Asia,
and Latin America were making overtures, often as a result of becoming
acquainted with the Department's work through its journal.

Back in Germany, DVV was making institutional, organizational,
and personnel adjustments, in order to cope with the expanding work
load and the fast pace at which the realities of the various countries,
projects, and partners were changing. At the beginning of the 60s, most
of the work remained under the close supervision of the office of DVV's
Director General. When the two long-term training seminars started,
however, it became necessary to employ specialists for the exclusive task
of administration and teaching at each center. Nevertheless, it was not
until September 1969 that DVV set up a special division to handle the

international dimensions of its work. Initially established under the designation "Department for Adult Education in Developing Countries," the division became the "Department for International Cooperation" in 1977, and was renamed the "Institute for International Cooperation of DVV" at the 1993 DVV General Assembly.

GUIDELINES AND PRIORITIES

An early attempt to define the role of DVV and its work with partners in the development of adult education in Africa, Asia, and Latin America was a memorandum written in 1962 to outline the aims underlying the training of adult educators from developing countries. While arguing for an adult education concentrating on basic education and community development, it took the position that adult education must be viewed as a dimension of technical development assistance. The decisive point of intervention was held to be basic and advanced training of community developers, ministry officials, and extension workers so as to prepare them for participation in development.

The first set of principles formulated as guidelines for the work of DVV in Africa, Asia, and Latin America was developed and published by the Department in 1969. These guidelines described the Department's purpose and potential, at the same time pointing out the limitations of adult education and related international aid on development. They reflected the stormy ideological debate that arose in the wake of growing evidence that independence ending colonialism had been replaced by new mechanisms often scarcely concealing neocolonial forms of oppression and exploitation. They also reflected insights from the first years of experience in development policy and aid, and discussed important findings on education, in particular the hitherto often neglected area of adult education, and its restricted role in fostering development.

These guidelines have been revised and adapted several times since the first draft. As priorities changed, based on experience accumulated in the course of cooperation with partners in Africa, Asia, and Latin America, some major modifications were elaborated and incorporated in a new draft in the late 80s. In 1989 they were adopted by DVV's Board of Management. The following passages from the chapter "Guidelines and Priorities" should provide a better understanding of their framework, precepts, and focus:

- Man's capacity to learn and the necessity for life-long learning justify the need for adult education, and, indeed, make it possible. Adult education provides orientation and know-how as tools for the individual to better comprehend and influence processes of personal and social development. In doing so, it responds to the demands and challenges faced by man and society in a constantly changing world.

- Adult education takes on many forms depending on the particular historical and cultural background of its setting. It is influenced by the prevailing economic, social, religious and value systems. It occurs wherever adults find themselves in the process of learning how to better satisfy basic nutritional, housing, clothing and health needs, but also when they endeavor to learn how to ensure a greater degree of social justice and more active participation in the cultural and political life of their communities.

- Adult education in an emancipating sense is motivated by the wants and needs of its target group, and as such requires a participatory form of program selection and organization, in other words, active involvement on the part of the participants in the choice of topics and methods for their learning. This can occur in a formally structured learning situation, or through individual or group action, provided that the participants are afforded the opportunity to analyze their conditions and become conscious of the course and outcome of their actions.

- Organizational forms, content and methods for adult education can only be fully comprehended within a social context. The rich stores of knowledge and experience together with the established structures for traditional and non-formal education already existing within DVV's partner countries provide the obvious point of departure and focus for developing programs that correspond with contemporary needs.

- As a professional adult education association in a large industrial country, and aware of the moral foundation for its solidarity, DVV offers its assistance and cooperation to adult education organizations in its partner countries. DVV does not consider itself to be a donor organization, but rather a professional partner which can contribute its long years of experience in the field and its numerous international contacts to supplement the expertise, comprehensive knowledge and grasp of local conditions, and dedication brought into the partner relationship by its national counterparts.

- In view of the diverse and changing nature of adult education, DVV is committed in its cooperation with partner organizations to an approach which is varied both in terms of method and content. Accordingly, its description of activities is extensive, and includes:

  - Basic and continued training of adult educators at fundamental, intermediate and advanced levels,
  - Development, production, distribution and application of printed and audio-visual teaching and learning aids,
  - Research and analysis of programs for the preparation, supervision and evaluation of adult education and social development,
  - Reinforcement of the institutional and material infrastructure available to partner organizations,
  - Work at the grassroots level in rural and urban areas, taking into particular consideration the existing forms of production, distribution and gainful employment,
  - Vocational training to strengthen earning power,
  - Promotion of cooperative ventures,
  - Development and implementation of appropriate technology, within the various work sectors,
  - Community development as an integral approach to adult education encompassing the spheres of family, health, agriculture, crafts and trades, as well as culture,
  - Dialogue and exchange of experience among adult educators on local, national and regional levels.

- Beyond professional cooperation, DVV can lend financial assistance to its partners upon agreement with them to support their work in adult education, e.g., to implement basic and advanced training programs, to produce educational materials and to purchase equipment. . . . This technical cooperation is defined not by the interests of the donor, but by the needs of the partner (German Adult Education Association, 1992).

PARTNERS AND APPROACHES

Institutions and organizations providing adult education in Africa, Asia, and Latin America are very diverse in background, role, programs, and activities. It is predominantly from within the international network of professional adult educators and their institutions that DVV receives applications and proposals for future cooperation. Most come from members of the regional adult education associations.

Since its inception, DVV has been cooperating with national NGOs, government departments for adult education, parastatal institutions, university centers, and the regional organizations for adult education. The NGO sector is the most frequently represented on the list of partners in current project activities in Africa, Asia, and Latin America.

In regard to the practical implementation of local adult education programs, DVV mainly relies on cooperation with numerous committed NGOs, private and independent agencies as well as university institutions. These can be associations or grassroots organizations, and may differ in size or importance. Their scope of influence can be local, regional, or national. DVV believes that these organizations are in the best position to initiate activities on the community level, and, whether alone or together with other organizations, to gather and appraise experiences on a higher level, confront government officials and departments with their demands, and offer their professional services. However, DVV also realizes the need for governmental involvement in the development of adult education, and not merely for the sake of legislation and resources.

DVV currently employs three major operational approaches:

The first category includes those situations where, upon agreement with the partner, DVV opens project offices in designated countries out of which it can collaborate with national associations and development organizations, adult education departments of government ministries, and adult education centers at universities.

Under the second approach, consultations in a particular country lead to joint ventures with one partner in clearly defined areas of cooperation. Most projects of this nature are limited in scope and time.

The third option encompasses DVV's cooperation with regional adult education associations and networks, including the form of institutional support as well as program funding.

For each form of cooperation we have developed instruments like formal agreements, yearly activity plans, annual reports, and project consultations, to monitor the collaboration with colleagues and partners in Africa, Asia, and Latin America.

Staff rotation constitutes a distinctive feature of DVV's organizational system. Senior staff members undertake assignments on a rotating basis for a determined number of years in the various project offices. Such arrangements allow partners the advantage of valuable experience in professional, management, and administrative matters. At the same time, program officers return to DVV headquarters with a wealth of new experience. Exposure of this nature has served to substantially improve professional understanding and cooperation.

FUNDING AND PLANNING

The year 1993 marked the thirtieth year of international cooperation funded by the Federal Ministry for Economic Cooperation and Development. The following table shows that a figure of more than 170 million German marks has been invested over that period in support of adult education in Africa, Asia, and Latin America. The current annual budget amounts to around 10 million German marks for these regions alone. Most of the projects and country programs run on annual budgets ranging from 300,000 to 600,000 German marks. An amount of 1.7 million German marks is channeled annually into support of the regional adult education associations and networks.

Normally there is a time frame of three years for agreements in which DVV assumes financial commitments towards its partners. Contracts are based on DVV proposals, subject to approval by the Ministry of Economic Cooperation and Development. This procedure calls for strong commitment to medium-term planning on the part of DVV and its partners. There is a general understanding between the association and the funding ministry that most of the projects require long-term involvement with continual reevaluation and appraisal of the development processes and the respective program orientations with their related projects and activities.

Owing to DVV's concept of professional cooperation in partnership and solidarity, most of our projects have a lifetime of from ten to fifteen years.

Table 6.1 provides a picture of the financial resources available over the last thirty years. The figures for 1991–1993 include the budget for projects in Central and Eastern Europe.

PROJECTS AND PARTNERSHIPS

The 1980s saw the successful completion of several projects launched years previously. Among them were national programs in the African

Table 6.1 DVV Financial Commitments

year	expended budget (DM)	number of projects	year	expended budget (DM)	number of projects
1963	236.120,00	1	1979	5.513.000,00	13
1964	718.548,00	6	1980	6.364.000,00	14
1965	1.090.993,00	9	1981	7.603.000,00	16
1966	1.327.199,00	12	1982	7.865.000,00	16
1967	1.361.458,00	7	1983	8.161.100,00	16
1968	1.361.400,00	6	1984	8.383.000,00	16
1969	1.871.760,00	13	1985	8.410.000,00	17
1970	1.881.100,00	8	1986	8.490.000,00	19
1971	1.969.600,00	9	1987	9.650.000,00	19
1972	2.379.950,00	12	1988	9.307.455,00	20
1973	2.666.890,00	14	1989	9.415.000,00	19
1974	4.427.672,00	12	1990	10.214.750,00	20
1975	3.325.200,00	6	1991	12.252.400,00	21
1976	3.488.300,00	6	1992	13.901.900,00	21
1977	4.655.300,00	10	1993	14.990.000,00	23
1978	5.717.610,00	15			
Total:				178.954.705,00	

countries of the Congo, Somalia, Tanzania, Zambia, and Zaire, as well as the effective partnership pursued with the Kerala Association for Non-formal Education and Development in the southern part of India. At the same time, consultations, thorough preparation, financial planning, and pilot phases led to the emergence of new nationally based programs. They fill the space left by the outgoing projects, and have been added to the list of ongoing partnerships. What follows here is an overview of the current situation as of early 1993.

COOPERATION IN AFRICA

Burundi

This project provides support to local initiatives, especially in rural areas, in an effort to ascertain their educational and developmental needs and attend to them accordingly. The Burundian NGOs maintain close ties with NGOs of neighboring countries, and one of the major aims and strategies of the program is to implement exchange and cooperation on a subregional level. Areas of focus include agriculture, health and nutrition, appropriate technology, and community development. The training of adult educators and the production of teaching and learning materials incorporate efforts of ecclesiastical groups and governmental agencies engaged in adult education.

Madagascar

The major partner in this project, since its inception in 1987, has been the Department for Popular Education and Literacy of the Ministry for Population, Social Services, Youth and Sports. More and more NGOs working in rural areas are providing training for literacy tutors, producing teaching and learning materials, offering orientation in agricultural and health education, and conducting project evaluations. Experimental centers have been started in several parts of rural Madagascar.

Lesotho

There are three partners who figure in the work of this project: the Institute of Extra-Mural Studies at the University of Lesotho, the Lesotho Association of Nonformal Education and the Lesotho Distance Teaching Center. Here again, the training of adult educators and the production of teaching and learning materials play a central role. Research and evaluation are also supported and scholarships are provided for certain programs. Assistance is further channeled into infrastructural development of partner headquarters and rural outposts.

Sierra Leone

This program has been selected for a more extensive presentation below.

Uganda

At the beginning, in 1985, DVV was cooperating with the Centre for Continuing Education of Makerere University, the National Adult Education Association, and the Kiira Adult Education Association. Since 1991, the Department of Community Development of the local ministry has joined the partnership. The university center is mainly concerned with training, teaching, and research at the university level, whereas the national association, working through some fifty branches, concentrates on the grassroots level. The Kiira Association places strong emphasis on rural crafts and income generating activities.

AALAE

DVV began cooperating with the African Association for Literacy and Adult Education in 1987. Assistance goes into institutional development and the various AALAE networks created to address the areas of literacy, specific needs of women, the environment, participatory research, and university work. Other activities involve the development of management techniques for African NGOs, publications, and an exchange program between African adult educators on a country-to-country basis.

COOPERATION IN ASIA

India

Major partners here are the Society for Participatory Research in Asia (PRIA), which works on a regional basis in India and Asia as well, and concentrates on training, research and publications; SEVA MANDIR, a foundation concerned with rural and urban development in the state of Rajasthan; and the Society for the Promotion of Area Resource Centres (SPARC), a dedicated initiative working with pavement dwellers in Greater Bombay. Through PRIA, DVV channels input into several other educational and developmental institutions in India.

ASPBAE

The Asian-South Pacific Bureau of Adult Education has been a partner of DVV ever since 1976. Program support is used for regional, subregional and in-country activities related to training, research, and publications. Complementary efforts include special action learning programs and study exchanges. Priority areas include literacy and education for all, women, environmental, and workers' education. Institutional support backs the growing organizational and consultative structures.

COOPERATION IN LATIN AMERICA

Bolivia

When cooperation was initiated in 1986, there was one partner, the Department for Adult and Nonformal Education of the Ministry of Education. The partnership has been extended to include several private, ecclesiastical, and non-governmental organizations involved in adult education. The work of the partners has a strong bias in the direction of productive and income generating activities, and, accordingly, substantial support goes to outfit workshops and centers with equipment and tools, as well as to provide training in relevant areas. Radio San Gabriel uses the mass media and publications to reach the Aymara-speaking population.

Colombia

For more than twenty years, several partners in various provinces of the country have been cooperating with DVV. While government departments in the provinces were the major partners in the 1970s and 1980s, DVV's project office meanwhile also concentrates on smaller institutions with a nongovernmental, ecclesiastical, or private background in the field of training, learning and teaching materials, and productive as well as income-generating activities. These efforts serve to complement governmental work in adult education.

Mexico

A dominant focus in this project is the support of national NGOs that mainly serve marginal and indigenous groups. The sphere of cooperation includes several states. Integrated initiatives in the education and training sector, as well as in social and rural organization, are related to production, marketing, and income generation. These activities are expected to help strengthen the Indian communities in their struggle for recognition of their cultures. The process is supported by literacy efforts in the indigenous vernacular.

CEAAL

The Latin American Council of Adult Education entered into an agreement of cooperation with DVV in the mid-eighties. Since then, DVV has provided substantial support for their institutional structures, as well as for program areas such as adult education for democracy, literacy and basic education, health, grassroots economy, communication, and ecology. Additionally, DVV supports CEAAL's model center, "El Canelo de Nos" on the outskirts of Santiago de Chile.

SECTORAL PROGRAMS

Training of Trainers

This project combines several activities with strong spin-off effects. The scholarship program currently covers ten institutions in Africa alone, and was able to provide support to more than 500 students in 1992. The study course on adult education in the Federal Republic of Germany takes place every year and invites about fifteen adult educators from Africa or Asia to learn more about adult education in an industrialized country. Very important side effects are the exchanges between participants from various countries, who also teach German adult educators about their work.

A strong feature of this program is the distribution of important reading materials, which DVV buys in bulk and sends to institutions in need. Smaller projects of cooperation with partners, which currently include Zimbabwe, Zaire, Ghana, Lebanon, Argentina, Angola, Guinea, and Senegal, have in several cases generated stronger interest on both sides, so that former pilot projects eventually resulted in larger country programs.

Journal Publication

Adult Education and Development is a semiannual journal for adult education in Africa, Asia, and Latin America. It is a forum for dialogue and the exchange of information among adult educators. It contains discussions of new experiences, and developments in the theory and practice of adult education. It is designed to assist adult educators working at so-called middle levels in teaching, organization, and administration. It is published in English, French, and Spanish editions. The mailing list includes more than 15,000 addresses throughout the world, more than 90% of which are in Africa, Asia, and Latin America.

Some of the themes in past issues included environment, gender, democracy, agricultural extension, and the quincentenary debate. In 1993, the journal celebrated its twentieth year of existence.

Table 6.2 Scholarships in Anglophone and Francophone Africa (1992)

Country	Number	Course
Botswana	9	Diploma
Ghana	45	Diploma
Lesotho	155	Diploma
Nigeria, Calabar	40	Diploma/Certificate
Nigeria, Ibadan	30	Diploma
Sierra Leone	89	Diploma/Certificate
Swaziland	45	Part-time/Certificate
Tanzania	25	Certificate
Tanzania	20	Diploma (1st year)
Tanzania	5	Diploma (2nd year)
Tanzania (Zanzibar)	4	Diploma (1st year)
Tanzania	8	Third-country students Diploma 2nd year
Zambia	7	Certificate
Zimbabwe	12	Part-time/Diploma
Institut Panafricain pour le Développement/Cameroun	10	Diploma
Total:	**504**	

Table 6.3

Geographical Distribution of the journal as of 12/31/1992 (figures for 12/31/1991 appear in brackets)

Africa	7,503	(7,314)	=	52.67%	(52.19%)
Asia	3,297	(3,288)	=	23.14%	(23.46%)
Latin America	2,089	(2,085)	=	14.67%	(14.88%)
FRG, Europe, Australia, Canada, USA, Japan	1,356	(1,327)	=	9.52%	(9.47%)
Total:	**14,245**	**(14,014)**	**=**	**100.00%**	**(100.00%)**

Proportion Developing Countries: Industrialized countries

Developing Countries	12,889	(12,687)	=	90.48%	(90.53%)
Industrializing Countries	1,356	(1,327)	=	9.52%	(9.47%)

Development Education

This project was launched in 1977 to assist local centers of adult education in the preparation of courses on the peoples and cultures of Africa, Asia, and Latin America. Accents include issues of development aid and the world economic (dis)order, the North-South conflict, handicraft techniques inherited from Africa, Asia, and Latin America, intercultural learning, ecology, and the "one world." The area represents an important aspect of our work. It has organized more than one hundred training seminars for adult educators in the field of development education, produced more than forty different handbooks, and provides comprehensive advisory services for DVV local centers. Moreover, it incorporates feedback from program officers who are continuously gathering experience from counterparts in the various partnerships in Africa, Asia, and Latin America.

AN EXAMPLE FROM AFRICA

The following consists of a closer examination of DVV's program in Sierra Leone. The intention here is not to present that program as a model for other countries, but rather to illustrate one of the options for organizing cooperation by relating how professional interests were approached a decade ago by adult educators in Sierra Leone in collaboration with DVV.

Beginning in the mid-seventies, DVV began providing support and advisory services on a small scale to several partners in Sierra Leone. Those efforts led to the opening of an independent project office in Freetown in 1981. The partners on the Sierra Leonean side were the Adult Education Unit of the Ministry of Education, the Department (now the Institute) of Extra-Mural Studies of Fourah Bay College at the University of Sierra Leone, the Sierra Leone Adult Education Association and the People's Educational Association. Pursuant to the agreement signed by DVV with the Ministry of Foreign Affairs of the Government of Sierra Leone, which had commissioned the partners in question to implement the planned adult education program in the rural and urban regions of Sierra Leone, the main areas of cooperation included training of adult educators on different levels, the development of teaching and learning materials, research and evaluation, as well as institutional support and the provision of equipment.

The constellation of the cooperation is obviously an interesting one. DVV, as an NGO, signed an agreement with a government institution. As an NGO, DVV receives government funds to cooperate with Sierra Leonean partners, who in turn represent their own government, as well as the NGO sector and the university. This helps to ensure that the governmental and nongovernmental sectors join the university in a concerted effort, all with the mutual realization that each must fulfill special functions and responsibilities.

What are some of the underlying principles of DVV's work in Sierra Leone? DVV recognizes the role that each partner has played, is currently playing, and will continue to play, in the national development of adult education. It respects their efforts to expand their areas of operation and to improve their services. Bearing this in mind, the DVV project office works with the partners on professional matters. It collaborates in the training of adult educators at different levels and the preparation of teaching and learning materials, and assists in setting up small scale projects for community development. As a matter of policy, DVV never plans, implements, or evaluates any program in Sierra Leone on its own, but always in conjunction with at least one partner. Cooperation must be a joint venture from the start!

Over the years, the following elements of the program have been important, directly or indirectly, for the development of adult education in Sierra Leone: negotiations on the part of the various partners and DVV with the government to develop a national policy on adult education; mobilization of resources—material and human—under the regular national budget; stimulation of dialogue towards more and improved literacy work through publications; research on women-specific issues and literacy; motivation for literacy in varying cultural contexts; evaluation of literacy programs; development and printing of primers on various levels, with diverse contents, and in different languages; research into traditional forms, contents, principles and institutional arrangements for education and their modern-day relevance; collection of stories and songs, riddles and proverbs, their transcription, translation, and publication; compilation and distribution of a national directory on providers of adult education; research on the informal sector and social services, in order to identify already existing mechanisms of training and education, and explore possibilities for intervening in the areas of writing, arithmetic, and bookkeeping skills; advocating and lobbying for adult education and literacy, by approaching members of parliament; promotion of adult education at the diploma level to prepare professionals for the tasks of planning and coordination; organizing workshops and seminars to inform and mobilize traditional and political authorities at different levels (national, regional, and tribal) for their support of literacy and adult education; promotion of interagency cooperation among the country's providers of adult education and development agencies; qualifying senior personnel and staff of partner organizations in management and organizational skills; providing scholarships for the training of adult educators, librarians, and scholars of African studies; furnishing institutional support, equipment, and material investments to develop the infrastructure and institutional base of partners.

Dialogue among DVV and its counterparts in planning these different activities, and networking to implement them, have constituted prominent features in the partnership arrangement in Sierra Leone. NGOs operating at the grassroots level conduct most of the classes and activities related to literacy, but they recurrently resort to the cooperation of government schools and their teachers in the implementation of their programs. The NGOs know that they often need government backing and support, and government knows that all the larger and smaller NGOs can service areas not accessible to the government. Through its various departments of education, linguistics, and sociology, the university has been instrumental in carrying out research related to adult education and in developing standardized orthographies and a national language policy relevant for literacy work.

DVV brings a professional background from the work of adult education in Germany into the partnership with Sierra Leone, needless to say without intending to export German structures or contents. Besides this, combined with its international experience, it fortunately also has a budget for different expenditures. Current financial constraints in Sierra Leone preclude DVV's Sierra Leonean counterparts from matching sufficiently that budget with their own national resources. This problem, which is due to current national and international economics and politics, tends to undermine the policy to "support" the partners' activities, preferably sharing equal responsibility with them instead of assuming the greater part of the burden. Nevertheless, DVV considers it advantageous to be open about the amount of seed money it can provide for a certain period. This allows all parties concerned the room they need for concentrated planning of programs and activities and permits each partner to contribute in coordinating the joint ventures.

Cooperation between professional institutions, in a spirit of partnership and solidarity, requires dedicated participation and administrative solidity on both sides, a commitment that includes the sound allocation of funds and accounting procedures. Where conscientiousness is missing in the latter respect, time and energy are more apt to be spent on clarifying financial matters than in concentrating on professional details. This is particularly important in periods of transition, such as the one now occurring in Sierra Leone, where all partners have jointly opened a coordinating office. This is in line with the closing of the DVV project office during 1993. The new arrangement will serve mutual interests and function as a liaison office for the cooperation with DVV and, it is to be hoped, with other international partners.

STATEMENT ON LITERACY

Increasing the rate of literacy, either through the school system or in adult literacy programs, is not an easy task and only one aspect in the process of producing a literate culture. It entails the transition of predominantly oral to predominantly written language; it requires parallel or interrelated institutional and technological backing which goes far beyond DVV's educational possibilities. Important considerations in this respect are the standardization of language, its use in administration, the production of paper and printing. This involves an evolutionary process that does not take years or decades, but rather centuries.

Many of the problems involved in literacy and postliteracy work are related to a misunderstanding of that process, in which literacy activities play only a restricted role. Over the years, DVV has been requested by partners in most of its projects to cooperate in such activities. As a consequence, during the early 1980s it decided to formulate its position. There were many functional literacy projects and campaigns going on at the time, and international organizations and national governments in particular were still proclaiming the need "to wipe out illiteracy." DVV's experience in literacy work, both on national and international levels, led it to attempt to focus the debate on a more sensitive approach to literacy. Four of its members (Jakob Horn, Wolfgang Leumer, Rolf Niemann, and the present author) elaborated a statement for presentation at an international conference in 1983. As the comments are still relevant, some passages from that statement, entitled "Cooperation or campaigning for literacy: Let's remove doubtful promises and cope with the practicable," follow:

Illiteracy=ignorance=indignity: a wrong equation

Active as we are in the field of adult education and development, we deplore the fact that many of our colleagues are increasingly referring to illiterates as ignorant, to illiteracy as an indignity to mankind, and at the same time assuming that illiteracy is the cause of oppression, exploitation and further impoverishment. It is even more deplorable to find this attitude in official declarations, reports and so-called research pamphlets that pretend to offer insight and guidance, but which, in fact, are misleading in many respects.

The kind of *despair* felt by many of us in the face of the ever-increasing misery in the world and ever-widening gaps between the haves and have-nots should not become an excuse for a wrong analysis, and can never become a justification for the mere repetition of slogans that will not hold water when confronted with a thorough examination of our insights and day-to-day experiences.

Causality: Appearances Are Deceptive

As far as the presumption of causality is concerned—correlation and interdependence are not equal to causality—there is no generally proved evidence that literacy

in historical terms was a prerequisite of economic and social development. In fact *historically* in Europe and other industrialized countries widespread literacy *followed* the industrial revolution, and they reinforced each other.

Nor is there any general evidence that *literacy efforts by themselves* have diminished exploitation and poverty in the so-called literate societies.

The fact that the frequently cited *maps of poverty and illiteracy* coincide is no proof that literacy is the determining factor for the distribution of wealth within a given society or between nations.

Many examples have shown that ever-increasing efforts for and large expenditure on literacy did *not necessarily* lead to a *reduction of poverty*.

Literacy and intelligence are both context bound. Literacy is not a prerequisite for intelligent understanding and handling of life. Literacy becomes a necessary, or at least an enabling skill, for the individual in a literate environment.

There is also no direct relationship between *literacy and the attainment of participatory structures* and general human values, literacy is not the exclusive or even self-sufficient skill for liberation and self-realization, or for the abolishment of oppression (German Adult Education Association, 1983, pp. 1–5).

Literacy: The Good, The Bad and The Ugly

Those who still propound the argument that literacy finally leads to the enlightenment of individuals and/or mankind should keep in mind that the terrifying arms race and destruction of unrenewable natural resources, which endanger the existence of our world, are not perpetrated by illiterates, but are only possible through literacy and highly literate specialists— although again, this should not be mistaken as a causal relationship.

We should also bear in mind—without taking a romantic view of illiterate communities—that *non-literate societies* have produced and still produce positive indigenous values and techniques for the satisfaction of basic needs and human enrichment, which are important and appropriate now and may become more decisive in the future. Are we fully aware of and concerned about the harmful and often *destructive potential of our literacy endeavors* and the indirect, negative influences and repercussions on developmental processes which are apparent in phenomena like rural exodus, negligence of traditional skills and cultural heritages bound to non-written transfer from generation to generation?

We do see a perspective for *integrated literacy work* as part of a more comprehensive concept of adult education and development which takes adults—literates and illiterates alike—seriously in their realization of their lives, and which remains open to the question of whether literacy can be meaningful or even a tool for change. Whether literacy is a necessary or helpful tool for the improvement of living conditions can only be assessed *according to the specific prevailing situation.* Assessment and decision have to be based on the experience and knowledge of those who are concerned and directly involved.

Our experience shows clearly that adult education and local development can often be effected *without* literacy skills and that the need for literacy may only arise *during or even after* the performance of activities by a given community or the society at large. In imposing literacy above all as a precondition we could be opposing our own objectives by demotivating the learners and leading to failure; the demotivation effect may be permanent and irreversible.

Literacy, like any other means in the development of the individual, the community and the society has to be a socially appropriate "technology". A largely literate environment produces the necessity for additional literacy efforts. Adult education must make provision for motivated learners and try to satisfy their demands.

Reality Versus Wishful Thinking

Let us be honest and realistic: No matter what efforts are made—unless the world, North and South, West and East, and the rich, elite and powerful within countries are prepared for an alternative orientation and a total shift of financial resources from arms' budgets to basic services—illiteracy will be a fact of life even after the year 2000. Therefore the call for "eradication of illiteracy by the year 2000" is misleading and an *unrealistic objective*. It is an illusion and not a meaningful utopia. Moreover, it is a discrimination and an insult for those who will continue to master their lives as illiterates or non-literates.

Illiteracy is not a fatal disease which requires a "vaccination program" for its eradication. On the contrary, literacy work needs a careful, sensitive and sensible choice of pedagogical approaches. Neither hand-outs nor injections will help.

As can be imagined, many of the points that were raised were met with bitter protest, especially from sources that still preferred propaganda over analysis. At the same time, however, criticism came from individuals who firmly believed in literacy as a prerequisite for human development. Nonetheless, DVV deemed it necessary to pursue the issue in an open dialogue with organizations and initiatives that concentrated on improving literacy statistics in terms of numbers and time span, because it felt that such organizations were underestimating the complexity of a process that tends to create new systems of communication not readily accessible or relevant to nonliterate communities. For years, to that end, the journal has maintained a special section called "The Literacy Corner," in which letters and articles addressing the literacy debate are published.

In retrospect, DVV has encountered many people and institutions whose education and training programs stress other needs of the individual and the society—such as, the acquisition of skills needed for employment or the organization of income-generating activities—needs which are at least as important as literacy itself in an understanding of integrated educational work aimed at lifelong learning. Such an approach lends more substance to literacy work and at the same time helps people and communities to cope with other real problems.

PERSPECTIVES

Adult education on its own is not capable of solving the world's crisis. On the other hand, without the lifelong disposition to learn in informal and formal educational settings, people—and this refers particularly to adults—will not be in a position to comprehend, reflect upon, and modify the permanently changing conditions and situations both in a local and global context.

International aid to adult education in Africa, Asia, and Latin America can only contribute to the efforts undertaken on a national level, and if possible, in a context conducive to regional cooperation. However, as much as the successful developments in several countries in the field of adult education should be appreciated, it is important to recognize the growing reality of an international crisis endangering the life of more and more people and destroying indigenous cultures, and the growing influence of destructive technologies inducing a global environmental crisis with disastrous effects on the local level.

With the breakdown of the Soviet Union and the creation of so many new national states, and the breakup of the former Eastern Block, the Department for International Cooperation of DVV is receiving solicitations for assistance from adult education organizations located in those countries. In this situation the question arises as to whether much of the world that was formerly known as the "East" now belongs to an extended "South"? As an example, is not Kazakhstan, now a member of the Commonwealth of Independent States formed by successors of the former Soviet Union, at least under a regional perspective part of Asia? Will adult education institutions of Kazakhstan eventually become members of the Asian-South Pacific Bureau of Adult Education?

As interesting as such speculation may be, however, requests for international cooperation cannot wait. During the past three years, DVV, in the spirit of professionalism and solidarity, has entered into several new partnerships with colleagues and institutions in the East. Fortunately, once again the Ministry of Economic Cooperation and Development has provided special funds over and above the aid DVV continues to receive towards support of adult education in Africa, Asia, and Latin America.

BIBLIOGRAPHY

German Adult Education Association (1983). *Adult Education and Development* 21. Bonn, Germany: DVV/German Adult Education Association.
German Adult Education Association (1992). Annual Report of the Institute for International Cooperation. Bonn, Germany: DVV/German Adult Education Association.

CHAPTER 7

Japan: Cooperation in Adult Education in Developing Countries

KEN MOTOKI AND YASUMASA HIRASAWA

Adult education programs and activities are referred to as "social education" in Japan. Social education is defined as "systematic out-of-school education activities for the youth and adults." The scope of social education in Japan is wider than that of adult education in the United States and Europe and should better be compared to the concept of "nonformal education."

Social education programs are centrally supervised by the Ministry of Education. A number of such programs, however, are run by other ministries and agencies, and many vocational skills programs are operated by the Ministries of Labor, of Transportation, of Agriculture, of Forestry and Fishery, and others. International cooperation programs for adult education in developing countries, in particular, are promoted primarily by ministries and agencies other than the Ministry of Education.

It needs to be mentioned that out-of-school nonformal education activities for nonschooled children has much significance in developing countries. However, the definition of adult education in Western societies does not really cover this aspect.

In this paper, adult education activities are defined in broad terms and Japan's international cooperation activities are described in the context of nonformal education initiatives.

JAPAN'S CURRENT INTERNATIONAL COOPERATION

UNESCO was the first international organization that Japan joined after the war (in 1951), even before becoming a UN member. Japan's

115

international cooperation activities expanded since then, as it joined the World Bank and the Colombo Plan. Japan set up the Overseas Economic Cooperation Fund (OECF) in 1961, and the Overseas Technical Cooperation Agency in 1962. (It was renamed Japan International Cooperation Agency in 1974.) Her Official Development Assistance (ODA) ranked second in 1986, next to that of the United States, among the Development Assistance Committee (DAC) members. Japan's ODA ranked first in 1989, amounting to about 9 billion U.S. dollars.

Its bilateral grants (gratuitous financial assistance) reached 200 billion yen (1.7 billion dollars) in 1990, covering mainly such fields as medicine, health, agricultural development, education, research, and the securing of decent living standards. Its priority recipients were Asian countries, including Bangladesh, the Philippines, Thailand, Indonesia, and Pakistan.

Budgeted in the category of economic development assistance, these grants are classified as a general grant, a fishery-related grant, a disaster-related grant, a cultural grant, and a food production-related grant.

Cultural grant activities began in 1976, as part of international cultural exchange programs, and have been provided to promote education and research in developing countries, to preserve cultural assets and historic sites, to extend money to purchase necessary equipment and materials for cultural exhibition and public performance. The amount of cultural grants, on the average, is about 50 million yen (440 thousand dollars) for each project. Among the pieces of equipment purchased recently, using this money, are the astronomical telescope for the Chulalongkorn University, the archaeological earth probe for the Ministry of Education, the machinery to restore the ruins of Sukhothai for the Ministry of Education (Thailand), the apparatus and materials for learning scientific principles for the Children's Museum of Science and Technology and Japanese language education programs for the University of the Air (China), the machinery to restore cultural assets for the National Museum, and the information processing equipment for the National Central Library (Philippines). The above equipment was purchased in the recipient countries.

There are also technical assistance programs. Technical assistance is aimed at "improving the knowledge, skill and technical know-how and productive capacities of the people in developing countries," and "improving the capacities to utilize existing resources more effectively." This is more or less software aid targeted at cultivating manpower resources. We may call this a form of adult education or nonformal education activity.

Some technical assistance programs are wholly government-sponsored, others are privately-sponsored using government subsidies, and the others are wholly privately-sponsored. Wholly government-sponsored programs, based on bilateral agreements, are executed by the Japan International Cooperation Agency (JICA), a special government-affiliated corporation under the jurisdiction of the Foreign Ministry. Some programs are cosponsored with the Ministry of Agriculture and Forestry and the Ministry of International Trade and Industry. About 60% of technical assistance in the bilateral ODA expenditures, as shown in the DAC statistics, are administered by JICA. The remaining 40% of assistance, also government-sponsored, is executed by other agencies and organizations. This includes a program for exchange students from developing countries (Ministry of Education), international research cooperation programs (Ministry of International Trade and Industry), and tropical agricultural research programs (Ministry of Agriculture and Forestry).

JICA conducts a number of programs, such as receiving trainees, dispatching experts, supplying equipment, in addition to project-based technical cooperation, overseas youth cooperation, development research, development cooperation, and grant aid promotion. Its budget in FY 1990 amounted to about 130 billion yen (1.1 billion dollars).

This illustration indicates that Japan's educational cooperation with developing countries is mainly taking place in the field of technical education, through economic and industrial cooperation programs, rather than through projects under the jurisdiction of the Ministry of Education.

TECHNICAL AND SKILL TRAINING PROGRAMS OF JICA

JICA receives a large number of promising trainees from developing countries and provides them with opportunities to acquire knowledge and skills in fields such as public administration, agriculture and forestry, mining and manufacturing, energy, health and medicine, and public utilities. These trainees are mostly public servants and government-affiliated researchers, because JICA's programs are planned according to bilateral government agreements. The number of trainees received in FY 1989 was 7,500, and the cumulative figure to this date is 90,000. Trainees in the field of public utilities account for 25%, agriculture, forestry and fishery 20%, mining and manufacturing 13%, health and medicine 10%, and public administration 10%. The majority comes from Asia

(60%), and others are from Latin America (20%), Near and Middle East, and Africa. The number of trainees has increased year after year. It has increased five-fold in the past twenty years and two-fold in the past ten years.

Training is divided into "domestic training (in Japan)" and "third-country training." The domestic variety consists of group and individual training. For individual training, a site is chosen and curriculum is arranged so that the needs of the students are met properly. For group training, details of curriculum, a plan of execution, and required qualifications for participants, are shown to the governments of developing countries at the time of soliciting for participation in the courses. Several to a dozen participants are received for each course.

JICA, in collaboration with local governments, private enterprises, public corporations, research institutes, and ministries and agencies concerned, offers more than two hundred training courses. It operates eleven training centers nationwide, including those in Tokyo, Tsukuba, Osaka, Nagoya, Kobe, and Kita-Kyushu.

Recently, third-country training programs have gradually expanded. Sponsored by Japan, these programs take place at the sites of large-scale technological projects in developing countries. Expenses for traveling and lodging of trainees are mostly borne by Japan, and the host countries share some direct and indirect expenses. As of 1991, forty-seven third-country training programs were offered in eighteen countries.

Some non-JICA technical cooperation programs receiving government subsidies are run by the central government and others are run by local governments and NGOs.

Central government programs include support for government-sponsored exchange students from developing countries (Ministry of Education), and feasibility studies by private research organizations commissioned by various ministries and agencies.

Local governments extend significant support and cooperation directly and indirectly to government-sponsored technical cooperation programs carried on by JICA. They provide inputs to training programs which reflect unique features of their local industrial activities. Sometimes they independently offer programs to accommodate trainees from overseas. Since they supplement technical cooperation programs of the government, they receive some financial assistance. Such local initiatives started in 1971 in the prefectures of Yamanashi, Hyogo, and Kumanoto, and today they are seen in all prefectures. The cumulative number of trainees accepted in these programs reached 4,229 in 1989.

ACTIVITIES OF RESEARCH AND DEVELOPMENT
ORGANIZATIONS

Japanese involvement in adult education activities in developing countries has been illustrated, featuring technical cooperation. Programs are mostly sponsored by the Ministry of Foreign Affairs, the Ministry of International Trade and Industry, the Ministry of Agriculture, Forestry and Fishery, etc. There are not, however, many programs under the jurisdiction of the Ministry of Education.

International activities by the Ministry of Education are carried on in cooperation with UNESCO, which Japan joined in 1951. Such programs, led both by government and by private organizations, were seen as the symbol of Japan's return to the international community. In 1952 the Law on UNESCO Activities was enacted and the Japanese National Commission for UNESCO was established. The following year, Japan became a member of the executive committee, and its contribution to UNESCO—after United States withdrawal—is now the largest. Japan has been a particularly active participant in educational, scientific, and cultural programs in the Asia Pacific region.

The Asian Cultural Center for UNESCO (ACCU) was established in 1971 as a foundation under the control of the Ministries of Education and Foreign Affairs. (Its predecessor was the UNESCO Publication Center in Tokyo.) It aims at preserving and developing Asian culture and promoting publishing activities, following the basic guidelines of UNESCO. Its major activities include joint projects in the region, and training courses. ACCU serves as a coordinator in the new system of joint project operation which UNESCO member countries collaborate to design and manage on an equal footing. The outcomes of such activities are supposed to be brought back to their respective countries for innovative use. The training consists of publication courses, held several times a year in Tokyo and Asian countries for librarians from Asia, and leadership training courses for cultural activities. ACCU is engaged also in the non-Latin letter design improvement project, consciousness-raising activities for the preservation of Asian cultural assets, publication of bulletins, and management of its affiliated libraries. The libraries house all UNESCO publications and other publications, particularly books and textbooks for Asian children, as well as slides, photographs, and films.

ACCU has a strong commitment to the solution of literacy problems. It produces study materials and books, and trains instructors for literacy education at the Regional Office for Education in Asia and the Pacific, in

Bangkok. Currently, representatives from more than twenty countries participate in the literacy projects, including India, Bangladesh, Thailand, Indonesia, Papua New Guinea, the Philippines, and China.

In publishing projects, a model English version is first produced, in discussions among representatives from the various countries, and then pictures and language are changed so they accurately represent the situation in respective countries. In the training of experts, emphasis is placed on the examination of the relationship between literacy and everyday life, between literacy and oral traditions, and between literacy and the enjoyment of stories, as well as the use of puppet shows, slides, and illustrations.

Literacy instructors often find themselves removed from the everyday life of the mass of illiterate people. "Walk along the paddies" programs are included in the training, and picture book authors with experiences in settlement work are asked to serve as technical advisors. Discussions are encouraged, to illuminate the relationship between local dialects/minority tongues and official language.

ACTIVITIES IN DEVELOPING COUNTRIES

(1) Involvement of International Cooperation Experts

International cooperation is not just a matter of providing financial support and receiving trainees. Experts are dispatched to the sites of overseas development projects. They are sent to developing countries by the UN, the Japanese government, or private sector organizations, to provide technical support, and to promote nation building and manpower resource development.

The Asian Productivity Organization (APO) is one such body that assigns cooperation experts. APO was founded in 1961 as an international organization with headquarters in Tokyo, for the purpose of promoting economic activities in various countries and of improving people's living standards through mutual cooperation among member countries. The areas of APO activities are broadly classified as research and planning, manufacturing, agriculture, and publication.

In most cases, experts in manufacturing techniques are sent. They facilitate management rationalization in individual companies and disseminate technical know-how. They are invited from APO member countries, the United States, and Europe. In the past, 75% of them have been Japanese experts. Thirty-six experts were sent from Japan in FY 1990.

The program of the Japanese government is managed by JICA. JICA's overseas activities consist of dispatching experts, supplying equipment and materials, providing project-based technical cooperation (social development, health and medical services, family planning, agriculture, forestry and fishery cooperation, and industrial development cooperation), and making feasibility studies. JICA's expert dispatch program will be described in detail below.

Private sector organizations also send experts to developing countries. A typical example is the Japan Overseas Trade Development Council (JODC) program, under which engineers with sophisticated industrial technical skills and professional consultants are sent. Founded in 1970 as the Asian Commerce Development Association, it was renamed JODC in 1972. It is under the jurisdiction of the Ministry of International Trade and Industry. JODC promotes industrial activities, trading, and technical cooperation in developing countries, by providing loans from the small business cooperation fund for overseas investment and the import promotion fund, and by dispatching private sector experts. Requests for the assignment of experts from the private sector are received by local offices of the Japan External Trade Organization (JETRO) and communicated to JODC. As of 1990, there were 876 registered experts at the JODC, and so far 1,096 experts, for both long-term and short-term projects, have been sent in fields such as organizational development, marketing, labor management, business management, diagnosis of small business management, plant design, financial management, and on-the-job training. Ninety-one percent of them have been sent to Asian countries.

Many young international cooperation experts have been sent as private sector volunteers to developing countries by the Organization for Industrial, Spiritual and Cultural Advancement International (OISCA), which was founded in 1969 to promote Japan's industrial development cooperation project for developing countries. With headquarters in Tokyo, OISCA has member organizations in ninety-eight countries. Major activities include dispatching international cooperation volunteers and training development volunteers, and receiving technical trainees from overseas. It also organizes international conferences, sends out development research groups, and promotes development education, tree planting, and international exchange activities. International cooperation volunteers are sent as a group, consisting of experienced senior leaders and young engineers. By March 1991, 1,536 experts had been sent to eighty-seven projects in thirteen countries.

(2) Experts Assigned by JICA

JICA has sent abroad experts in two major categories since 1955: training experts and project experts. The cumulative number of those sent reached 30,570 by 1990. They have been assigned to Asia (18,914), Central and South America (5,483), Near and Middle East (2,589), Africa (2,373), and to other areas.

JICA first sent 28 experts to five South East Asian nations in 1955 under a special program of the Colombo Plan, called "expert dispatch." The program was designed specifically to help promote manpower training in recipient countries so that economic and social developments would be carried out effectively, utilizing local human resources. The cumulative figure of experts in this program reached 14,501 by 1990. They have helped the development of necessary manpower locally, in such fields as public administration planning, public utilities services, agriculture, forestry and fishery industries, mining and manufacturing industries, health and medical services, social welfare services, human resources development, and others. To be more specific, for instance, the category of "human resources development" aimed at promoting science education, Japanese language education, vocational training, technology education and audio-visual education. In this category 3,317 experts had been sent by 1989.

In addition to these experts, others have been sent to perform other functions (16,069 in total by 1990). For instance, JICA has sent experts to carry out project-based technological cooperation activities in five categories: social development; health and medical services; family planning; agriculture, forestry and fishery development; and industrial development. Also it has sent experts to conduct feasibility studies and to offer consultation services for development projects.

Thus, the cumulative figure of experts sent out under the initiative of JICA in all categories of development aid was 30,570 from 1955 to 1990.

(3) Participation in Literacy and Adult Basic Education

Above, the current status of Japanese international cooperation in developing countries has been described, featuring JICA programs. The Ministries of Foreign Affairs, International Trade and Industry, Agriculture, and Forestry and Fishery, have mainly been involved in manpower development in economic and industrial activities of developing countries. Japan's overseas cooperation has taken place mostly in these areas.

In this section, adult education programs under the jurisdiction of the Ministry of Education will be highlighted.

In the past, Japan's overseas cooperation in the field of education, as compared to economic and industrial cooperation, was rather limited. Recently, however, several projects related to literacy and adult basic education have attracted much attention.

First, the Ministry of Education has directly financed activities of the Japanese National Commission for UNESCO. Also, Japanese contributions account for over 20% of the entire budget of the organization. A certain amount of this contribution is appropriated for UNESCO's literacy and adult basic education projects. Japan contributed 1.4 million dollars and 0.7 million dollars, in 1990 and 1991, to the "Asia Pacific Regional Programs toward Education for All," promoted by the UNESCO Regional Office for Education in Asia and the Pacific in Bangkok. Japan has founded the "Literacy Education Trust Fund" to assist staff training and educational materials development, so as to eliminate illiteracy in the Asia Pacific region.

The National Federation of UNESCO Associations in Japan, affiliated with the Ministry of Education, has led the campaign for the "World Terakoya Movement," since 1989 supported by the Japan Committee of UNESCO. "Terakoya" was the name of a voluntary elementary school in the premodern Edo period, and its spirit reflected deeply the wishes of the people. The movement has collected funds from all over Japan, to establish Terakoya-like classes in developing countries, through UNESCO Headquarters in Paris, in close collaboration with NGOs. By the end of FY 1990, 180 million Yen (1.5 million dollars) had been collected.

Thus far, mainly Japanese government-related activities have been discussed, but NGOs have played important roles, also.

A Citizen's Committee in Japan for Overseas Support—named SHAPLA NEER ("white lotus flower")—opened its office in Bangladesh in 1974 to promote literacy campaigns. It organized cooperatives and developed dietary improvement programs. Tied with these activities, literacy education has been promoted in night schools and community classes for women. Group discussions on important daily concerns, drama performances, and handicrafts, are included in the literacy programs. One of the objectives is to develop leaders for cooperative and literacy campaigns. Every August SHAPLA NEER organizes a study tour, during which many young people from Japan have opportunities to learn the reality of life in developing countries.

The Sotoshu Volunteer Association (SVA) has carried on cooperative activities, including literacy education in refugee camps and urban and rural slums, since the Indo-Chinese refugees massively migrated into Thailand in 1975. At the Banbinai camp in the northeastern part of Thailand, adjacent to the Laotian border, the Association has collected folk tales of the Mons, a mountain minority population, and produced picture books, using the traditional Mon embroidery to teach the children of the area. It has also mimeographed and disseminated children's books written in Lao (the official language in Laos) and in Thai (official language in Thailand).

The Japan Committee for Negros Campaign is another voluntary organization, established when the sugar price collapsed in the Negros Island in the Philippines, leading to starvation of agricultural workers and tenant farmers. UNICEF designated the island as a target of relief aid. Collaborating with the Negros Relief and Recovery Center (NRRC), the Committee has undertaken projects to supply milk, purchase water buffaloes, and teach agricultural skills. NRRC conducts literacy education in the mother tongue of the mountain people, hoping to develop self-reliance by using the tasks of their everyday lives as teaching material.

CONCLUSION

The postwar social education administration was supposed to follow the principle of "support but no control," emphasizing the administrative responsibility to assist and encourage citizens' voluntary learning activities. In reality, however, administrative control was rather strong in many programs. This was one major reason why nongovernmental organizations were slow to develop in Japan, and even today the country does not have strong international NGOs. As a result, international cooperation projects are mainly government-run and the involvement of NGOs is limited.

Furthermore, Japanese society does not evaluate a person's experience in overseas cooperation activities in a positive manner, for the practice of lifelong employment is still dominant. This reality, therefore, discourages such participation.

In this chapter, Japan's international cooperation in adult education—that is, nonformal education—in developing countries, especially in Asia, has been illustrated. Its international contribution, however, has been the object of much criticism, both within Japan and outside.

First, Japan's ODA financial contribution ranks first or second among DAC countries. Its per capita figure (10th among 18 DAC countries) and percentage figure, relative to GNP (12th), are, however, rather small.

Second, improvement in the quality of assistance has been called for. Grants figure at less than 50%, the lowest of all DAC countries.

Third, it is often pointed out that Japan's international cooperation has mainly developed in economic and industrial spheres, while education and culture-related cooperation has not been as extensive. This picture is particularly true in adult education. The financial base of the Asian and South Pacific Bureau of Adult Education (ASPBE), an adult educators' NGO in Asia, is largely supported by Germany, which contributes as much as half a million dollars a year, while Japan, an Asian country, provides no financial support at all. While Japan invaded and did much harm to Asian countries during World War II, she has been criticized for not compensating sufficiently for these past acts.

Fourth, there is a lack of support domestically for active cooperation with developing countries. There is a great shortage of labor in industrial circles in Japan currently, and it is expected that the era of "absolute shortage of labor force" will come soon, marked by a decrease in the number of young workers and an increase in the aged population. The "strong yen-weak dollar" situation has triggered an increase of persons from abroad seeking jobs in Japan. The Japanese government, however, has not accepted the entry of unskilled labor, which has led to the increase of illegal workers and disguised refugees.

As one result, the Ad Hoc Council on Administrative Reform has come up with an "OJT Scheme for Foreign Labor." Training workers on the job is expected to meet partly the needs of small business that is constantly troubled with labor shortage, as well as the needs of foreign workers who hope to acquire technical skills while working to earn some money in Japan.

The fundamental issue here is whether Japan has cultivated social foundations resilient enough to accommodate the multicultural reality. For instance, Japan has so far accepted only a limited number of refugees, and their life in Japan has been marked with much instability and uncertainty.

Japan has long maintained a strong homogeneous culture, with a predominant majority of Japanese nationals. The Western concepts of human rights have not made a strong impact, as yet. The country is now deeply concerned with "internationalization from within," in view of rapidly changing international circumstances. The issue of accommodating foreign workers has reminded Japan of the need to face a growing multicultural reality. The common thinking and mind-sets of Japanese people in the past have to be changed, as well.

Recently, the need to promote "development education" has been advocated for schools and social education programs. Groups of such curriculum developers have emerged and some schools practice new curricular ideas. Whether this initiative will succeed or not will determine Japan's position in the international community.

BIBLIOGRAPHY

Higuchi, Sadao (1991). *Seifu kaihatsu enjo* (Official development assistance). 2nd printing. Tokyo: Keiso Shobo.
Inoue, Terumasa (1992). *Kokusai kyoryoku senmonka to iu shigoto* (The work of international cooperation experts). Tokyo: Perican-sha.
Sasagawa, Koichi (1991). Shikiji ni okeru kokusai-kyoryoku no doko to kadai (Issues for international cooperation in the field of literacy), in Nihon Shakai Kyoiku Gakkai/Japan Society for Study of Adult Education (ed.) *Kokusai shikiji junen to Nihon no shikijimondai* (The decade of international literacy and Japanese literacy problems). Tokyo: Toyokan.
Koido, Yuji et al. (eds.) (1992). *Gaikokujin rodosha seisaku to kadai* (Policy matters and issues of foreign workers). Tokyo: Zeimu-Keiri Kyokai.

CHAPTER 8

Sweden: Adult Education for Democracy

GUNNAR RYDSTRÖM

"Sweden is to a great extent a study circle democracy."

—Olof Palme

In the December 2, 1991 issue of *Newsweek*, Sweden was put at the top of the international list of adult education nations. Why this honor?

When the various popular movements gained ground at the turn of the twentieth century—the labor movement, the temperance movement, the nonconformists, the cooperative movement—they found that education of ordinary members was crucial for their strength, success, and development. But they needed knowledge of a kind that the formal school system of the times could not provide. The lower, compulsory levels were elementary indeed, the higher levels academic and Latin-oriented, and the university world was hostile to the very concept of popular education, to the extent that extramural studies did not emerge in Sweden until very late, in the 1960s. The popular movements (or, as some would prefer, the folk development organizations) wanted to build their own educational tradition, to shape a new kind of culture: participatory and democratic (Albinson et al., 1984, p. 2). This included the setting up of small, local libraries, presently to be incorporated into the public library system.

A number of *study associations* were formed. That of the labor movement, ABF, was the pioneer in the field, being founded in 1912, but many others followed suit. Regardless of their ideology and political orientation, they all were subsidized by the government from early on; that is, they were both accepted by, and independent of, the ruling establishment that was pretty conservative during the first three decades of the twentieth century.

A characteristic pedagogical feature was "the study circle," which is a study group without a teacher. Instead, the group is monitored by a "study circle leader," who administers it and leads its discussions, but in other respects is merely another participant, a *primus inter pares*. Originally, this grew out of sheer necessity, but soon developed into a general philosophy that everybody has got something to contribute, from his or her own experience as a member of society and humankind. This ties in quite nicely with Freire's methods, and it is not surprising that this kind of egalitarian adult education study group is an ideal that Swedish organizations and educators are keen to transfer to other countries.

A very Scandinavian form of adult education is the folk high school. (This is an unfortunate translation of the Swedish "högskola," as it is no high school at all but a residential college for grown-ups.) The first schools were opened in the latter half of the nineteenth century, essentially to give relevant training to the sons of an increasingly wealthy class of farmers who were about to dominate for half a century the municipal government then in the process of being established. The folk high school institution was later partly taken over by the labor and nonconformist movements. These schools offered—and still offer—a wide range of subjects in long and short courses. The individual schools define their own curricula, and, traditionally, the trainees have a big influence on the contents of studies. Today there are about 130 folk high schools in Sweden. Two thirds of them are run by the organizations mentioned above, and about one third by county councils.

Another adult education sector that gave Sweden good marks in the *Newsweek* league was the labor market retraining program provided by the AMU Group. (A table of abbreviations will be found at the conclusion of this chapter.) (That program used to be entirely state-run but was turned into a limited company in 1993). The basic concept is to offer courses for people made redundant, to give them new or improved skills in more promising fields of work. From the labor market perspective, it is a matter of channeling the work force from sectors in decline to sectors in ascendancy and expansion. From the individual's point of view, of course, it is a matter of landing a job to be able to lead a productive and meaningful life, instead of living on the dole. The program is financed by grants from the National Labor Market Board (AMS). At SEK 4.5 billion, this is more than all other Swedish adult education put together.

Adults who for some reason previously have missed out on their schooling opportunities, can reenter the formal school system through *Komvux* (municipal adult education). The main objective is to qualify people for studies at higher levels. Courses are given in the daytime, or in the evenings, at the local school, or at a separate unit, at the levels of upper comprehensive school or upper secondary school.

Finally, there is no formal training in adult education in Sweden, no authorized adult educators with precedence to certain posts. Research in adult education is of recent date. There is a department for further training of folk high school teachers at Linköping University, but, by and large, all adult educators in Sweden are trained on the job, attending in-service training courses, open to people of very different backgrounds. Study circle leaders are quite often volunteers.

All in all, some one-and-one-half to two million Swedes take part in some form or another of adult education each year, that is about 40% of the adult population. There is no doubt that, over the years, this has been an important platform for discussion of vital issues in the constantly changing society which is twentieth-century Sweden, and a means to adjust to these changes. The voluntary study associations, the folk high schools, and all other forms of adult education, have constituted one of the mainstays of the "Swedish model" and of the country's democracy, more important than the mass media.

Recent economic stagnation and a shift in politics have put a strain on popular education. Private enterprise in-service training has grown, to become dominant in the field, while publicly funded adult education has met with increasing difficulties in maintaining its standard.

How has the classical Swedish popular education model fared when put out in the Third World? There follows a review of some selected areas, mainly from Africa, where Sweden has been most active.

STUDY CAMPAIGNS

The Institute of Adult Education (IAE) in Dar es Saalam was, at first, a center for extramural studies along traditional British lines. When the Swedes entered in strength in the latter half of the 1960s, it was transformed into an institution for training of adult educators, and an organizer and coordinator of mass study campaigns (and made a parastatal in 1970).

The general outline of these campaigns—radio programs, a text book, study group meetings, sometimes combined with distance education—had been used before in cooperative education, both in Tanzania and (later) in Zambia (see below). These campaigns also got their inspiration from the literacy work being carried out during the same period in Tanzania, and they were very much part of the national mobilization effort, a sign of great expectations for the future. When Tanzania ran into serious economic difficulties towards the end of the decade, the mass study campaigns also petered out.

Another reason for the campaigns to stop was that SIDA pulled out of the IAE in the middle of the seventies. Perhaps it acted prematurely, but those were the days when early take-over was an encouraged and desirable goal. Up to then, the IAE had carried out an organizational expansion, opening several branches in all regions, making use of the cadre of adult educators being trained during the golden years, and a complete distance education department. The IAE was now left with a big set-up and meager funds. To survive, they had to run courses that paid their way. That meant evening courses that yielded a certificate which enabled people to sit for exams and to reenter the formal school system. And the diploma course, developed by the IAE in Dar es Salaam around 1970, changed from a one-year practical course to a two year theoretical, stiffly academic course. The element of folk development had all but gone in the 1980s, the egalitarian study group leader replaced by the rather conventional teacher.

FROM FOLK HIGH SCHOOLS TO DEVELOPMENT COLLEGES

An official Tanzanian delegation visited a number of Swedish folk high schools in 1971. They were duly impressed. Their favorable report resulted in a political decision to erect similar institutions in Tanzania, one in each district. In the end, 52 out of a total of 103 districts actually got a Folk Development College (FDC), often a converted former Rural Training Center.

An FDC was to serve the local community by running courses that could improve the quality of life in the surrounding villages. These courses were supposed to pick up the new literates, although they were not, strictly speaking, postliteracy courses. (That was taken care of elsewhere.) The FDCs were to have three financial sources: the villages in the area, income-generating activities at the colleges themselves, and grants from the Ministry of Education (MoE). In fact, the first two sources have

The first study campaign was called *To Plan is to Choose*, based on Tanzania's second Five Year Development Plan. A simple study guide was cyclostyled, referring to important sections of the official document and with hints on how to carry out discussions in group ("study circle"). It was distributed to two pilot areas where the IAE had branches at the time. The outcome revealed a lot of hang-ups (with the use of Swahili in some parts of the country, with distribution, with the training of study group leaders).

The first full-scale campaigns were called *The Choice is Yours*, as a preparation for the 1970 general election, both in practical and ideological terms, and *Time to Rejoice*, as part of the independence celebrations in December 1971. Both led up to the country's *tour de force* in this field of adult education:

Man is Health in 1973, with about two million participants, at the low cost of US $ 0.10 per head. To carry it out some 75,000 study group leaders had to be trained. This was done in three stages: regional trainers were instructed centrally in Dar es Salaam, and they in turn prepared trainers of local study group leaders (a model later used for the crash training of 35,000 new teachers in five years, when General Primary Education was introduced).

The campaign got a nationwide response, and evaluation showed that it actually led to changes in people's attitudes and everyday behavior. Apart from the regular SIDA support to the IAE (mainly staff and equipment) a special grant made it possible to print the textbooks in a sufficient number of copies and spread them.

In 1975 a fifth campaign followed, *Food is Life*, equally comprehensive in geographical scope and participation.

The sixth campaign was *Forests are Wealth* in 1981, about aforestation. Few study groups were actually formed, but many trees were planted.

Figure 8.1 Six Study Campaigns in Tanzania

been pretty dry most of the time, leaving the public vote, topped up by SIDA funds, to cover most expenditure.

Another problem was the lack of rapport between the various FDCs and the villages. The villagers had rather vague notions of what courses to demand and what they actually could get. The villages had no infrastructure either for the selection of candidates or for making use of the trainees once they returned with their new skills.

The result was that the FDCs gradually developed into a formal kind of learning institution, catering to primary school leavers. The pedagogical methods used were appalling, according to Swedish consultants who evaluated the project towards the end of the 1980s (Norbeck in Albinson, 1984, p. 2). The whole concept of a school, run for the benefit of the rural population and geared to their needs, had evaporated in ten years.

Instead of leaving the FDCs in the doldrums, SIDA (Swedish International Development Agency) put up more money, in an attempt to revitalize the FDC scheme. A two-pronged strategy was chosen: pairs of fifteen principals and fifteen study organizers were retrained in the FDC philosophy and practice, and a number of teacher trainers, selected from the same colleges as the administrators, were simultaneously trained at Kibaha, the FDC main center outside Dar es Salaam (once established as the Nordic Tanganyika Project in the early 1960s). The principals and organizers were asked to do some donkey work: to go out into the neighboring villages, to collect information on their educational needs and wishes, as a prototype for doing the same investigation "at home;" this they did, presenting model surveys with careful analyses and realistic proposals. Teachers at these FDCs were given a pedagogical rerun during the same period of time. In the end, seven FDCs were selected, situated in various parts of the country, and these are meant to become model schools for the FDCs in the regions.

The shake-up of the FDCs is being performed by the adult education center at Linköping University, on contract with SIDA.

The Swedish folk high schools have also worked directly with popular education projects. Latin American refugees in Sweden have been assembled for seminars and courses, and, when returning to their home countries, they have started work, e.g., within the framework of CEAAL, a regional umbrella organization that has received support from the solidarity fund of the Swedish Association of Folk High Schools and funds directly from SIDA. Also, after the collapse of the Soviet Union, individual folk high schools have struck up cooperation with groups in the Baltic states, especially Estonia, where fifteen folk high schools were opened in the course of one year.

NGOs

The total amount of development assistance money channeled through Swedish NGOs has increased rapidly during the last few years, from SEK c. 330 million in 1985 to c. 875 million eight years later. (If emergency assistance is added, it amounts to approximately SEK 1.5 billion, about 20% of all Swedish bilateral aid.)

The allocation is done in basically two ways:

A dozen major organizations, such as the confederation of the trade unions, the Swedish Cooperative Center (SCC), and a number of religious (mission) bodies, receive a lump sum that is negotiated every year with SIDA. The Authority does not scrutinize the proposals from these organizations in detail but demands careful and continuous evaluation.

All "other organizations" interested in carrying out development projects, must apply each time and present a detailed plan and a budget. Adult education takes up only a small portion of their aid.

Among the major NGOs, trade union and cooperative education get the biggest share of grants for adult education purposes, while religious organizations, although receiving a great slice of the total grant, do not spend a lot of the money on formal adult education projects.

LO (the Swedish Trade Union Confederation) and TCO (the Swedish Central Organization of Salaried Employees) have formed a joint Council that handles all international cooperation in their field. Practically the whole budget consists of grants from SIDA. A characteristic feature is the great number of projects: 140 in Africa, 67 in Asia, 113 in Latin America and 26 projects in former communist countries in Eastern Europe (in 1991/92). Most of the money is sent via the International Trade Secretariats and not directly to trade unions in the Third World, although the "movement to movement" cooperation is slowly gaining ground.

The objective is to make members of trade unions more active, better informed, more inclined to, and insistent on, democratic procedure and accountability in the trade union movement itself and in society at large. In other words, the primary aim is ideological, not economic (to eradicate poverty or raise the GNP of any particular country). It is stated in unequivocal terms that "the pedagogical method to be used is the study circle," as an integral part of creating "sustainable and democratic development." In practice, this can be hard to achieve, since formal education has a considerable influence on what participants expect from education and to the extent that educators have been irrevocably formed by the school system.

One general requirement stipulated by SIDA, in order for it to grant money to any NGO project, is that it be sanctioned by the authorities in the recipient country. As trade unionism in many Third World countries is in opposition to the government, this clause would cripple most cooperation and LO/TCO have been exempted from it.

As early as 1958, the cooperative movement started a solidarity fund, called the Without Boundaries Fund. It is still in existence, since 1964, handled by the SCC (Swedish Cooperative Center). This provided money to seminars offered in Sweden to cooperators around the Third World. Up to 1983, when the seminars were suspended, a total of 442 board members and staff from thirty-five countries had participated in the twenty-four seminars that had been held.

They were discontinued for several reasons. It was felt that Sweden as a venue could not offer the conditions and experiences that could be useful and appropriate for these participants. During this period of time, regional training centers had been set up in Delhi (India) and Moshi (Tanzania), and, it was believed, they could and should take over responsibility for this kind of education.

The SCC has been particularly active in Zambia, where a cooperative college opened in 1979. This is a powerhouse, where campaigns are planned, staff trained, material written and produced, documentation gathered. It possesses one of the best cooperative libraries in the whole region of Southern Africa. The actual work in the field is done by annual study group campaigns, partly carried out by mobile teams. The participants are recruited by the district organizers, who have been trained in study group methodology, which they impart to study group leaders.

The cost of cooperative education has been covered by the SCC, and, ultimately, by SIDA. In the case of Zambia, the cost has been covered not only out of the NGO purse mentioned above, but also by a slice of the SIDA sector grant.

The Swedish Mission Council is an umbrella organization of twenty-one churches and mission societies. Its main aim is to strengthen cooperation and fellowship in the religious community, but it also receives a large annual sum (SEK 170 million in 1990/91) from SIDA, for distribution among member organizations running development projects in the Third World. Most of the money goes to community development (education, health, water supply, agriculture, etc.) in some eighty countries, often backed up by volunteers. In the educational sector, most money goes to primary education (construction of schools, for instance) and to vocational training of young people, while only a minor part is allocated to adult education as such.

DIAKONIA is the aid and development organization of seven free churches ("free" as opposed to the Church of Sweden, which is funded by taxation, governed by politically elected laymen, and into which you up to 1994 were born as a citizen automatically becoming a member).

Out of a total SIDA grant of SEK c. 40 million (1990/91), about 11 million was spent on adult education (half of it on vocational training) in fifty countries. DIAKONIA does not run projects under its own name, always working through existing, well-established local structures, not necessarily parishes of sister churches.

During the difficult years when South Africa was in the grip of apartheid, it was not possible to implement a program of development assistance to the black population of the country. It was not even possible openly to give support to organizations working in South Africa or to the banned liberation movements, such as the African National Congress (ANC). Instead, an unspecified "humanitarian aid" was clandestinely distributed to various charity organizations, via a set of international bodies. The World University Service (WUS), based in Geneva, became the most important of these. This humanitarian aid grew in scope and sophistication over the years. In 1991/92, it had reached SEK 310 million. Out of that, 78 million was intended for education (including a substantial scholarship program for black South Africans in exile).

Many of the South African organizations receiving support were involved in political work against the apartheid regime. They are now reorienting themselves along professional lines. They have developed good networks and they are in high esteem among people because of their anti-apartheid record, whereas ministries and private enterprise have low credibility due to their previous involvement. On the other hand, support to the ANC will tail off, as the former liberation movement is transformed into a political party.

This means that for a long time to come adult education programs will be organized by NGOs, not by the Ministry of Education (or ministries, since, at the moment there are nineteen of them). SIDA will lend a great part of their support to adult education through WUS, which now has an office in Cape Town, better to monitor the work.

For 1992–93, there were about sixty projects that could be labeled "adult education." Many of these were literacy projects aimed at a particular area or a certain group of people. This can pay off immediately, as the wage system in South Africa is very rigid, and very much tied to formal criteria, such as the ability to read and write. A worker who acquires that skill is automatically upgraded a number of steps on the wage ladder.

The LO/TCO Council has given support to COSATU, the main trade union confederation in South Africa. Because of the unique situation, it did not carry on much education of members, but rendered social, economic, and also legal aid, to victims of apartheid.

Table 8.1

Basic Facts and Figures, 1989/90 (in millions, SEK)		
Total foreign aid budget	11,661	
Bilateral assistance via SIDA	6,190	
Education assistance	319	
Breakdown:		
— primary	180	
— vocational	75	
— adult	32	
Over a six-year period, 1984-90		
— primary	50%	
— vocational	20%	
— adult	10%	
Accumulated Swedish education assistance up to 1990:	3,500	
(To Sub-Saharan Africa)	3,000	
NGOs:		
Total assistance to education	262	
Formal education	84	
Nonformal Education	168	
— trade union + coop.	109	(40% of total)
— vocational	30	(12%)
— literacy	5	(2%)

(Annual Joint Review of the Swedish Support to General Education 1990/91, 1992, p.2)

LITERACY

Some of Sweden's program countries in Africa have carried out massive literacy campaigns. One of the most successful was that of Ethiopia, faced with a 93% illiteracy rate in 1974. Between 1979 and 1986, about nineteen million people were taught in fifteen indigenous languages by roughly one-and-one-half million "campaigners," volunteers who worked without pay in the villages. Nearly fifteen million reached Standard II proficiency in reading and writing. Most of the costs were met by the 25,000 Farmers' Societies. SIDA became involved at a later stage.

In two other African countries, Mozambique and Tanzania, also using literacy programs as part of an overall national mobilization effort, SIDA, on the other hand, made considerable contributions from the start. To quote from an evaluation report on Mozambique:

> SIDA has been the major contributor of finance and equipment to adult education, having provided 7.6 million Swedish crowns (SEK) over the period 1977–84. SIDA aid has been made use of in almost every sphere of operation, and has often been of crucial importance to many of the adult education programmes taking place at all. It has been exceptionally flexible, permitting some urgent reallocations of funds to cover special needs (Johnston, 1984, p. 17).

In the beginning, people enrolled quite enthusiastically, and the illiteracy rate actually dropped from 90% in 1975 to 72% in 1980 (no mean achievement), but in the 80s there was a drastic decline in participation. Quite apart from the civil strife and the disintegrating economy afflicting the country, the reasons were also intrinsic. The volunteers charged with the task had very few incentives to carry on the work, and they gradually got tired of this sustained sacrifice, as "almost no-one received any real recognition for their labour" (Ibid., p. 22). Some rewards had to be given, in order to recharge their batteries of motivation. Prizes in the form of radio sets and bicycles were set up for the best performers, and a T-shirt and a pair of shoes (hard to come by in Mozambique at the time) were handed out to everybody as a general encouragement. Simple things, but important in the context.

Tanzania embarked on a very ambitious program in 1970, proclaimed "Adult Education Year," followed by the "Literacy Year" of 1971, when a pilot project was carried out in six districts, where illiteracy was to be eradicated by the 9th of December, as part of the Independence Day celebrations. During the same period UNESCO launched its work-oriented adult literacy pilot project (WOALPP) in the Lake Victoria region. This "functional" approach combined literacy skills with discussions on improved agricultural methods. For instance, primers on various crops were used. This approach had a great influence on the large scale literacy campaigns of the 1970s. Over a ten-year period, SIDA gave about SEK 107 million in support, a substantial sum.

Botswana also ran an ambitious national literacy program in the 1980s. The objective was to make everyone literate in the official language, Setswana, by 1984. But, time was too short for the staff available to reach the target of 250,000 new literates. The program had been handled as a shot in the arm exercise, financed as an investment, not as a long-term commitment on a recurrent budget. After reorganization, the new target year was set at 1994.

The latest mass literacy campaign for SIDA to get involved in is the one newly-launched in Namibia. After the start in 1992, with textbooks in eight languages, and a much higher demand than supply, SIDA support will peak in 1993/94 (SEK 15 million), "as it is now that matters" (Johan Norbeck, interview, March 31, 1993).

In what ways has Sweden's bilateral aid, channeled through SIDA, been used for literacy work? A number of distinct fields can be listed.

Deliveries of paper for printing primers and other study materials is one big item. Two examples are 6,000 tons over a five year period for the literacy program in Tanzania, and a similar quantity for the Mozambican program. In Tanzania, a special Adult Education Printing Press was set up, and writers' workshops have been organized to boost the production of suitable reading material.

Another vital area is transport. Many adult education centers in rural areas cannot function, and many adult educators just do not take part, if vehicles are not provided. This involves anything from heavy duty lorries and Toyota land cruisers to motorcycles and quite ordinary bicycles. Of course, there are other problems. The roads are rough and spare parts are used up at a fast pace, in the end making the machines immobile. Often the "SIDA car" is the only means of motor transport in the area, which makes it vulnerable, it being co-opted by bigger shots, who claim priority. This means that these cars are not always used for the stated purpose of distributing adult education materials, supervision of study groups, and bringing participants to seminars at various training centers. Still, without these vehicles, many programs would never get going at all.

Apart from various teaching aids, much equipment is required for efficient literacy work. Take the rural training centers in Mozambique, for example. These were generally housed in abandoned mission stations which had been stripped of most of their fittings and gear. SIDA granted funds for equipping the centers with sheets and blankets, locally made wooden furniture, crockery and cutlery, etc., to make life a bit more bearable for the trainees, thus improving the quality of training. Unfortunately, most of these centers have been destroyed in Renamo attacks.

Finally, the training of professional adult educators, such as organizers and administrators, as well as literacy teachers—be they called promoters, volunteers, or campaigners—is a vital part of SIDA support to adult education. Even a small honorarium (as in Botswana, Tanzania, and Namibia) can be an incentive to keep the flame when the original enthusiasm has flagged.

POSTLITERACY

It is a well-known fact that new literates always run the risk of losing their newly-acquired skills of reading and writing, unless these are sustained by constant practice. They must be motivated to do so, and they must be given the opportunity. There are basically two ways of carrying out "postliteracy" activities: one is to provide reading material to predominantly illiterate environments, such as the rural areas in most African countries; another is to offer follow-up courses. A combination of the two is the most common approach.

In Tanzania, the setting up of rural libraries was part of the UNESCO literacy pilot project (WOALPP). With the completion of the pilot, this was expanded to cover several regions. The original plan was to set up a library of at least 500 titles in each and every village in the country (estimated at more than 8,000). In the event, some 3,000 were actually installed, normally in primary schools. Each library was manned by a librarian, who got some rudimentary training and a small honorarium to keep the library open a few days a week.

One of the major contributors to the scheme was SIDA, which also cooperated with the Swedish Library Association, matching money on the usual 80–20% basis, for purchasing books for rural libraries in Zimbabwe. Meanwhile, the Royal Library in Stockholm took on a very big project in Nicaragua and the Swedish Volunteer Service sent out librarians as volunteers in a number of countries.

The publication of rural newspapers in Swahili was tried out in the WOALPP project, quite successfully. Seven more were launched in the beginning of the 1970s, with support from SIDA, among others. They were generally four-column, four-page tabloids, with a print run of between 25,000 and (at best) 100,000 copies, to be distributed via adult education centers, rural libraries, and various organizations, such as the Institute of Adult Education. The retail price was very low. These simple papers, carrying local, national, and even international news, and always a relevant feature article and letters to the editor, became popular. Most people in an area knew about "their" newspaper, and many also read it.

To be able to read in peace is not a matter of course for many Africans. Their dwellings are seldom fitted with a study, or even a quiet corner. Women—who nearly always dominate in literacy classes—have a lot of chores around the house, and may not be able to read, at least not in daytime, even if they have the necessary books. Thus, a common reading room in the village can become a sort of haven for readers, and also a meeting place.

In Botswana, a number of these have been installed in the villages, with SIDA support. About fifty of them have been fitted with solar energy, a reliable source of light in a desert country. The reading room is often the only house in the village that has got electricity. Another way of solving the problem of night reading (and classes) is the provision of kerosene lamps. Over a decade ago, 750 such lamps were part of the adult education SIDA grant to Mozambique.

In Tanzania, an extensive program of postliteracy courses, in a number of subjects, at different levels, was organized in the wake of the national literacy campaigns of the 1970s. Some subjects were compulsory: Swahili, mathematics, political education, and agriculture. Some were offered only at certain centers, such as home economics and agriculture, while some were optional.

After about ten years of operation, this program was phased out in 1988, as it was far too academic, above the level of the learners, the gap too great between the functional literacy and the postliteracy curricula. These programs were also too expensive to run on a long-term basis on MoE funds. Instead, a more learner-oriented curriculum was introduced. Forty per cent of the time was allocated to theoretical work and 60% to practical matters. The objective was eventually to convert these courses into income-generating activities. There was no direct link between the postliteracy system and the formal education system.

Ethiopia was faced with a similar need among the millions who had taken part in the successful 1979 national literacy campaign. Community Skill Training Centers (CSTC) were erected (cf. the Tanzanian FDCs) and provided with arable land by the local communities. The aim was to have one in each of the 591 districts. By 1987, 408 districts actually had one.

Here people could learn crafts, such as carpentry, pottery, leather work, or weaving, but also modern agriculture, accountancy, etc. The centers were run by the nearly 25,000 Farmers' Societies (Cooperatives).

Unfortunately many of them were in a sorry state because of bad equipment, poorly trained staff, bad administrative routines, and general lack of funds.

In 1986–87, SIDA decided to undertake the fitting out of the centers and a training program for staff. This was well under way when the final phase of the civil war crippled many of the activities, including adult education. The Farmers' Societies had been the lowest level of the power structure, responsible for keeping local law and order and for collecting certain taxes, for instance, and they had gradually become very unpopular. Mengistu, having registered the wind of change in the communist world, tried to change his ways and lifted the farmers' obligation to belong to the societies. Farmers then claimed back the land they had allotted to the CSTCs and these lost their economic foundation. Some of them became targets of public wrath and were vandalized.

Also in Mozambique, another country ravaged by a long and bitter war, shored up by the Republic of South Africa, adult education has suffered but not disappeared altogether. Courses are held and adult education is still very much on the Mozambican agenda. One serious hampering factor has been the lack of trained adult educators.

In recent years, SIDA has mainly supported the Manga training center in Beira, with Linköping University as an intermediary. Modest plans for putting up a number of centers along the FDC-CSTC lines have met with SIDA approval. (A similar, but much grander project in Namibia, after some soul searching, was turned down for lack of realism.)

The Tanzanian postliteracy program was evaluated by a team in 1991. Their findings were alarming and their verdict was devastating.

This was a comparative study of five districts in different parts of Tanzania. The postliteracy program was said to be in full swing in all of them, but in fact was visible only in the most advanced of them, a coffee-growing district in the north of Tanzania. It had the only functioning library, well equipped and well run at that. Enrollment in courses was quite satisfactory, and retainment of literacy skills was at a distinctly higher level than in the other four districts. In those, activity was low. Less than a fifth of the population was attending classes, less than a third had ever done so. The libraries were closed. A third of the respondents said that they never, or hardly ever, read anything, over fifty per cent said that they hardly ever made calculations on paper. The rural newspapers were not distributed, or were spread in a capricious fashion. The adult educators seemed demoralized.

It is obvious that literacy as such does not lead to prosperity or even economic progress. The opposite seems more true: when a community has reached a certain level of economic development, the need for reading and writing will become evident, and then the actual skills in their turn can add to further advancement. When the conviction that literacy leads to prosperity is no longer there, and when the political momentum—the driving force in any literacy program—is lost, any program can deteriorate very fast.

The evaluation concluded: "It is clearly inappropriate for the project to continue with fictional classes, fictional learners, and fictional teachers" (Carr-Hill et al, 1991, p. 327). Therefore, the SIDA grant was suspended in 1992, "until such a time as a new strategy has been developed in the Ministry" [of Education] (Agneta Lind interview, April 1, 1993).

SUMMARY

In an international comparison, Sweden has always allocated an unusually large amount to basic education, adult education included; most donor countries concentrate on higher education. How did this come about?

One reason is that the popular movement element has been strong in Swedish foreign aid since its inception, which was not a political decision but grew out of the international solidarity work among the popular organizations. A joint committee handling this work was eventually remodeled into the civil service department that in 1965 became SIDA. Some of the committee members who were ardent adult educators became, as SIDA bureaucrats in disguise, "apostles" of adult education in the various aid programs.

A strong commitment to support basic education was also in harmony with the social democratic ideology, then prevalent in Sweden, pledging solidarity with the underprivileged and equal opportunities to education. This also found inspiration, or expression, in the strategy to meet basic needs, stating not only the right to food and clean water but also to knowledge, with reading and writing as instrumental skills. In some of the newly liberated countries Sweden found a political will and egalitarian aspirations it could recognize and encourage, although the one-party structures that evolved at times could be felt as an embarrassment, since Swedes are used to functioning in a pluralistic society.

It can be said that Sweden found a "niche" that it has continued to

occupy. There are no signs that it will abandon it. The Jomtien conference in Thailand in 1990 saw a shift in the assistance policy of Germany
and the Netherlands, but hardly in that of Sweden, which again stressed
the importance of education for *adults* in the global onslaught on igno-
rance. It should also be said that it is a small niche, adult education getting roughly ten per cent of the total education assistance, which already
is a small share of the total aid budget.

If adult education is so important, Sweden being one of the main
actors, why is not more money allocated to this purpose? Government to
government aid is between Sweden and a number of African countries.
SIDA took care of half of the recurrent adult education budget in Tanzania for several years. As we noted above, the SIDA support was crucial
for the literacy program in Mozambique, and is going to be so in the
Namibia program.

Few Swedes have been directly involved in field work, for the simple
reason that they have no expertise in literacy to offer. Instead, the Swedish role has been that of backing up with "logistics," such as transport,
training, textbooks, forks, and sheets. Sometimes SIDA has influenced
the direction of a program; for example, in Mozambique original plans
to teach in Portuguese were dropped in favor of local languages, following recommendations from SIDA.

The NGOs have a much wider geographical coverage than government programs. They give support to a great many small projects around
the globe. This presents a problem for SIDA: How to handle all these
projects in a rational and professional way? The solution has been to
lump them together and trust the good intentions and sense of responsibility of the nongovernmental organizations. On the whole, this has
worked well over the years. In some cases, such as South Africa, where
the Swedish record of staunch opposition to apartheid is something to be
proud of, this was absolutely necessary to avoid political fuss and jeop-
ardizing people's lives.

SIDA has also given support to several international and regional
bodies, such as the ICAE, the CEAAL in Latin America, the AALAE in
Africa, and has provided financial support to various studies and campaigns, such as the International Literacy Year.

Of course, it can be asked if it is an entirely good thing to try to
export a concept, born and bred in Swedish circumstances, to societies
with quite different cultural backgrounds. In many places, this has
failed, mainly because formal pedagogical methods have proven too

strong. There is always the tendency for an educational setup to become a world to itself, cut off from the surrounding community. Why is it so difficult to build an educational activity for adults from bottom-up? Because there are always forces in a society that co-opt such ambitions and one has to start all over again. Democracy is not a gift forever; it is something people must achieve again and again.

In that sense, Swedish folk development education is a method that can be emulated, rather than imitated. It should be regarded as an inspiration and not as a blueprint. Seen in this light, education can be said to be Sweden's best export commodity, far better than Bofors guns.

ABBREVIATIONS USED IN THIS CHAPTER

ABF, Arbetarnas Bildningsförbund, the Workers' Educational Association

AMU, Arbetsmarknadsutbildning, National Employment Training Agency

CSTC, Community Skills Training Centre, Ethiopia

FDC, Folk Development College, Tanzania

IAE, Institute of Adult Education, Tanzania

Komvux, Kommunala Vuxenskolan, Municipal Adult Education

LO, Landsorganisationen, the Swedish Trade Union Confederation

SCC, the Swedish Cooperative Centre

TCO, Tjänstemännens Centralorganisation, the Swedish Central Organization of Salaried Employees

WOALPP, Work-Oriented Adult Literacy Pilot Project, Tanzania

WUS, World University Service, Geneva

BIBLIOGRAPHY

Interviews

At the Center of Adult Education: Linköping University: Stellan Boozon-Johansson, Director; Hans Hoverberg, Consultant (former teacher trainer); Johan Norbeck, Head of International Cooperation.

At SIDA Education Division: Ingemar Gustafsson, Head of Division; Margareta Husén, Senior Program Officer; Agneta Lind, Head of Section; Christine McNab, Program Officer; Britt Sjöstedt, Program Officer. At the Swedish Council of Adult Education: Peter Engberg, Director. At the LO/TCO Council of International Trade Union Cooperation: Kerstin Wallin, Project Director.

Consultant with more than ten years of adult education experience in the Third World: Folke Albinson.

Published Sources

Abraham, Kinfe (1992). *Swedish education assistance: A statistical review of education, culture and public administration aid and some global pointers.* Document No. 55, SIDA Education Division, 1(1989/90–91/92). Stockholm: Swedish International Development Authority.

Albinson, Folke (1990). *Regional seminars for strengthening the CSTC Programme: Report from two evaluations.* Addis Ababa, Ethiopia: Ministry of Education.

——— (1988). *Report on a study visit to adult education programmes in Tanzania.* Dar es Salaam, Tanzania: Ministry of Education.

——— (1990). *Ministry of Education/SIDA cooperation in adult education, 1986/87–1989/90.* Addis Ababa, Ethiopia: Ministry of Education.

——— (1993). *Training for cooperative leadership: A study of SCC's international cooperation seminars, 1962–83.* Stockholm: Swedish Cooperative Centre.

Albinson, Folke, Tyko Holgersson, Johan Norbeck, and Rolf Sundén (1984). *Swedish folk development education and developing countries.* Document No. 18, SIDA Education Division. Stockholm: Swedish International Development Authority.

Albinson, Folke, and Charles Kabuga (1985). *Education and training plan for the cooperative sector in Zambia: Proposed guidelines 1986–90.* Stockholm: Swedish Cooperative Centre.

Blid, Henry (1990). *Education by the people: Study circles.* Ludvika, Sweden: ABF, Workers' Education Association.

Carr-Hill, Roy A., Mikael N. Kweka, Mary Rusimbi, and Rustica Chingelele (1991). *The functioning and effects of the Tanzania Literacy Programme.* Stockholm: Swedish International Development Authority.

Interfund (1992). *Education updated: The Interfund briefing on education in South Africa.* Pamphlet. Johannesburg, South Africa: Interfund.

Johansson, Anders I., Kjell Nyström, and Rolf Sundén (1983). *Adult education in Tanzania: A review.* Document No. 9, SIDA Education Division. Stockholm: Swedish International Development Authority.

146   ADULT EDUCATION THROUGH WORLD COLLABORATION

Johnston, Anton (1984). *SIDA support and other international support to the adult education sector in Mozambique.* Stockholm: Swedish International Development Authority.

Lauglo, Jon, and Mmantsetsa P. T. Marope (1987). *Education in Botswana 1981-86 with Swedish support.* Document No. 35, SIDA Education Division. Stockholm: Swedish International Development Authority.

Lind, Agneta, and Anton Johnston (1990). *Adult literacy in the Third World: A review of objectives and strategies.* Stockholm: Swedish International Development Authority.

LO/TCO Council of Trade Union Cooperation (1992). *Trade union international assistance.* Annual Report 1991/92. Stockholm: Swedish Trade Union Confederation & the Swedish Central Organisation of Salaried Employees.

——— (1992). *Trade union international assistance.* Pamphlet.

Löfving, Anna (1992). *Sammanstallning av de undervisningsprojekt som 1990/91 fick stöd av SIDA via svenska enskilda organisationer* (Survey of educational projects receiving SIDA support via Swedish NGOs). Stockholm University.

Ministry of Education and Culture, Namibia (1993). Fact finding report on the ministry literacy programme. Internal memorandum. Windhoek, Namibia.

——— (1991). *Guide to the National Literacy Programme in Namibia.* Windhoek, Namibia: Ministry of Education and Culture.

Norbeck, Johan, and Anton Johnston (1984). *Projects of the professional training of adult education cadres in Mozambique.* Consultancy Report. Linköping, Sweden: Center of Adult Education, Linköping University.

Pehrsson, Kajsa (1990). *Rätten till kunskap. Kampen för läskunnighet i tredje världen* (The right to knowledge: The battle for literacy in the Third World). SIDA pamphlet. Stockholm: Swedish International Development Authority.

SIDA (1991). *Education statistical digest 1989/90-1991/92: Country profiles, 2.* Stockholm: Swedish International Development Authority.

Warr, David (1987). *Zambia Cooperative College national study group programme 1983-85.* Evaluation Report. Cambridge, U.K.: International Extension College.

Åberg, Ingrid Puck (1992). *Att skapa något slags hopp. Om svenskt humanitärt bistånd i Södra Afrika* (To give some kind of hope: On humanitarian aid in Southern Africa). Stockholm: Swedish International Development Authority.

CHAPTER 9

The Netherlands: Dutch Viewpoints on Adult Education in Developing Countries

KEES P. EPSKAMP

Educational activities within the context of development and change aim at linking up content with the participant's learning needs. Education always intends, one way or another, to accomplish a process of change. This process, in the first instance, is related to the level of awareness of individuals and/or groups. In short, next to the accumulation of knowledge and the acquisition of skills, learning is aimed at awareness raising. However, such processes of change do not come about in a vacuum. Changes in individual consciousness cannot be disconnected from the social context in which they take place, not even in situations of informal learning.

What do we mean by informal learning? In general, it can be defined as the process by which the members of a target group are provided with a frame of reference, through which they can interpret and handle their own experiences in a more adequate way than they did before. In this way, learning has a broader meaning than schooling, although the two concepts overlap to a certain extent. We start from the principle that schooling aims at the acquisition and transfer of a certain body of knowledge and of certain skills. In practice, however, it is quite difficult to maintain the distinction between schooling and informal learning. Most schooling includes a broader educative function as well, whereas school-like transfer of knowledge and skills can be detected in informal learning situations. Accordingly, the distinction made concerns only differences in emphasis.

147

In essence, informal learning is "learning from each other." This has certain consequences, especially in the case of permanent education. The solution for the clash between regular formal education and certain branches of permanent education, which aim at minorities in society that have poor chances and are beyond the reach of formal education, is sought in an integration of informal learning and formal schooling. Theoretically, little can be said against this, insofar as real integration is concerned and educative activities are not merely used as a resource to motivate participants to take more education. Real integration, however, can only be apparent from the attitude of the tutors and animators.

As said before, educational activities aim at linking up the learning contents with the participants' learning needs. Hence, for example, there are no rigid curricula and required examinations, as is often the case with formal schooling. Gradually animators, facilitators, and social workers in the educative field became aware of large differences in the views on society held respectively by the target groups and themselves.

MORE ATTENTION TO AFRICA IN THE NINETIES

The North Atlantic nations, as well as the Third World, have long since searched for non-Western development models. They discovered, gradually, that these models actually do exist, and are directly related to non-Western development thinking. In the case of many indigenous peoples, this thinking is not based on a Western linear view of history and progress. Other development models are based on a completely different value system, as inspired by the great world religions of Islam, Hinduism, or Buddhism, as in Iran, India and Thailand, China or Japan. From a worldwide economic point of view, these non-Western development models are slightly inconvenient for the implementation of development cooperation policies from donor countries.

If we regard development as a process in which society gains increasing control over the environment, and growing control over its own political fate, and offers its members increasing control over themselves, then, according to Inayatullah (1967, p. 102), it is ironic that the North Atlantic world, which has developed itself with the help of innovations in the areas of science, technology, and the social organization, expects the Third World to copy or adopt this course without violating the creative monopoly of the West. However, no development process benefits from thoughtless copying.

When, in the mid-eighties, Africa south of the Sahara was declared more or less bankrupt by the World Bank, this continent became of more interest to all North Atlantic donor agencies, including the national ones. The goal became to abolish the nightmare of poverty from Africa in the nineties. A number of studies showed that the development efforts of the past years have not brought Africa actual structural and sustainable socioeconomic changes, least of all to the Poorest of the Poor (POP). External reasons for this were, of course, the international drop in the price of raw materials, the growing international debt, and the decreasing influx of capital from industry and donor agencies. Moreover, droughts and desertification increased as well.

In addition, there are internal factors, such as the failure of almost all countries to reach the necessary policy reforms. In the early eighties, it became clear that the African one-party state (ruled by the military or otherwise) did not function well when confronted with such external tensions. It also appeared that the internal political problems in almost every African country amount to cultural or ethnic problems. Domestic wars, in the eyes of North Atlantic governments, resembled the old tribal tensions, so familiar in the Africa of colonial times, and maybe even characteristic and endogenous of kingdoms, states, and cultures that have long been used to shifting borders and changing leaders.

The former colonial governments, the majority of which constitute the current donors in development cooperation, and which are united in the European Community (EC), are finding this very difficult. The Europeans, more so than the Americans who declared Africa economically bankrupt, are struggling with the formulation of an African cultural bankruptcy. The more so because the EC, as yet, is an unwieldy administrative system in which the preparation and formulation of policy often takes a number of years before it can actually be implemented.

In the long-term perspective study, *Sub-Saharan Africa: From crisis to sustainable growth* (1989), which was conducted by the World Bank, attention is paid not only to schooling at primary and tertiary levels, but to training for employment. It provides a design for the efficient management of human resources programs, which are of interest to the informal economic sector and the small-scale entrepreneurship. In adult education, this requires the providing of basic knowledge and skills for trade activities, and more attention to the principles of apprenticeship.

While, on the one hand, the World Bank and the European Community set structural socioeconomic requirements for African countries before they can even look forward to the least financial support, on the

other hand, within the framework of the World Decade for Cultural Development (WDCD), a great deal of attention was paid to the cultural
difficulties that may be encountered with integrated rural development
projects or other income-generating projects in Africa. According to Serageldin (1991), Japanese donors, in particular, try to stimulate African
ideas on group dynamics through the Quality Circle Concept (QCC), in
order to increase competition and greater efficiency in management,
in public administration, and African businesses. These are new trends
in development thinking that the World Bank welcomes.

Yet, besides the interest in new developments in the formal sector of
industry, interest also remains in the informal sector of economic life, as
a part of the development at grassroots level, and as a phase in the transition to a modern economy. At this level particularly, the cultural component of local development can be given a tailor-made interpretation, as
Mutanda Ntumba (1991, pp. 37–38) clearly indicates for the projects
that involve the Centre of Bantu Civilisations (CECEBA) in Central
Africa.

EDUCATION FOR ALL IN 2000: THE DUTCH GOVERNMENT POSITION

The World Bank organized the World Conference on Education for
All, in cooperation with the multilateral UN organizations UNESCO,
UNDP and UNICEF, in Bangkok, in March 1990. The guidelines for
Education for All have been adopted by many governments in the North
as part of their policy and funding of development cooperation. From the
sixties onward, international development circles have taken the position
that human resources are the basis of development. In that development
process, according to the Dutch government policy note *A world of difference; A new framework for development co-operation in the 1990s*
(1991, p. 175), education fulfills two important social functions: a socio-
economic and a sociocultural one. In addition, Dutch policy clearly emphasizes the development of all types of basic education.

Basic education for all in developing countries implies a combination
of formal, nonformal, and informal education. This combination is
aimed at imparting essential knowledge, skills, values, and attitudes
needed for a decent existence. This policy encompasses children, as well
as adults who have had insufficient access to education.

In brief, according to Dutch policy, the first priority is to comply with basic learning needs. Meeting these basic needs is, in fact, a form of poverty prevention. At the same time, it is a tool that reinforces the cultural identity of the people, and provides them with knowledge and basic skills to enable them more easily to gain access to health care, to information on food and nutrition, and to provisions of better housing and hygiene.

During the World Conference in 1990, mentioned above, one of the objectives set for future aid was that in the year 2000 formal education should be accessible to all. Aid to Africa especially deserves the highest priority, because here, percentage wise, education is least accessible to the population. This is true, to a lesser extent, for Asian and Latin American countries; the improvements of education striven for there are of a more qualitative nature. On these two continents, education is inaccessible mainly to the poorest people in society: the lower castes, the poor, women, nomads, indigenous peoples, refugees, and ethnic minorities.

To be able to realize education for all in the magic year 2000, a restructuring of educational systems is to be striven for; a reallocation of government funds must be accomplished; and the necessary savings must be made. This applies to formal education received through schools and similar educational institutions, in particular.

Furthermore, the government note mentioned above also acknowledges a number of traditional and nonformal educational types of transfer of knowledge and schooling that may contribute significantly to the development of society and the individual, such as fighting illiteracy; providing training of skills in the fields of nutrition, health, and hygiene; stimulating traditional types of professional training; providing types of on-the-job training; and extending forms of distance education via radio and television.

In the Dutch policy note, *A world of difference*, mentioned above,[1] one of the starting points was that the support to education in developing countries will be intensified. In nonformal education this support is mainly translated into special programs and projects designed for women and small farmers, through (semi) government as well as private channels. The education of trainers and information officers is essential. Within the integrated rural development programs, attention will be paid to functional literacy and the teaching of basic skills, such as reading, writing, arithmetic, food production and processing, health care, nutrition, hygiene, earning of income, etc. In brief, the nonformal educational activities serve to reinforce the cultural identity of the poorest of the poor, and to increase their chance of a productive life.

In this note, culture is regarded as " . . . whatever characterises a community, or the combination of mentalities and ways of life, including the tangible and intangible products of that community" (1991, p. 190). However, in practice, in development cooperation, the concept of "culture" is of relevance to various issues such as, (1) the sociocultural setting within which the development activities take place; (2) the ways of living and thinking within a community that are subject to processes of social change; and (3) cultural manifestations which are preserved (such as temples), promoted (such as theater), or exchanged (such as pictures or texts) through international cooperation.

Hence, in Dutch development cooperation, culture is not at all regarded as irrelevant or as an obstacle. On the contrary, technological and economic developments cannot be separated from the cultural context.[2] Furthermore, in Dutch policy, culture is not regarded as invariable, or "sacred," but as developing constantly. That is why the tying in of development activities with current processes of cultural change is advocated.

ADULT EDUCATION AND THE DUTCH OFFICIAL GOVERNMENT POLICY

Dutch government support of adult education projects and programs in the Third World is formulated and coordinated by the Directorate-General of International Cooperation (DGIS), also referred to as the Department of Development Cooperation, which is a part of the Ministry of Foreign Affairs. Besides incidental contributions to special projects, the structural management and the allocation of funds for the financing of small-scale projects in the area of nonformal and adult education have been contracted out to four Dutch nongovernmental organizations (NGOs), each having its own networks and contacts with counterpart organizations in the Third World. These four NGOs are the CEBEMO, the ICCO, the HIVOS and the NOVIB.[3]

Each of these four organizations has its own view on development aid. This is not surprising, considering the fact that CEBEMO and ICCO are, in fact, clerical organizations that used to take care of the aid to the Catholic and Protestant missions. HIVOS is also based on a philosophical view on development and cooperation: a humanistic philosophy. NOVIB claims to be a neutral NGO, but has long since been slightly left wing. In spite of these differences in background, all four organizations are of the opinion that development projects in the area of adult education should not be imposed from the outside, should be small-scale, should benefit the poorest of the poor, should be target group oriented, and should promote a participatory approach in the formulation, the execution, and the evaluation of the development projects.

And yet, over the past few years, the general national flow of criticism of development aid has pressed these four Dutch NGOs hard.[4] A study of the impact of the work of the four hit home, and specifically addressed the need for a clearer cost-benefit analysis, and for professionalization of the organization of each of them. They were also criticized for lacking internal communication and cooperation. According to Van de Veen (1991, p. 8), the criticism was aimed at the pretentious slogan of the four organizations in particular: "Where Dutch government fails to reach the poorest of the poor, we succeed."

However, this study showed that in the past twenty-five years the best results were achieved with the financing of elementary social provisions in health care, water supply, and educational activities. These provisions reached the poorest people best. It appears that in economic programs the benefits of a project usually reach those in society who already are doing better. Projects that are aimed at increasing awareness of power relations, or that offer political schooling, often show disappointing results.

In accordance with the Dutch government position, the policy report, "Development Cooperation and Education in the Nineties," appeared in 1992. It includes a specific paragraph about adult education. The report is based on the view that the most striking characteristic of nonformal adult education is the voluntary participation in the learning programs.[5] This makes certain demands on the setup of these programs, and the way in which the transfer of knowledge and social and professional skills takes place. Therefore, the programs should tie in with the learning needs of the target group. The programs are arranged in such a way that they emphasize knowledge and skills that can be applied immediately. Every element in these programs is aimed at increasing the accessibility of the education offered.

This report is based on the fact that the need for nonformal education gradually evolved because many young people are not able to follow all the successive phases of formal education. Sometimes they lack material means. Sometimes they lack the intellectual capacity to meet the requirements of the different levels. Students who drop out of school often display a measure of illiteracy.

Following UNESCO, the Ministry of Development Cooperation judges an illiterate to be someone who cannot read or write and understand a simple text about everyday life. The statistics on illiteracy vary considerably per area. It is certain that, in almost every area, the highest number of illiterates can be found among older people and women.

Besides the large-scale national literacy campaigns, the real work falls to NGOs that often set up literacy courses on location, and remain to support these for specific target groups, such as the "untouchables," women, refugees, ethnic minorities, landless laborers, etc. In spite of the fact that literacy may be seen as a goal by itself, in these educational programs learning to read and write is linked to the acquisition of useful professional or social skills, a type of functional literacy.

Not only do they try to make the nonformal educational activities match the immediate learning needs of the target groups, thus giving them better access to the labor market, they also try to make adult education tie in with the local culture in general.

> This applies especially to the use of bulletins, visual and written materials for people who have only recently learned to read and write, and to the use of educational radio programmes that tie in with prevailing traditions. The use of locally present performing arts (among which narrative art, theater, mask and puppet play, dance and music), as a means of education in developing countries, also increases. These tools tie in well with the local culture, and enable one to illustrate things in such a way that they become clear and accessible.[6]

For that reason, in the past the Dutch Department of Development Cooperation cofinanced two international seminars to give birth to, and support, the International Popular Theatre Alliance (IPTA). Both initiatives received technical assistance from the International Council for Adult Education (ICAE) in Toronto. The first meeting was held in 1982 in Koitta, a small Hindu village not far from Dhaka, Bangladesh. The second meeting was organized in 1991 in Rehoboth, Namibia.

Research in educational strategies and adult education in developing countries is conducted on a continuing basis, at the levels of formal and nonformal education. In addition to a number of individual researchers affiliated with Dutch universities, a large part of Dutch research potential has been assembled within a unique research center, known as CESO.

CENTER FOR THE STUDY OF EDUCATION
IN DEVELOPING COUNTRIES

The Center for the Study of Education in Developing Countries (CESO) was founded in 1963 to do interdisciplinary research. Its general objective is to make a scientific and practical contribution to the improvement of education in developing countries and to development cooperation. That is why CESO aims at solving various educational problems. It may, therefore, be described as a small research institute, the specific activities of which are determined by demands that arise from the actual development processes in the Third World.

CESO's central function consists of a national and international exchange of scientific information about education in developing countries, in the process collecting research materials, studies and documentation. The research activities contribute to the solving of fundamental problems in education, problems that hinder human development in today's and tomorrow's world. Because of this practical attitude, research and studies are often intertwined with advisory work. The tasks CESO has set for itself are: conducting research; providing advice; monitoring documentation; providing education, training and guidance; and, finally, maintaining networks, at home and abroad.

Besides these tasks, which are characteristic of the activities undertaken and maintained by its staff and secretariat, there are, of course, the more substantial or thematic activities that can be distinguished, four of which have priority in the CESO planning: (1) description and analysis of educational developments and systems; (2) education and productive life; (3) education and cultural identity; (4) evaluation of educational activities.

In adult education, research into education, culture, and a productive life is especially important. CESO tries to make its ideas on research and capacities match the national and international trends and questions as formulated, for example, at the World Conference on Education for All (Jomtien 1990).

CESO's general view on the educational situation makes the relationship between education and development more explicit. On the one hand, CESO pays attention to the development within formal educational systems; yet, on the other hand, it acknowledges that a human being is formed by a diversity of complementary or conflicting learning situations. It regards education as a central element in human culture. That is why its research is geared towards the interface between education and society, in which, in principle, research and the provision of services are not limited to the level of education.

Since its foundation, CESO has paid a great deal of attention to basic education. Initially, this concerned formal basic education and related socialization and education at home. Later, the activities, stimulated by external demand, were geared more towards various forms of education for specific, often deprived, target groups: the rural population, women, job-seeking youngsters, and minorities. CESO has always approached these "education lacking" groups from their sociocultural background and history. Examples are the "Territorios Nacionales" (Colombia), "Delsilife" (South East Asia), the refugees issue in Central America, and studies relating to "Education and Production."

Following the Dutch government position, CESO pays special attention to the two important social functions of education: the socioeconomic and the sociocultural. This attention permeates the research themes "Education and a productive life" and "Education and culture." It is clearly recognizable in the surveys on "indigenous learning" and the activities dealing with "popular education" in Latin America.

The cooperation between the governments of the Netherlands and Colombia (1981–1983) in the experimental application of an educational model in the Territorios Nacionales of Colombia, in the project areas of the Vaupes and Vichada, showed how vulnerable an adult education program is, when it comes to promoting consciousness-raising projects among deprived population groups. This bilateral project was started in 1978 and was aimed at developing an educational model for the indigenous population.

Until the end of the sixties, these Territorios Nacionales seemed of no importance in the policy of the Colombian government. Only the church, because of her mission posts, had a better insight into social life in this area, and in the common learning needs. However, according to Oltheten et al. (1992, p. 336), reliable data about the demographic structure, the indigenous lifestyle, and natural surroundings were lacking.

In view of the increasing border conflicts with neighboring countries, and infiltration by cocaine barons and guerrillas, the central government felt compelled to get a better grip on this area, and to give the local people the feeling, through adult education, that they were, at the very least, Colombian citizens. During the five-year plan 1978–1983 the initial impetus was given to achieve this goal. It later grew into a large-scale project among the Indian communities in the jungle and the savannas.

The educational model was clearly placed within the social context of the rural communities, stressing that education should be seen as a permanent process. That is why the first priority was to investigate how the education offered could be adjusted to the social system and the educational needs of the Indian population. To map these needs, the local people were actively involved in the assessments studies.

SOCIO-ECONOMIC DEVELOPMENT	SOCIO-CULTURAL DEVELOPMENT
PRODUCTIVE LIFE	CULTURAL IDENTITY

Figure 9.1: Two social functions of education and their intended outcomes

The needs demonstrated an ambivalence the researchers had not expected. People wanted to identify more with the national society, yet, at the same time, they felt the need to reinforce their own indigenous identity. This showed particularly in their wish for literacy. Learning Spanish as the official language, and learning basic arithmetic for trade activities, were much appreciated. Yet, the indigenous language also deserved more research. In addition, they wanted more insight into and control over the rich natural resources, and a new and autonomous way of exploitation that would make them less dependent on large landowners, mining and oil companies, etc.

This participatory way of working, which would lead to the objectives mentioned above, was not well received by either the Roman Catholic Church or the Colombian government. The Church lost her monopoly on providing education through the mission schools, and, with it, her grip on the population. The Colombian government was afraid the local population would become too emancipated. The elections in 1983 provided the Ministry of Education with a reason to cut down on the project.

INFORMAL LEARNING: INDIGENOUS KNOWLEDGE AND TRAINING IN VOCATION SKILLS

Each society has a social organization in which individuals take their places. Whereas the biological gratification of the need for food existed in hunting animals and the collecting of edible plants, the options and preferences concerning edibility and preparation were determined by the cultural context. The knowledge, skills, ideas, and attitudes were transmitted from one generation to the next through the upbringing of children. "Such knowledge, skills and values have been transmitted to succeeding generations through techniques and methods arising from the native people's own ingenuity and tradition" (Soriano, 1981, p. 61).

According to Soriano, despite the fact that it is a question of "different layers of indigenousness, vertically and horizontally," indigenous learning systems have a number of characteristics in common (*Ibid.*, pp. 61–64). The most important of these is probably that learning is a holistic experience. According to Bennagen (1985, p. 20), this holistic experience can be accounted for by the fact that during the learning event no distinction can be made between the affective, the normative, and the cognitive elements. Because the distance between apprentice and master is defined as optimum, on the basis of an ascribed or achieved status, the involvement of all participants (kinsmen, peers, friends, and other members of the community) is optimum, too. The learning event, therefore, aims at a consistency in which values and goals are related to actual economic opportunities. "This way, the holistic character of indigenous learning systems is retained by maintaining the consistency between content (e.g., productive science and technology), method and personnel (e.g., community participation) and goals (e.g., increased production and equity)" (Bennagen, 1985, p. 21).

The setting of such indigenous learning processes, therefore, is life itself. The learning situation is almost always immediate; that is, work and learning situation are closely knit together. The aim is not a career, a future. People work "here and now" in order to learn, and they learn "here and now" in order to work.

The pedagogics of traditional learning systems are mainly oral and performative. They are a life-long process of "learning by doing." Written sources describing these pedagogics are negligible. Only in the last hundred years have ethnographers and anthropologists done research in this area.

The content in indigenous learning processes changes with age and especially with sex for each social group. The content is partly determined by the position the child will have in the community when an adult.

As the division of labor increases, the indigenous learning processes get a more explicit character. The transference of knowledge and learning of skills will no longer be solely dependent on the seasons and the individual's age. At the same time, particular people are assigned the role of instructor.

For the transference of knowledge, these teachers make use of performative pedagogics. Indigenous learning processes are made up of demonstration by the teacher and copying by the pupil, and also by casual learning that takes place as pupils observe adult actions and then later perform them when at play.

With a further increase in division of labor, indigenous learning processes become more specific and explicit. Learning skills and knowledge are assigned to particular stages of life. Special people are appointed to act as instructors, or tutors. Customary didactic methods include observation of what was being demonstrated, repeatedly trying out what had been observed, through simulation and imitation, followed by a test period in which the individual seeks to prove his or her competence.

As the social organization of a society grows still more complex, owing to further division of labor and increasing technological progress, professional sectors become ever more specialized, and basic skills become increasingly diverse. The training of skills becomes more and more technical. Apprenticeship systems come into being.

In the course of 1985, CESO undertook a long-term study of indigenous learning processes. This meant the familiarization of people in a certain sociocultural unit with knowledge and skills that tie in with a certain manufacturing sector, as it takes place outside the training or information programs that have been developed for this particular purpose. This study is aimed at the Southeast Asian region, and initially focused on the food production sector.

In 1988, the preparation of a workshop on indigenous technological knowledge, and the way in which this knowledge is acquired, resulted in a modest conference called the "Southeast Asian Regional Workshop on Indigenous Technological Knowledge," which was organized jointly by the Social Research Institute of the Chulalongkorn University (CUSRI) and CESO.

The workshop was followed up by regional contacts with the Mountain People's Culture and Development Education Foundation (MPCDE), in Chiengmai, Thailand. This resulted in the setting up of a small research project, starting in 1990. The project's goal was to test a fieldwork method aimed at gaining insight into the acquisition of knowledge in productive activities, and the relationship between the different (formal, nonformal, and informal) ways of acquiring knowledge, and the teaching of skills in a number of trades.

POPULAR EDUCATION

It is generally known that education in any society transmits current values and behavioral patterns in order to maintain the existing social organization. Yet, at the same time, it is generally accepted that education contributes to social change. Continuously present is a tension between the conservative and the innovative nature of education. A second fundamental contradiction in education is that it treats people equally, yet it also makes them different because it is geared to training specialists.[7]

In Latin America, popular education aims to increase the awareness of oppressed groups, and to change the conditions under which they live. Therefore, it has political implications—albeit not explicitly so. "Popular education" is an instrument that is used in a process of liberation. Among other things, it opposes the current adult education programs that have been imposed from the outside, and that aim to change the "pupil" without changing the sociopolitical system in which the "pupil" lives. Popular education tries to break through this barrier by stimulating and monitoring initiatives at a local level and by letting the local population determine their own history and development. For this purpose, the community needs to organize itself before undertaking joint actions. This requires a high level of participation of the entire population.

Much of this development is based on the ideas of Paulo Freire, developed in the 1970s.[8] His opinions about consciousness-raising, and the opposing of the instrumentality of the current adult education programs, form a common denominator of all "popular education" initiatives. However, in the various Latin American countries, a variety of popular education models are applied in slums and rural communities and among the marginal groups. Popular education uses the minimal action of socially oppressed groups and spontaneous initiatives. One of the objectives of popular education organizations is to make the people trust their own initiatives.

The most striking characteristics of popular education are the following: it has a concrete point of departure, because it works in, and originates from, common sectors in society; it is a process in which knowledge is created because the people themselves participate in its development; it is an action-oriented development which aims to change reality; it is a collective approach, and not a manipulative initiative developed from above. Popular education is practice-oriented, because it consists of initiatives taken by the people to meet their own basic needs in the area of education. It is by definition nonformal education and mainly aimed at adults.

Finally, an important characteristic of popular education is that it promotes and strives for, the recognition of the autonomous "popular culture," and, consequently, upgrades the cultural identity of the people concerned. The people and organizations involved are made aware of the importance of indigenous and independent knowledge systems and forms of expression as valuable alternatives to a culture introduced from outside. The existing local culture is then used for the development of locally produced learning and transference materials.

Even though popular education as a pedagogic movement is appreciated, there is a clear need for a systematization of its educational practices. An increase of systematic knowledge renders the possibility to train better educators, and to achieve higher efficiency in the projects.

To contribute to this, in the first half of the nineties, CESO cooperated with a group of Latin American researchers that conducted research based on a number of concrete activities in various countries, around the following sub-themes: the quality of the educational processes; characteristics of the pedagogical relationship; the relationship between the activities and politics and policy.

In the course of 1992, CEBEMO, HIVOS, and ICCO contributed financially, which made the execution of this research program, "Systematization of Popular Education in Latin America," possible. It was carried out in cooperation with the Centro de Investigación y Educación Popular (CINEP) in Santafé de Bogotá.

INFORMAL LEARNING IN THE DELSILIFE APPROACH

The Delsilife project is an acronym for "Development of a Coordinated Educational Intervention System for Improving the Quality of Life of the Rural Poor through Self-reliance." Its aim is to develop an intervention model which is basically educational, in order to improve the position and living conditions of the deprived rural population. The project is carried out by the Regional Center for Educational Innovation and Technology (INNOTECH), Manila, a specialized organ of the Southeast Asian Ministers of Education Organisation (SEAMEO).

The Delsilife approach aims at improving sustainable problem-solving capacities in communities, by activating a process of learning among the rural poor, thus enabling them to alter their own circumstances. The Delsilife project is an educational experiment which has been tested and examined in selected pilot-communities in Indonesia, Malaysia, the Philippines, and Thailand. One of the core elements of this educational intervention system is the training of instrumental skills and basic life skills, both primarily aimed at increasing income.

The most important role that basic life skills has assumed in the Del-

Table 9.1 Characteristics of conventional and participatory projects

	Conventional projects	Participatory projects
scale	large-scale	small-scale
cooperation	top-down vertical hierarchical authoritarian outside-in nonparticipatory	bottom-up horizontal cooperative democratic inside-out participatory
attitude	paternalistic	equalitarian
change (seen as)	improvement/progress	transformation
development (criteria for)	exogenous criteria to growth and progress	endogenous criteria to growth and progress
solutions (kind of)	incidental	structural
problem-approach	problem-solving	problem-raising
dissemination	campaigning	awareness raising
communication (kind of)	monologue, one-way	dialogue, two-way
media used	macro media 'big media'	micro media 'little media'
research	feasibility studies inception studies	participatory research action research
development (of)	sectors (food, nutrition, health care, family planning)	target groups (children, women, youth, landless labourers, slum dwellers, refugees, indigenous people)
leadership	project manager project coordinator	animator, promotor, facilitator, catylist, front-line-worker
participation	as a means to an end	as an end in itself
objectives	product-focused	process-focused
budget	high budget	low budget
planning	closed planning	open planning

(Source: Kronenburg, 1986, pp. 209-212)

silife project is based on a coincidence. The need for these basic skills originated from the transformation process that had been started in the pilot communities. The basic life skills thus became explicit aspects of social change. Whereas the technical or instrumental skills originally were part of the training package of this educational intervention system, the training of basic life skills did not come to the surface until later, as a derivative. That is why "Basic Life Skills" has been given a very specific interpretation within the Delsilife project.

In the Delsilife project, "Basic Life Skills" comprises various skills. Kraak (1987) took the following inventory:

1. literacy and command of a language;

2. numeracy and its fields of application;

3. the entire problem-solving process;

4. dealing with risks and uncertainties;

5. social skills in negotiating;

6. communication techniques;

7. learning to deal with a new general technical level.

The need for these skills became a part of the Delsilife project from the bottom up; that is to say, from the pilot communities. The project management team complied with this specific request for training in skills.

In spite of the fact that mobilizing the poorest of the poor across the world remains an immensely difficult problem, the Delsilife approach tried to reach them by: a) taking the community (or a part of it), rather than the individual, as the starting point for its pedagogics; and, b) improving the quality of life in the community, by way of highly motivated local initiators. The idea behind the Delsilife project, which offers the poorest of the poor a chance to improve the quality of their life, has not yet been confirmed.

It may be that the idea is too ambitious, and that the expectations are unrealistic. After all, development initiatives in the area of self-actualization usually flourish best with people whose basic needs have already been met. The lower strata of society profit from this kind of middle class initiative as soon as jobs become available for unskilled people.

Thus, their chances of income are determined by the decisions made by others.

Therefore, it would be unjust merely to assess and judge the Delsilife approach on the basis of its target group strategy. It not only stimulates the setting up of small-scale economic activities, it also helps to solve a number of community problems in the areas of health care, hygiene, infrastructure, water supply, cooperation, and planning. Both initiatives imply provisions that benefit the poorest people. However, it remains a fact that special attention needs to be paid to the poorest groups, especially when illiteracy creates a barrier to participation in sector-oriented learning groups.

DELSILIFE AND TRAINING IN SKILLS

The basic idea of Delsilife is that the villagers should be stimulated to improve their circumstances through their own efforts, and that the acquisition of new knowledge and skills plays an essential part in this. Learning groups are set up within which those skills are learned that may help solve problems—problems that are regarded as important by the villagers. The groups also address the improvement of the so-called "horizontal" skills that may come in handy in social and economic relationships, such as providing leadership, problem analysis, planning and management, reading and writing, simple bookkeeping, etc.

Different learning programs contain, besides instrumental knowledge and skills, a number of basic life skills, which are sometimes explicit and sometimes implicit. Developing learning materials relating to the basic life skills proved to be essential, as this is a relatively underdeveloped area in learning programs for adults. The groups were confronted with planning a learning program, solving problems and conflicts, financial management and bookkeeping, organization, management, approaching and negotiating with public and private services.

Some examples: the cooperatives for the distribution of medicine in Thailand had to learn to maintain accurate bookkeeping; the food production group in the Philippines had to learn to consider the markets for their goods. This latter also held true for other groups that produced goods for markets, such as the fishing group in Thailand; the tailors group, the mat weavers, and the banana growers in Malaysia; the duck breeders in Indonesia; etc. Almost all the groups that were involved in the production of goods for markets had to deal with marketing, sales, planning and organization, management, cost accounting, and financial management.

In various cases, the participants started their own businesses, after having sufficiently mastered the concept. Participants in tailoring programs, for instance, managed to get contracts with various manufacturers of clothes, or with institutions that take care of school uniforms. One participant in the electricity learning group in the Philippines started a repair shop in the village.

The effects of the confrontation with Delsilife and with the basic life skills become apparent in a number of practical examples. The main issue is the social-psychological impact which indicates a growing level of independence. The community council makes sure that people form learning groups, and that, if necessary, these groups get outside assistance for the carrying out of learning programs.

The results of the Delsilife method, which was tried out in a limited number of villages for a period of two years, are extremely positive, and, as a result, the participating countries wanted to apply the system on a large scale. For the Delsilife partners, during the eighties, finding the right dissemination strategies and techniques became an important point of attention. Many agents will have to be trained in the Delsilife method, and the demand for efficient training and information material will be considerable.

During the two-year testing period, long discussions took place on the essentials of the method. Sometimes this gave the impression that one was dealing with a complex and difficult concept, which would not be easily transmitted to others who work with it. However, recent experiences have shown that the basic ideas are relatively easily understood. In brief, it is a problem-solving approach applied within the context of a specific organizational strategy, with the small learning group as the core unit. In the final analysis, Delsilife is a method consisting of a number of steps which should be taken and which can easily be understood.

Because of its general applicability, and through the gradually growing number of government staff and other persons who have become familiar with the method, tracing the number of instances in which Delsilife has been applied is becoming more and more difficult, even though INNOTECH tries to record and report the cases as much as possible.

In due time, Delsilife has been adopted as a method for development in other programs, notably in the SEAMEO Human Resources Development Project funded by the Canadian International Development Agency (CIDA). Elements of Delsilife have been adopted in the Quality of Life Promotion Program in Thailand.

So far the method has spread as a self-propelling phenomenon, through the efforts of the original Delsilife staff in the countries and INNOTECH (Center for Educational Innovation and Technology), and through requests from "the market," i.e., institutions, programs, and communities which had heard about the method.

Apart from these "spontaneous" developments, however, already during the testing period, it was felt necessary to make more systematic efforts to disseminate the Delsilife method in the countries concerned.

FINAL REMARKS

Taking a broad definition of adult education as a point of departure, including informal and formal educative activities, as well as all sorts of training and human resource development, the Netherlands governmental and nongovernmental agencies in development cooperation strive to be of help to the poorest of the poor in the Third World on a continuing basis. The main contributions cover sponsoring, monitoring, and investigating adult education projects. The main donor is the Dutch government, financially contributing to multilateral as well as to bilateral projects, and also to local activities in developing countries, by making use of mediating Dutch NGOs.

In correspondence with the most recent policy paper in Dutch development cooperation (1991), the Department of Development Cooperation is in favor of financing research projects in adult education which are going to be realized in a collaborative way. Two examples of collaborative research projects sponsored by the Dutch government have been presented. The first was realized during the seventies in Colombia under the name of "Territorios Nacionales," and the second one, which was called "Delsilife," took place during the eighties in the Southeast Asian region.

Delsilife has proved to be a potentially effective method to improve the quality of life in poor rural communities. In short, the Delsilife approach aimed at "improving sustainable problem-solving capacities in communities." In this, it has demonstrated its ability to activate a process of learning among the rural poor, thus enabling them to alter their own circumstances.

Next to Dutch governmental policy lines for the nineties, attention has been paid to the cultural dimension of development in adult education projects and to the way in which adult education projects contribute to a more productive life, linking up educative activities to the needs of the local labor market. Furthermore, Dutch development cooperation is focused at specific target groups involved (children, youth, women, indigenous people) and favors participatory didactic approaches in adult education projects in the Third World.

A renewed vision and approach, better targeted attention, and support of "basic education for all" in the year 2000 are needed, according to the Dutch point of view. It is not only in the national interest of each country, but also in the international interest. It is important that adult education is approached in close and sound cooperation between governments and organizations. International cooperation and exchange of experiences and information is needed. For this, good coordination between donors and professional organizations, in which each contributes according to ability and expertise, is essential.

NOTES

1. In the Dutch version, pp. 192–93; in the English version, pp. 179–80.

2. These policy views on culture may be found in the Dutch version, p. 205; in the English version, p. 192.

3. CEBEMO stands for Catholic Organization for Joint Financing of Development Programs; NOVIB stands for the Netherlands Organization for Development Cooperation; HIVOS for the Humanistic Institute for Cooperation with Developing Countries; ICCO stands for Interchurch Coordination Committee for Development Projects.

4. General criticism on development aid is as old as the area itself. For a critical reflection on foreign aid in the late sixties and early seventies, see Brandon Robinson's article, "Foreign assistance and national decisions," in the *International Development Review*, 15 (1) (1973): 13–16.

Initial criticism, which was aimed in particular at the adult education activities of the four NGOs mentioned above, broke out in 1990. Max van den Berg, General Secretary of the NOVIB, gave an interview to Wio Joustra, entitled "Ontwikkelingshulp wordt te veel bekeken vanuit de polder," which appeared in *De Volkskrant*, 16 May 1990 (p. 15). On 23 May 1990, an article by Theo Klein appeared in that same newspaper, which stated that the Philippine embassy in The Hague complained about the fact that not only the ICCO, but other MFOs (co-financing organizations) also financially support the purchase of weapons by armed rebels in the Philippines. Not long after, this was followed by a letter to the editor, published on 20 June 1990 in *De Volkskrant*, by the town planner Jan

168   ADULT EDUCATION THROUGH WORLD COLLABORATION

de Boer, who agreed wholeheartedly with NOVIB's General Secretary Max van den Berg, that North Atlantic societies should take a step down economically, to prevent the poorest of the poor in developing countries from getting even for their misery. This entire discussion was settled by an article by Theo Ruyter, "Het ontwikkelingsdenken op de helling," which appeared in *Onze Wereld*, 33 (6) (1990): 27–32.

Around 1990, not just in the Netherlands, but within the EEC also, a relatively negative point of view was held on the role of development aid. Yet an optimistic approach was taken in an article by Michel Chauvin, "Three Decades of Development: Failure, but No Grounds for Despair," in *The Courier*, 137 (1993): 59–61.

5. This statement is taken from the Dutch policy report which is not available in English translation, "Development cooperation and education in the nineties," p. 16. See *Nota ontwikkelingssamenwerking* . . . in Bibliography.

6. Ibid., p. 18.

7. For more general information about "popular education", see Emilio Morillo, "Educación popular; mito y realidad," *Autoeducación*, 10 (29) (1990): 44–47. See also "Controversies and assertations of popular education in Latin America," by Jorge Osorio in the *Participatory Formation Newsletter*, 3 (1) (1989): 29–35.

8. In the meantime, Freire's ideas have been criticized extensively. See particularly Alan Rogers, "Training for literacy: The problem with Freire," in *Adult Education and Development*, 39 (1992): 132–42.

BIBLIOGRAPHY

A world of difference: A new framework for development co-operation in the 1990s (1991). The Hague: Staatsuitgeverij/Ministry of Foreign Affairs.

Bennagen, P. L. (1985). Indigenous learning systems among the Kankanaey: A pilot case study, in *INNOTECH Journal 9* (1).

Boeren, A. and A. Kater (eds.) (1990). *Delsilife: An educational strategy to fight poverty* (CESO Paperback, No. 9) The Hague: Centre for the Study of Education in Developing Countries.

Een wereld van verschil; nieuwe kaders voor ontwikkelingssamenwerking in de jaren negentig (1990) The Hague: Staatsuitgeverij/Tweede Kamer der Staten Generaal.

Epskamp, C. P. (1983). Getting popular theatre internationally organised, in *Sonolux Information* 11: 19–21.

—— (1993). Playing in a sandpit: International popular theatre meeting in Namibia, in *South African Theatre Journal* 7 (1).

Inayatullah (1967). Toward a non-Western model of development, in D. Lerner and W. Schramm (eds.) *Communication and change* (Honolulu, Hawaii: East-West Center), 98–102.

Indigenous knowledge and learning (1988). Papers presented in the Workshop on Indigenous Knowledge and Skills and the Ways They are Acquired (Cha'am, Thailand, 2–5 March 1988). Bangkok & The Hague: Social Research Institute, Chulalongkorn University/Centre for the Study of Education in Developing Countries.

Kraak, J. H. (1987). Basic life skills onder de loupe. Paper gepresenteerd tijdens de CESO-retraite 1987. The Hague: Centre for the Study of Education in Developing Countries.

Kronenburg, J. B. M. (1986). *Empowerment of the poor: A comparative analysis of two development endeavours in Kenya.* Amsterdam: Royal Tropical Institute (KIT).

Mutanda Ntumba, A. (1991). Culture and rural development projects in Central Africa, in *The Courier* (International Centre of Bantu Civilisations) 126 (March-April): 37–38.

Oltheten, Th., J. Ooijens and T. Thybergin (1992). Participatief onderwijs en culturele identiteit: de case van de inheemse bevolking van het Colombiaans Amazone-gebied, in *Volkseducatie en basisonderwijs in Latijns Amerika* (CESO Paperback, No. 15) The Hague: Centre for the Study of Education in Developing Countries.

Nota Ontwikkelingssamenwerking en onderwijs in de jaren negentig (1992). The Hague: Staatsuitgeverij/Ministerie van Buitenlandse Zaken.

Serageldin, I. (1991). Banking on culture: The director of the World Bank's Africa department discusses the issue, in *UNESCO Sources* 25 (April): 10.

Soriano, L. B. (1981). "Indigenous learning systems for deprived areas," in *INNOTECH Journal* 5: 59–64.

Sub-Saharan Africa, from crisis to sustainable growth: A long-term perspective study (1989). Washington, D.C.: The World Bank.

Van Dam, A., S. Martinic and G. Peter (1992). *Popular education in Latin America: Synthesis of the discussion themes.* (CESO Verhandeling, No. 50) The Hague: Centre for the Study of Education in Developing Countries.

Van de Veen, H. (1991) Impactstudie haalt zekerheden ontwikkelingswerk onderuit, in *Onze Wereld* 34 (11): 8–9.

CHAPTER 10

The United States: Adult Education within the Foreign Aid Program

JOHN P. COMINGS

The United States program of foreign aid began after the second world war with the Marshall Plan. The Marshall Plan provided assistance to countries in western Europe, which had been both the allies and the enemies of the United States, helping them rebuild the infrastructure and industry that were destroyed during the war. Within a few years, the Marshall Plan was viewed as a great success, and it became, therefore, the model that the United States would adopt for foreign aid to the developing countries of Asia, Africa, and Latin America (Method and Shaw, 1981).

By the time Harry Truman won election as the U.S. President in November 1948, the role of the Third World as a battleground between the capitalist and communist blocks was already evident. Truman's advisors believed that a Marshall Plan for the Third World could produce the same economic growth that was occurring in western Europe. The Department of State developed a plan to expand foreign aid to support economic growth in the Third World, with the hope that this growth would cause these countries to align themselves with American interests. In his Inaugural Address (January 1949), Truman emphasized four points of action in his new administration. The fourth point was a Marshall Plan for the Third World.

The first name for the U.S. foreign aid program came out of Truman's speech, the Point Four Program. In the 1950s this became the International Cooperation Administration (ICA). The experience of the Marshall Plan was the model for the early efforts of the ICA. The early ICA program focused on assistance to build infrastructure and industry, but the effect of these efforts was less dramatic than it had been in western Europe.

The assistance to western Europe had been given to societies that had recently been as advanced as the United States. The devastation of the war had damaged infrastructure and industry, but the trained and experienced human capital was, for the most part, still intact. Though there were many creative and well-trained people in the Third World at that time, they were a very small percentage of the population of their countries. The work force was largely uneducated and illiterate, and most of the population had little experience with the modern economy.

By the end of the 1950s, ICA had come to see education and training as a key element in the process of development and began funding programs that built the human capital needed to take advantage of the infrastructure, agriculture, and industrial development activities it was also funding. A good deal of this education funding went to bring Third World people to the United States to study at the undergraduate and postgraduate level and to build higher education capacity in their countries. This effort produced a well trained technical elite, but did little for the great mass of the rural poor.

In the early 1960s ICA became known as the Agency for International Development (AID) and by then focused all of its efforts on the Third World. Education for the rural poor was acknowledged as important to the success of AID's development program and to improve social equity within the countries where that program was taking place. Throughout the 1960s, approximately 5 percent of AID's budget ($150 million per year) went to assist education. Most of AID's education budget during the 1960s supported elementary, secondary, and higher education. Only about 1 percent went into adult education. Uncounted in this number, however, was the adult education taking place within other sectors, such as agriculture, health, family planning, and rural development.

Into the early 1970s adult education continued at a slightly higher 2% of the total education budget, but in the middle of the 1970s a new approach to education, nonformal education (NFE), was articulated by Philip Coombs (1973). AID began to see NFE as a way to provide relevant, useful, education to the large population of rural poor who still had no access to formal school at a unit cost that could be sustained by most Third World countries.

In the middle of the 1970s, AID staff went through a process of rethinking their development assistance program. Development strategies, which had been operating for more than a decade, were not producing the impact that had been projected. The donor community was beginning to acknowledge the need to target aid to the rural poor. At the same time, Third World governments had entered the development debate and were demanding that foreign aid build capacity and independence. By the middle of the 1970s, AID had formulated a policy of meeting basic human needs that included adult nonformal education. By the end of the 1970s, funding for NFE had reached 8 percent of AID's total education budget.

Statistics on the disparity between educational levels of men and women clearly argue for a special emphasis on women for all education programs, and especially for adult education. In AID, the attention to gender issues began in 1973 when Arvonne Fraser of the Women's Equity Action League, Wilma Heidi of the National Organization for Women, Irene Tinker of the Federation of Organizations for Professional Women, and Virginia Allen of the State Department, formed an alliance with Senator Charles Percy, a liberal Republican, to introduce an amendment to the foreign assistance act that required all U.S. bilateral assistance to be administered to give particular attention to programs, projects, and activities that contribute to integrating women into the national economies of developing countries, thus improving their status and assisting the total development effort. This led to the establishment within AID of the Office of Women in Development (Staudt, 1985).

The WID office works by supporting research and pilot projects that address the constraints on including women in development programs. In some cases, the WID office also supports other projects. For instance, the Office of Education is supporting an international project called Advancing Basic Education and Literacy (ABEL). The WID office has added funds to this project to support specific activities that focus on women and girls. The WID office also acts as a policy advocate within AID that continually supports the inclusion of women's issues in all AID projects (USAID, *User's Guide*, 1991).

The WID office has education as one area of focus, but has given very little support to adult education. Most of the education funding goes to support projects that focus on increasing access to primary, secondary, and tertiary schooling for girls. The WID office programs have supported nonformal education projects that focus on income generation, small business development and agriculture (USAID, *Women in Development*, 1991).

AID funded universities, consulting firms, Third World institutions, and U.S. nonprofit organizations with grants to pursue NFE activities. These institutions were provided with funds for research, experimentation, fellowships, information gathering and dissemination, and pilot projects that were meant to produce models for NFE and the capacity for technical assistance and training to replicate those models. The University of Massachusetts, the University of California at Los Angeles, and Michigan State University received institutional development grants that supported their faculty and students, and now many professionals in the field have degrees from these three institutions. With AID support, Michigan State maintained what was probably the most comprehensive collection of materials on NFE and published a newsletter with part of its grant.

An evaluation of AID's experience in NFE between 1970 and 1980 found great promise, suggested ways to improve AID's program of support, and recommended that AID continue building on its experience during the 1980s (Krueger and Moulton, 1981).

Funding for adult education and NFE peaked in the early 1980s and began to decline. This decline coincided with a change of administration in Washington, D.C., that brought into the education management team of AID people who felt that formal primary education should be the sole focus of U.S. support to education in the Third World. The high hopes for NFE never had a chance to be realized. Even so, a good deal of adult education activity was funded by AID in the 1980s in the form of health education, agriculture extension, family planning, adult literacy, and microenterprise development that are not identified as adult education. Two AID officials once estimated these activities as accounting for almost $62,000,000 per year of project support in fiscal year 1977. By the end of the 1980s, most of AID's support to NFE and adult education had evaporated. In AID's 1992 *Congressional Presentation* (USAID, 1992) NFE and adult education received very little mention, just a few words in several hundred pages.

In its earliest days, adult education in AID programs meant adult literacy. In the 1970s the concept of family life education, in which literacy was brought together with family planning, became popular. At the same time, adult education was taking on a wider definition within community development and integrated rural development schemes. Adult education was then seen as both literacy and a tool of other development efforts, such as agriculture and health.

In the late 1970s the new concept of NFE added adult literacy training that was influenced by the problem-posing methodology developed by Paulo Freire (1968). Thus, empowerment and consciousness raising became part of the curriculum. In the 1980s, adult education moved away from the basic skills of literacy and the political objective of empowerment and focused more on content that could improve daily life, such as income-generating activities that helped rural poor acquire skills and capital to set up and run microenterprises.

The World Conference on Education for All (WCEFA) held in Jomtien, Thailand, in 1990 provided an opportunity to redefine adult education. Adult literacy was acknowledged again as an important goal, along with education and training in the essential skills required for better living and sound and sustainable development (WCEFA, 1990). AID was a cosponsor of the WCEFA and supported the goals set out in the *World Declaration on Education for All*. AID is now supporting education efforts meant to meet those goals. Adult education, however, is not a priority in AID's budget, and most of its basic education effort is focused on formal primary school.

CASE STUDIES

Although the total share of its education budget that goes to support adult education is small, AID has had a significant effect on the field. AID-supported programs have developed innovative methods, materials, and structures that have been adopted by other donors, governments, and nongovernmental organizations. In this chapter, three projects will be presented as case studies of the work that AID has supported. In each case, a discussion of how AID goes about its work will be presented as well.

The Ecuador Project

The Center for International Education (CIE) at the University of Massachusetts was one of the projects funded by AID through institutional development grants in the 1970s. AID's interest in CIE came out of experiences in Ecuador. In 1970, informal contacts between CIE, the Ecuadorean Ministry of Education, and the AID mission in Quito produced a five-year project that CIE implemented with the Ministry of Education (CIE, 1975).

The Ministry of Education and AID were interested in experimenting with new ways to provide basic education. The formal school system was not serving the poorest communities well, and its curriculum was considered irrelevant to rural life. The Ecuador Project was charged with meeting two objectives: (1) to create new methodologies that would produce learning and personal growth; (2) to demonstrate that these methodologies were valid as instruments for social change, even when used in a nonformal atmosphere independent of the formal school system.

The project design was influenced by the writing and work of Paulo Freire, and that of Ivan Illich (1972).

The director of the project was an Ecuadorean, and only one North American advisor was a resident of Ecuador at any given time. The rest of the staff of the project was Ecuadorean, from the same linguistic and cultural background as the rural poor who were to benefit from the project.

Though AID staff participated in the design, the project itself was turned over to an autonomous institution, the University of Massachusetts. This is common practice for AID. AID staff is involved in setting priorities and strategies for U.S. assistance within a country, and AID monitors the programmatic and financial aspects of a project.

AID staff is rarely involved in project implementation, technical assistance, or training. The adult education projects that AID funds, therefore, are significantly influenced by the institutions that manage the implementation. In this case, CIE was committed to a Freirean educational process and a collaborative, institution building approach, and these were represented in the project design.

The project functioned in twenty-six villages on the coast and in the highland of Ecuador. Each community identified between one and five facilitators who managed the educational processes in the village. They were trained by the project staff but were managed by the people they served.

A project staff member would visit a village and in a general meeting present the facilitator concept to the community. A few qualities of a good facilitator were presented and the community was left to decide if they wanted the project and who they wanted as their facilitator. Once the project was functioning, the first group of facilitators took on the role of the field workers in this process of identifying villages and selecting facilitators.

In the beginning of the project, the facilitators were trained by the CIE team, but later the more experienced facilitators became the trainers. The training process followed a learning cycle that included experience, reflection, conceptualization, practice, and internalization. Though each training program was different, it usually contained activities that focused on the following: trust building in the group, negotiation of course objectives and schedule, team building, Freire's concept of problem-posing education, literacy and numeracy teaching methodology, learning games, community goal setting, problem identification, problem solving, and evaluation.

After training, the facilitators worked with their communities to identify needs and to organize educational processes that met those needs. These processes took many different forms but all supported an active, problem-posing educational experience. Learners were expected to think critically and discover knowledge through a process of group discussion. Action to improve their lives was always the goal of these processes, not simple acquisition of skill or knowledge.

The project put on dramas that portrayed common rural problems. At the conclusion of the play, the actors led the audience in a discussion that focused on the action of the drama and then moved to the reality of their own lives: questions about ways in which they could solve their problems and barriers to appropriate action. The project used songs, puppet theater, and even sociodramas that involved the audience directly in the action of the play.

The facilitators also organized small group processes that drew inspiration from Freire's concept of culture circles. Photographs or drawings were presented as stimulus and then the facilitator helped the group through a process that allowed people to identify problems, discuss causes, and suggest solutions.

The project developed several educational games. Some were focused on consciousness raising, while others were meant to develop literacy and numeracy skills. Simulation board games were used for consciousness raising. They dealt with aspects of the lives of the rural poor and served as a mechanism to promote critical thinking and discussion about key issues in their lives. To take one example: "Hacienda" was set up like the game Monopoly, with individual pieces moved around a board based on the throw of dice. As a player moved around the board, he or she encountered obstacles and possibilities common to rural life. Chance, as well as the decisions of the player, determined the outcome of the game.

Fluency games were used to support literacy and numeracy learning. These games followed the rules of common card games. Each allowed for practice of specific skills, such as multiplication, addition, syllable or letter recognition, and word formation. Groups of people would play the games for fun, but in the playing they would practice their literacy skills.

The project produced a series of fotonovelas as well. Fotonovelas are like comic books but use photographs instead of drawings. They are a popular entertainment medium in Ecuador, commercial fotonovelas usually focusing on romance and drama among the elite of big cities. The project produced fotonovelas that used actors and stories that were similar to those found in rural villages. They provided a way to explore rural problems and, like the dramas, were meant to lead to discussion and action.

Radio was used to broadcast the dramas and stories of the project, but also to involve learners in speaking to each other. Some programs were recorded in villages where people had gathered to do community work. These were broadcast or played on a cassette in other villages involved in similar work. In this way, there was an exchange of experience and encouragement of each other's work.

This brief discussion of the innovations developed in the Ecuador project makes clear the innovative nature of the effort. The CIE staff was free to experiment within the broad guidelines set out by AID and the constraints of their budget. Though the project ended after only five years, its innovations are still used and serve as a model for NFE in other countries.[1]

The Nepal National Literacy Program

World Education is a nonprofit organization that received a large grant from AID to experiment with innovations in NFE in several countries. In Nepal, it began with a broad mandate to experiment with NFE processes in rural villages. Many different ways to involve rural people in discussions about their lives were tried, but many villagers were asking specifically for literacy. World Education responded by working with the Ministry of Education of Nepal to design a set of materials and a teacher training package for a national literacy program. The AID Mission became interested in the development of this literacy program and assisted World Education with additional funding through a grant (World Education, n.d.).

AID has funds set aside for projects proposed by Private Voluntary Agencies (PVOs), such as World Education. The term PVO is interchangeable with the term Nongovernmental Organization (NGO), which is more commonly used in international development. The requesting agency is expected to prepare a proposal that describes what it plans to accomplish and how it plans to go about it. A budget that includes some cost sharing by the NGO must conform to AID's regulations, and the project must serve one of the local AID Mission's priorities. Through three separate grants, AID supported World Education in its work that developed and refined the adult literacy program, added a nonformal primary education program for out-of-school children, expanded the program both through government agencies and NGOs, and pursued research into the impact of the literacy effort.

The project produced a set of four adult literacy primers, *Naya Goreto* (The New Path), that teaches reading, writing, and simple math, and presents information on a wide range of development topics, such as health, family planning, reforestation, agriculture, and the importance of the education of girls. The materials use a problem-posing approach, similar to that developed by Paulo Freire, that encourages learners to discuss issues important to improving their lives.

The literacy program also employs adaptations of the fluency games developed in the Ecuador Project. Several card games are employed as ways to practice word recognition and decoding skills. The use of stories and drama, in the form of comic strips, was also borrowed from the Ecuador Project's experience with fotonovelas.

In developing the literacy program, the project involved a group of Nepalis who were hired by the project but who were to become Ministry of Education employees at the end of the project. This staff not only helped in the design of the program, they became teachers in the field test of the materials and methods. By the time the program was ready for expansion, they were accomplished trainers who knew the literacy program from the point of view of both the teacher and the administrator.

As the program began to expand, it became clear that the Ministry did not have the resources needed to serve all who wanted to join a literacy class. The Project helped form a collaboration between the Ministry and a large group of international and Nepali NGOs. The Ministry produced the materials and sold them at cost (a cost that was much lower than any single NGO could achieve, because of economies of scale) and provided free teacher training. Over time, each NGO developed its own training capacity. Now the literacy program is a collaboration between NGOs and government, and the NGOs are supporting more than 50 percent of the classes.

A staff member from the project left the Ministry and joined an NGO, Action AID. In that capacity, he began experimenting with providing a literacy class adapted for children. Nepal still has many children, particularly girls, who do not have a chance to attend school, and some of these children were accompanying their parents to literacy classes. Action Aid's decision to provide a separate program was logical, and they used the Ministry materials as the basis for the new child materials, *Naulo Bihana* (Bright Morning). The Ministry was impressed by this innovation and, along with World Education, revised and mass produced the materials. Now, the government and most NGOs use both the adult and child materials produced by the Ministry of Education.

By 1993 the program was serving about 250,000 people a year and was growing. As more people completed the literacy program, the need for something simple and interesting to read became apparent. With AID funding, World Education and the Ministry began producing reading materials that used the same graphic conventions, comic book format, and vocabulary as the literacy materials. The materials focus on health, family planning, agriculture, the environment, income generation opportunities, democracy, and a wide range of other topics. They usually have a story as part of the text so that even people who are not motivated to read the information contained in the materials are interested in reading the stories.

One particularly promising intervention came when an AID-supported health project asked for assistance in preparing training materials for illiterate female village health volunteers (CHV). The CHVs were being trained to act as health promoters and health educators with groups of women in their villages. Though these materials were successful, the project went on to experiment with a program that provided literacy instruction to each CHV and between twenty and thirty of the women with whom she was working. This literacy program used Ministry materials, with supplements that focused on health and family planning, with special health-related reading materials for use after the classes were completed.

As was true in Ecuador, AID officials were not involved in the implementation of the project. World Education prepared its own proposal for funds that were set aside for PVOs, and AID judged that proposal against the development plans of the government, its own priorities, and the merit of competing proposals. World Education was free, within the constrains of the budget, to pursue the objectives in the proposal in whatever way it deemed most appropriate. This allowed for a range of innovations that had not originally been planned.[2]

Lesotho Distance Teaching Centre

The LDTC was established in 1974 as a semiautonomous body, with core funding from the Ministry of Education and a governing board made up of representatives from several ministries. The mission of the LDTC was to explore the use that could be made of distance teaching methods. In its first years, LDTC produced low cost booklets with simple illustrations and photographs, and developed radio broadcasts for educational courses and for programs that provided information to rural communities. By the time AID became involved with it in 1976, LDTC already had thirty staff members and was working in four areas: distance teaching for formal school exams, community education, studies of literacy and numeracy in Lesotho, and a service agency for organizations involved in education of any kind. It was this last activity, the service agency, that interested AID (Hoxeng, 1989, Development Associates, 1986, Creative Associates, 1979).

The LDTC had staff that was well trained and experienced in materials development, training, research, community development, and adult education, and made its expertise available to other institutions and programs. These are all valuable skills needed by ministries of education, but they are also useful to ministries of agriculture, health, and family planning, and to NGOs as well. In this way, adult education experts were involved in providing consultant services rather than coordinating or managing projects.

The skills made available by the service agency were important to the success of other institutions. The Ministry of Health, for example, could have developed such skills in its own staff, but rather recruited on the basis of health background and training, and promoted individuals on criteria important to the field of health. There is no incentive for Ministry of Health staff to develop the educational skills needed to communicate effectively with rural people. When these skills do exist within the Ministry, the people who possess them are usually given management or administrative positions and have little time left over for other matters. The service agency acknowledges this situation and places the experts in adult education within a single agency. It recruits people with these skills, rewards them for having these skills, and keeps them free of management tasks.

The LDTC provided service to the Ministry of Health in the development of an awareness campaign focused on the use of oral rehydration therapy. It developed improved training materials in preventive health measures and trained community health workers in mass communication techniques. In another venture, the LDTC provided assistance to the Credit Union League by developing a series of participatory multimedia programs that drew inspiration from the Ecuador Project. These programs explained to potential clients exactly what the Credit Union League was and how it made decisions on extending credit.

An official from AID's central education bureau in Washington, D.C., visited Lesotho in 1975. He had been working on the concept of a service agency and was impressed to find a nascent example already functioning. This official provided a small grant to the LDTC to experiment with the service agency approach and plan for a larger project. The next year, AID funded the LDTC to experiment for three years with the service agency approach. That project provided the LDTC with funds to develop and market their expertise in materials development, training, and communications, but it also added a new component—funds to experiment with revolving credit for rural poor who want to start a small or microenterprise. Once the AID funding was used to develop capacity, the Service Agency was funded by the organizations and institutions that used its services.

AID'S ROLE IN THE ADULT EDUCATION SECTOR

AID's funds committed specifically to adult education grew until 1980 and then began to decline. By the early 1990s, an examination of a list of AID projects would yield only a few adult education activities. Adult education processes are still part of AID work, but most of them are found in projects that focus on other development sectors or in projects that support the activities of NGOs. Very little adult literacy is supported by AID funds, but in 1992 new language was added to the legislation that funds AID that opens up the possibility of new adult education, nonformal education, and literacy programs.

Even though there is a clear lack of interest at this time, the case studies indicate that AID funding was important in supporting innovative experimentation in adult education in the 1970s and 1980s. At that time, AID was a leader in the field of support to NFE, and its support was helping to define and develop the field. This experimentation was successful, in part, because of the way in which AID provided support. Though AID provided funds, its staff did not take responsibility for design of a project. Once funding began, implementation was the responsibility of the agency that received the funds. Although there were some restrictions on how the money could be used, the agencies were free to pursue the objectives of their projects in any way that seemed appropriate to them. This freedom of implementation provided an environment in which experimentation takes place. This kind of creativity has been particularly important in adult education that needs a multiplicity of approaches and techniques to be successful. This makes the lack of AID interest in adult education particularly troubling.

AID does have a strong commitment to basic education, but it has decided to focus its resources on the expansion of the formal primary school system and the improvement of its quality. At the same time, educators in the United States have accepted that improvements in schooling alone cannot produce an impact on learning achievement for many, if not most, students who are scoring on the low end of achievement tests. Conditions in the communities and the families in which children live are a contributing factor to learning achievement, and even very indirect family indicators, like the number of books in a home, have a high correlation with learning achievement. In the United States, educators now understand that without a way to improve the basic skills of parents, systems of formal education are limited in the level of aggregate learning they can achieve, but AID is not influenced by this recognition.

AID has moved away from adult education, in part, because it has fewer resources and higher costs now than it did before. It must allocate its funding to where it will get the highest return and the most host country cooperation. Adult education usually has the lowest priority and, therefore, the least financial and human resources in most ministries of education. This lack of support makes implementation difficult, and donor funds are more likely to be matched by government support for the formal school system. Viable models of adult education, such as those of Nepal, Ecuador, and Lesotho need AID financing to attract additional resources. If AID had not cut off funding for NFE in an untimely way, local governments might have become committed to it.

Any discussion of adult education in development should pay attention to the success AID was supporting in the 1970s and 1980s. The entire program of support that included universities, research institutes, and NGOs developed models that pointed the way to more effective adult literacy programs, basic education for out-of-school children, systems of community education in poor rural villages, and institutions that could make available the skills of adult educators to support the work of other ministries and institutions. Had AID continued spending eight percent of its education budget on NFE during the 1980s and 1990s, there might be many more effective programs for the world's one billion people who will never benefit from formal school. There might also be many more examples of adult education service agencies that were making the work of other development sectors more successful.

NOTES

1. The preceding section makes use of material in Center for International Education (1990), and Illich (1972).
2. The preceding section makes use of material in World Education, n.d.

BIBLIOGRAPHY

CIE (Center for International Education) (1975). *Nonformal education in Ecuador.* July. Amherst, Mass.: University of Massachusetts.

Coombs, Philip (1973). *New paths to learning.* Essex, Connecticut: International Council on Education and Development.

Creative Associates (1979). *Nonformal education activities at Lesotho Distance Teaching Centre: Evaluation report.* April. Washington, D.C.: USAID.

Development Associates (1986). *Final evaluation: Project structuring nonformal education resources.* April. Washington, D.C.: USAID.

Freire, Paulo (1968). *Pedagogy of the oppressed.* New York: Seabury Press.

Hoxeng, James (1989). The service center approach. *Reports* 28, Spring. Boston, Mass.: World Education.

Illich, Ivan (1972). *Deschooling society.* New York: Harper and Row.

Krueger, Chris, and Jeanne Moulton (1981). *A retrospective study of the DS/ED nonformal education program 1970–1980.* May. Washington, D.C.: USAID.

Method, Francis J., and Saundria Kay Shaw (1981). *AID assistance to education: A retrospective study.* 17 February. Washington, D.C.: Creative Associates.

Staudt, Kathleen (1985). *Women, foreign assistance, and advocacy administration.* New York: Praeger.

USAID (1992). *Congressional presentation.* Washington, D.C.: Government Printing Office.

USAID (1991). *User's guide: Office of women in development.* Washington, D.C.: AID.

USAID (1991). *Women in development: A report to Congress by the U.S. Agency for International Development.* Washington, D.C.: AID.

WCEFA (1990). *World declaration on education for all.* April. New York: World Conference on Education for All.

World Education (n.d.) *The Nepal national literacy program.* Boston, Mass.: World Education.

PART THREE

The International Council
for Adult Education

CHAPTER 11

Building a Global Learning Network: The International Council for Adult Education

BUDD L. HALL

"All excellent things are as difficult as they are rare."

—Spinoza

"Thinking must be high, but action must be down to earth."

—Narayar Desai

This chapter on the International Council for Adult Education (ICAE) is a modest contribution to broader sharing of a quite remarkable story of sustained international cooperation in the field of adult education.[1] The International Council for Adult Education is the major international nongovernmental organization in the field of adult education. With members in well over one hundred nations; major regional bodies in Europe, Africa, Asia and the South Pacific, Latin America, the Caribbean, North America and the Arabic speaking states; programs in critical areas of global importance; a respected journal, *Convergence*; a tradition of holding World Assemblies each four to five years; the ICAE is a vital network for adult educators and others concerned with learning in community and global contexts.

The structures of the ICAE have made it possible for people in many parts of the world to use adult education for democratic purposes through smaller and larger activities. The entire story of the Council and its past and present impact would take many books. These notes by one of the people who worked in the Secretariat of the ICAE from 1975 to 1991 are a mostly anecdotal start.

HISTORICAL BACKGROUND

It began in a discussion in a room in the Tokyo Prince Hotel in Japan on the evening of July 27, 1972.[2] Present were J. Roby Kidd and Gordon Selman of Canada; Arthur Stock of England; John Cairns and Paul Bertelsen of UNESCO headquarters; Mary Grief and Alex Charters of the United States; Paul Chu of the International Labour Organization; John Lowe of Scotland; Helmuth Dolff of Germany; Paul Mhaiki of Tanzania; and about twenty others who were participants at the UNESCO Third International Conference on Adult Education. Roby Kidd had just finished a year traveling around the world, with funds from the International Development Research Centre (IDRC) in Canada, writing a report on new innovations in learning. But as usual with Kidd, he was doing several others things at the same time. He was taking the message to as many countries as possible that the UNESCO International Conference on Adult Education was important and that a new international organization for adult educators was in the planning stages.

A smaller group, including Selman of Canada, Chu of the ILO, Bertelsen of UNESCO, Dolff of Germany, Charters of the United States, and Lowe of Scotland had met the night of July 25, after the first formal day of the International UNESCO Conference. This advisory group took on responsibilities for inviting key adult educators from each of the regions who were present at the Tokyo conference to a special meeting, assigning particular preparatory responsibilities to each. The members of this group shared the view that just as the cooperative movement, the libraries, trade unions, and teachers all had international nongovernmental bodies, it was time for the adult education movement to do so as well. As indicated, in that hotel room discussion on the evening of the 27th, a substantial number of adult educators with good geographic representation were assembled. Kidd shared his thoughts on the possibilities of an international association.

While there was support for the idea from each of the regions represented, a number of questions and criticisms were put forward. Would the new association detract from the workings of UNESCO? Bertelsen and Cairns of UNESCO assured the group that would not be the case. If we were truly into an age of "life-long" learning, was it appropriate to create a "sectoral" association for adult educators? And, if this were to be an association of individuals, would it not weaken the existing national and regional associations by drawing membership away from them? At the end of the evening, once the delegates had left, the smaller core group met again to take a "reading" of the meeting, and decided that the ICAE would be a confederation of national and regional adult education associations, not of individuals, so as not to draw resources from national associations. Because of new commitments to life-long learning, special support for adult education was needed. Therefore, UNESCO officers working within the Adult Education Division favored the new organization.

In light of the substantial support which had been exhibited, the decision was made to go forward with the idea. Those national associations which were interested in joining could do so, and it was hoped that those not ready would come in at a later time.

Some months later, people around the world were informed by Kidd of the existence of the ICAE and an invitation to cooperate was extended. Malcolm Adeseshiah of India, former deputy director-general of UNESCO, became the first president; J. Roby Kidd of Canada was the secretary-general; and vice presidents included Paul Lengrend of France, Paul Mhaiki of Tanzania, and Majid Rahnema of Iran. Helmuth Dolff of Germany was the first treasurer.

The Council, which was legally registered in Canada on February 14, 1973, was the second effort at creating a world body of adult education in the twentieth century. The first was by Albert Mansbridge, who was the person most associated with the founding of the Workers' Education Association of Great Britain in the early 1900s. Mansbridge did a lot of work, primarily in the former British colonies—particularly in Canada and Australia—spreading the idea of education associations for the purpose of providing quality education to workers in industrialized countries equal to that received by the dominant, elite classes. He and Morse Cartwright of the Adult Education Association of the U.S.A. took on the responsibility for organizing the first world meeting of adult educators in 1929 in Oxford, England.

The World Association for Adult Education brought together a remarkable number of people from many different countries—most of the "world." The world of the 1920s did not extend much beyond North America, Europe, Australia, and to some extent Japan. It did not recognize most of Africa, Latin America, the Arabic-speaking countries, or the Caribbean. But the World Association did bring together the strong Nordic tradition, the French early work in popular education, and the British conceptions in one place for the first time. There were delegates from Japan and China, as well as other important colonial links such as India, Canada, and New Zealand. (It is worth noting that the very words "adult education" do not have a direct translation in either French or the Nordic languages. The very formulation of the concept itself betrays certain cultural-linguistic biases.)

The World Association continued until the beginning of the Second World War, when all of the international and global associations were fragmented as a consequence of that conflict. It was not revived in the postwar period, although the legal structures of the World Association were held by Edward Hutchinson, the postwar secretary of the National Institute for Adult Education for England and Wales.

The postwar wave of international organizing in adult education was stimulated by the birth of UNESCO. Founded in the immediate aftermath of the war as the scientific, cultural, and educational structure of the United Nations, UNESCO placed importance on the role of adult education in the building of a new world with respect for human rights and as a means of strengthening the possibilities of permanent peace. The first UNESCO international conference on adult education took place in 1949, in Elsinore, Denmark. It brought together about two hundred delegates from forty-five countries, including Ned Corbett, who was the executive director of the Canadian Adult Education Association.

Ned Corbett was a dedicated internationalist and was convinced that adult education was an important contributor to world reforms. At about that time, Corbett had just taken on a new assistant director, a young man, J. Roby Kidd, who was fresh out of Columbia Teachers College in New York with a doctorate in adult education, who brought with him much experience from working with the YMCA and other organizations. He began his career in a field that was defining itself as international in an era of profound hope and global reform. As a result, when Kidd later took over the directorship of the Canadian Association, he already had a strong commitment to international, as well as Canadian linkages. His previous work with UNESCO resulted in Canada hosting the second UNESCO international conference on adult education at the campus of the University of Montreal in 1960.

Kidd and Alexander Charters, of Syracuse University in the United States, were already working towards getting some kind of nongovernmental linkages started. Meetings of university adult educators coming together in Montreal resulted in the creation of the International Congress for University Adult Education (ICUAE). This body is still very much alive, with a permanent secretariat in Fredericton, New Brunswick. Its main activity in the 1990s is the publication of a journal on university adult education.

Thus, by 1972 many personal networks and early patterns of international exchange and cooperation were well established. Kidd in the meantime had moved from the Canadian Association for Adult Education to the Ontario Institute for Studies in Education, as first chair of the Adult Education Department in the new Graduate Faculty of Education. When plans were announced for the third UNESCO International Conference, Kidd began to weave the various contacts and friendships together more deliberately.

INITIAL SUPPORT

The initial support came from Canada, the United States, Britain, and the countries of the Commonwealth. India, Tanzania, Ghana, Nigeria, Jamaica, Venezuela, and a number of other developing countries, were members from the beginning. France, Germany, and Ireland were also early European members. It was the combination of contacts in the national adult education associations with those in university adult education that provided the strongest base for the early development of the Council.

EARLY UNESCO SUPPORT

The choice of Dr. Malcolm Adeseshiah as the first president was an important appointment. India had a strong tradition in adult education. In addition, his recent past with UNESCO was a reassurance to others of its centrality in the mission of the Council. Adeseshiah was an active economist, who wrote and contributed to international development policy debates. UNESCO and the members of the staff at headquarters in Paris, who followed adult education matters, were most supportive of any efforts which were directed at strengthening the links among adult educators. They saw clearly the benefits of an organization which worked outside of government circles to stimulate discussions and even to put pressure on governments themselves to be more generous in national budgets to adult education programing.

THE TIME WAS RIPE

One of the things that made it possible to start the ICAE in the early 1970s was the new independence in the previous decade of so many developing countries. There was suddenly a much larger world of adult education interests, with more countries working in the international arena, and, importantly, there were new sources of funds for international cooperation. The birth of the bilateral aid agencies, such as the U.S. Agency for International Development (USAID), the Canadian Agency for International Development (CIDA), and similar bodies in many of the richer nations, meant broader possibilities for supporting the adult education work in many of the developing countries.

There was also funding and new political power. With newer countries represented in U.N. organizations, there needed to be programs corresponding to their needs. So the times provided for a much larger constituency than had previously existed; a constituency with both a political and economic underpinning to it. But the times also brought with them new kinds of global sensibilities.

The rather sudden appearance of so many new nations brought a sensibility and a visibility to differences in standards of living in parts of the world of which many people in the world were unaware. The times also carried with them a renewed and broader sense of internationalism, the idea that together all could help make a better world and it could only happen if the entire world were involved, not just the European countries, not just the rich countries. Also there developed the sense of obligations in the rich countries to support training, education, and infrastructure development in countries which were less rich.

EARLY MANDATE

The mandate was to strengthen linkages among adult educators working in various countries. In the report to the second meeting of the board of the ICAE, which met in Cologne, Federal Republic of Germany May 13 and 14, 1974, the organization was described as, "a co-operative enterprise in development—a means of sharing ideas, resources and experience in the development of adult education and particularly a way of utilizing adult education more effectively in many of the developing countries" (ICAE, 1974). In addition, the early mandate included the exploration of the relationship of adult education to the major social issues of the day—peace, development, democracy, food. It was expected to provide an additional voice to, and work in tandem with, UNESCO and other United Nations agencies with like interests.

THE CHOICE OF CANADA FOR THE HEADQUARTERS

Canada was chosen as the first headquarters because Roby Kidd lived there. It was as simple as that. Kidd was the spark plug, the organizer who was able to "pull off" the Council. It is doubtful that Kidd asked anyone in the first few years if they were happy with Canada. No one else was really very interested in putting in the energy that it took to get things rolling. The fact, however, that Kidd was a Canadian may have been one of the reasons why he was able to work as effectively as he did. If Kidd had been from the United States or the Soviet Union, for example, given the international climate of the 1970s, it is unlikely that support would have been so forthcoming. Canada had a good international reputation, for its support of the United Nations, development in general, and for issues around human rights. It was an acceptable country and Kidd was rendered more "acceptable" by being a Canadian. Most importantly, Kidd was prepared to find the funding for the Council.

TANZANIAN CONNECTION

My own first connections with the ICAE came about because of my position at the Institute of Adult Education at the University of Dar es Salaam in Tanzania from 1970 to 1974. I had been in close contact with Paul Bertelsen, the head of adult education at UNESCO prior to the 1972 UNESCO conference. He had worked in Tanzania for a number of years before taking up his position with UNESCO in Paris. Because of his urging, I agreed to do the research for a major paper on Tanzania's adult education program for the Tokyo UNESCO Conference. I wrote the paper with Paul Mhaiki, the director of the Institute of Adult Education. On the strength of this paper, Paul Mhaiki was able to convince the Ministry of Education that Tanzania should be represented in Tokyo. Once in Tokyo, the Tanzanian efforts were highlighted by the conference. Paul Mhaiki met Kidd and the others and was offered the vice presidency of the Council for Africa. Upon returning from Tokyo,

Mhaiki held a meeting to resurrect the dormant Tanzanian Adult Education Association. Later, when I was ready to leave Tanzania, Mhaiki recommended me to Kidd as someone who could help him get the Council going.

FIRST FUNDS

The early work of the Council was supported by students from the Ontario Institute for Studies in Education (OISE) and other volunteers in Toronto. Kidd was very creative in making the most of modest funds. For example, the first office space was at the downtown Kensington Market Campus of George Brown Community College, arranged by Doug Light who was the president of the College and a former student of Kidd's at OISE. Canadian government funds for training were among the first grants to the Council. I was still working in Tanzania when we received an unsolicited grant from Kidd for work in our Institute there.

I joined the Council as the research officer in August 1975, after one year as a senior fellow at the Institute of Development Studies in Sussex, England. When I was hired, the Council's budget was about twenty-five thousand dollars a year, with my salary accounting for fifteen thousand. Shortly afterwards, the Council was successful in getting a number of project grants, including a substantial one from CIDA, to begin exploratory work in Latin America. Paz and Knute Buttedahl of the ICAE staff traveled throughout 1975–76 in Latin America, seeking the best ways to support and link up adult educators there.

By 1975–76, through volunteer and part-time support, the ICAE had a strong team in the Secretariat. In addition to Kidd, the Buttedahls and Hall, there were Jackie Sullivan, Audrey Herrema and Margaret Gayfer of Toronto, Abdelwahid Yousif of the Sudan (an OISE student), Nsang O'Khan Kabwasa of Zaire (OISE student) and Rebecca Kabwasa of the United States (working on the Dar es Salaam conference). Kidd carried out his duties as secretary general as a volunteer, in addition to his job as a professor in the Department of Adult Education at OISE.

The most substantial early funds received were for the organization of the 1976 conference on Adult Education and Development in Tanzania. Approximately $300,000 were found for preparations, travel, translations, reporting, accommodations, and follow-up, from a broad cross section of foundations and agencies. ICAE also began to receive funds for the early work in participatory research in 1976, but it was not until

1977 that it received the first substantial grant for central organizing activities of the organization: a five-year grant of $750,000 from the W. K. Kellogg Foundation.

EARLY PARADIGMS

From the very first days of the ICAE, it drew from a broad set of ideas about the role of adult education in society. The strongest early influences included the rich social activist traditions of Canada, the British Fabian socialist association with adult education, the liberal and humanistic adult education perspectives in the United States, the British extramural tradition, which had been exported to most of the colonies, the Gandhian tradition of India, and the folk high school traditions of both Germany and the Nordic countries. Adult education was seen by most to be a strong responsibility of the state. Indeed, in those days, there were as many governmental officials in adult education present in Council events as there were persons from the voluntary sector, what we now call the nongovernmental sector. The education of adults was seen as a necessary supplement to the creation of fully democratic societies and as an important contributing factor in the "development" of poorer nations. The adult education community itself, whether governmental, nongovernmental, university or community-based, was seen to be a large and reasonably coherent whole.

The earliest days of the Council in the 1970s brought together persons from the social reform traditions, those who thought it important to professionalize the field through university training, and those who saw it as a component of the newer paradigms of international development. To some degree, these same tendencies are still represented in the framework of the ICAE. The underlying ideology of the Council has been one of people from different parts of the world working together to strengthen the structures of adult education and the role of adult education in the face of critical global issues. What the Council did, even in the early days, was to create a much broader definition of adult education, to expand the meaning of adult education, to demonstrate how that notion of adult education was critical to achieving any number of aims in different countries. The ICAE has reflected the shifts in emphasis over time, namely, international cooperation in adult education (1972–76), adult education and development (1976–1982), adult education and social movements (1982–1990), and adult education and democracy (1990–present) (ICAE, 1991).

EARLY WAYS OF WORKING

During the first few years, the ICAE corresponded with and worked primarily through the twenty to thirty national associations. It was not very difficult to maintain contact, as there were few associations and the key people knew each other fairly well. In fact, at the time, the ICAE was mostly an information network, with some modest projects which for the most part served to support the building of the Secretariat's capacity to communicate with the membership. The adult education associations which joined the Council agreed to correspond with the Council about events and ideas from their countries and to share international information with their national members. Up until 1979, the Council operated from year to year with meetings of a "Board," which consisted of one representative from every association. Only later would a strong programmatic base come into being.

The Council was intent on gaining visibility for the role of adult education in a changing world vis-a-vis the United Nations, and in a wide variety of circles. It was establishing what is called in Spanish its "poder convucatoria," which is the notion of "If you call, somebody will come."

THE 1976 WORLD ASSEMBLY
IN DAR ES SALAAM, TANZANIA

Because of the necessary economies of space, time, and funding, all the international assemblies are invitational. The First World Assembly of Adult Education and Development in 1976 marked the transition in Council history from "international cooperation in adult education" to "adult education and development" and put the Council on the map, so to speak. First of all, it demonstrated the ICAE's capacity to organize an international conference. Secondly, it demonstrated that important figures in adult education and development would participate, persons such as Lucile Mair of Jamaica, Paulo Freire of Brazil, and Julius Nyerere, Tanzania's president. Thirdly, it put the ICAE at the heart of the discourse linking adult education and development. It was an exciting, passionate, and stimulating conference. It set the agenda for much of the international movement for years to come (Hall and Kidd, 1979). It gave the Council a way of working and set parameters and frameworks which it was able to use in many different ways.

For example, the first international support for participatory research, a community-based approach, came together in Dar es Salaam. Paulo Freire met with a group of younger adult educators in discussions of their work. President Julius Nyerere brought his sense of the South, the strength of the South, and what poorer countries could do for themselves. He shared his vision of the centrality of adult education to government policy, and his commitment to international cooperation in adult education.

Lucile Mair, the Jamaican historian, had just completed her breakthrough study on the history of women in the Caribbean. Her keynote address was a clarion call for adult education to reexamine the role of women in its theory and practice. The *Design for Action*, which came out of the conference, pulled together the implications of scores of ideas and commitments made by those assembled (*Ibid.*).

THE ROLE OF THE REGIONAL ORGANIZATIONS

Dar es Salaam also marked the beginning of a special role for the regional organizations of the ICAE. Three major regional adult education bodies existed prior to the formation of the ICAE: the European Bureau for Adult Education (founded in 1953), the African Adult Education Association (1969), and the Asian and South Pacific Bureau of Adult Education (1964). In Dar es Salaam, the Council made, at least informally, a commitment to strengthen and work with the regional bodies which already existed, and to support the creation and development of such organizations for other regions. The Asian group, for example, held its first reorganization meeting in many years in Africa at that conference!

The structures of the Council now came to include national associations, cooperating NGOs from other fields, the secretariat itself, and, with a role that would grow in subsequent years, the regional organizations. The model of a council of autonomous and independent institutional members, each with its own financing and its own board, was reinforced. The ICAE is not a development organization; it is a federation of independent, nongovernmental adult education organizations. In the 1979 Helsinki constitution, which is still in place, the regional organizations nominate the vice-presidents of the Executive Committee (a thirty-two member governing body), and the national associations nominate thirteen or so other members. This provides for a sharing of power.

THE CHOICE OF JULIUS NYERERE
AS FIRST HONORARY PRESIDENT

Julius Nyerere, as first honorary president, brought enormous prestige to the Council. One of the most respected world leaders, he believed in, and understood, adult education probably more than any other head of state. Early visibility and credibility for the ICAE was in part drawn from the association with such well known figures of the day. Many of the early vice-presidents were chosen because of their reputations and credibility. Eventually the Council itself, through its mandate and programs, began to have its own credibility, so that it lends institutional recognition of its own to those who serve as officers. In the earlier days it was a small, struggling organization that, quite frankly, did not receive much attention. There were no turf wars as there was no turf! It was quite a relaxed, informal thing. As it has grown and become a much more important body, in terms of politics and policy, it begins to reproduce the tensions and conflicts that are found in a larger society.

THE HELSINKI MEETINGS

In June 1979, meeting for the last time under the founding constitution, the Board put a new one in place in Helsinki. While not on the scale of the world assemblies, the Helsinki meeting was critical, as it marked the first meeting to take place in one of the Nordic countries, nations which have had a long commitment to adult education and social movements.

Helsinki was also the transition year in leadership between J. Roby Kidd and myself. On the basis of my experience as the secretary of the Dar es Salaam World Assembly, my part in the establishment of an international research network, and my success in raising some funds, the Board appointed me as secretary-general, and Chris Duke, formerly of Australia, as associate secretary-general. Duke stayed in this position, taking major responsibility for Asian regional matters, organizing the first major world meeting in China in 1983, supervising a study on adult education and poverty in 1980, and providing welcome organizational support to the Council until 1985 and the Third World Assembly in Buenos Aires, Argentina. Dr. J. Roby Kidd stayed on as treasurer of the Council until his death at sixty-five years in March 1982. The J. Roby Kidd Award commemorates his life and is given each year in recognition of new adult educators from across the world who show particular promise.

THE BEGINNING OF "NETWORKING" IN THE COUNCIL

The Council's experience in building a research "network" in the years 1976–79 served as a model for the development of a great many other such activist and grass roots networks in the future. We had discovered the concept and structure of networking in the late 1970s and found it an enormously valuable organizational tool for spreading new ideas quickly, building notions of "horizontality," and working quickly in nonbureaucratic ways. We applied the notion of networking to the development of other programmatic areas.

Yusuf Kassam, formerly director of the Institute of Adult Education in Tanzania, and former coordinator of the African Participatory Research Network, joined the Secretariat in Toronto in April 1981 as the new director of programmes. His experience in the field, and solid reputation in the international community, were to prove critical to the expansion of the role of programing in the Council throughout the next decade. The Council's second network was developed in the area of adult education and peace.

Helena Kekonnen from Finland came to ICAE with the idea of an adult education and peace network similar to the participatory research networks. From that the Council developed the notion of decentralized programming, which is still a key characteristic of ICAE programs. Decentralized programming means that all initiatives do not originate in the headquarters; instead, international focal points for the networks can be found in various parts of the world. The peace network was coordinated from Helsinki, the participatory research network from New Delhi, and so forth. Two additional networks were in place by 1980, in primary health care and adult education and the beginning of the women's program.

Margaret Gayfer, the editor of *Convergence*, undertook a research study on women and adult education, which later developed into a women's network (Gayfer and Bernard, 1983). This research project raised many new areas for adult educators and, because the project itself was a participatory one, the actual work of the project laid the ground work for an extensive network which continues to be one of the most important areas of the Council's program. It underscored the under-representation of women in adult education research, writing, and programming and stimulated the Council to begin to think of the representation of women in the very structures of the Council itself.

ADULT EDUCATION AND SOCIAL MOVEMENTS

With the strong organizational support of the Council's French member, Peuple et Culture, and the personal involvement of its secretary general, Bernard Smagghe, France was chosen for the Second World Assembly. It was held near Paris in October 1982, at a residential adult education center in the village of Marly-le-Roi. The Council wanted to strengthen its francophone base and was keen on making links with Francois Mitterand, the newly-elected president of France, who, it was known, had a commitment to both "education populaire," and to internationalism. He was the keynote speaker at the opening, which took place in the new plenary hall of UNESCO in Paris.

Strategically, the Paris Assembly represented the first time that the old and the new networks of the Council came together. Although the official title of the Paris conference was "Adult Education and Authentic Development," it was already clear that the notion of development was unable to capture what most of the practitioners and activists were experiencing. What became clear, initially by thinking through critical social issues around which networks or programs might be developed, was that there was much to be gained by linking adult education to the work of various social movements. It was argued that adult education had its origins in Europe within the various social movements and reforms which followed the industrial revolution. By the early 1980s the women's movement, the peace movement, trade union movements, solidarity movements of the North with the South, movements of indigenous people, and other movements were gaining momentum. Beginning in 1982 in Paris and continuing until 1990, the Executive and the Secretariat of the Council, among many other activities, worked to strengthen the links between the adult education movement and other movements.

Importantly, Dame Nita Barrow of Barbados was elected president of the ICAE in 1982. Dame Nita had an extensive career in nursing, primary health care, the women's movement, Christian world solidarity, as well as deep links with people in every part of the United Nations. Her leadership from 1982 to 1990 coincided with arguably one of the most productive periods of international adult education collaboration and expansion. Edmund Gleazer Jr. of the United States, with a long career of strengthening community colleges in that country, was elected as treasurer.

Social movements were identified as primary means of transformation. For adult educators, this meant trying to understand the agendas of the peace movement, the women's movement, North-South solidarity, the worker's movement, and others, as well as trying to demonstrate the potential of their field in the service of these movements.

The 1982-90 period broadened the membership considerably, adding to the earlier base of university faculty members and professional adult educators to include many more from the growing number of nongovernmental organizations.

The 1982-90 period also reflected the more open understanding of the politics of adult education. The notion of the neutrality of the field was for the most part put aside and in its place was an understanding that it is socially constructed in the same way that the world is constructed and that one is constantly facing a set of choices about how to work and what to do. The Council, in the spirit of Paulo Freire, and similar to church workers in the theology of liberation, made a preferential option for the poor.

TENSIONS OR COMPETING POINTS OF VIEW

There has always been competition between various points of view. When community-based or activist adult educators first came into Council circles, there was some criticism of those who were engaged in professional or institutionalized forms of adult education. Over the years, however, those tensions lessened, in part because of the much greater participation of nongovernmentally-based educators and a decrease in the participation of government adult education departments and university structures. By the mid 1990s, the Council was by and large taken up by the NGO voice.

There was an anticipation of tension in 1982, the first time we brought together all the previous Council members from the associations

and the universities with all of these new network people, social movement people, and activists. We thought there might be much friction, but,
in fact, people were quite happy. The ones who had been there for a time
were delighted to see so many new faces and energies. The younger folk
were pleased to find so much support from the "old timers." The halls
of Marly-le-Roi rang with song and dance, as well as demonstrations and
evidence of deep differences. The spirit of the 1982 event was perhaps
best captured by the plenary report from the women's caucus, animated
by Lynda Yanz. In the place of a narrative report by one speaker at the
microphone, the plenary hall resounded to the music and words of a song
which was collectively written with the help of Arlene Mantle, an activist
singer and song writer from Canada. The words raised critical questions
about the official opening deliberations several days earlier, noting in lyr-
ics, "They said 'man' and 'he', but where were 'we', women who hold up
half the sky?"

THE POLITICS OF GENDER

An important issue with which the Council has struggled has been
the changing role of women. As with most social action organizations,
the 1980s have raised important challenges to patriarchal patterns deeply
embedded in the structures of the Council and its memberships. The
politics of gender within an international organization such as the Council is decidedly complex, because the various elements of the organization do not work with each other on a day-to-day basis, and because of
the differences in gender politics in the various cultures of the world.
    The Participatory Research Network, the Adult Education and Peace
Network, and the Women's Programme in the Council all shared a common notion that they were more than informational programs. They saw
themselves as "transformative" in nature and concerned not only with
sharing ideas with those outside the organization but with certain con-
stituencies within the Council itself. They took the Council seriously and
wanted it to be a model, as far as possible, of democratic ways of working. The women's program encouraged women to take up leadership responsibilities in their own adult education organizations, but eventually
those issues began to be raised about the other structures of the Council,
the Executive Committee, the Secretariat itself, and the committees.
Questions such as how many women there were on the Executive Committee, who the key decision makers were in the Council, and what was

the role of women within the Council. These have been important issues since they were informally raised as early as 1980, when Margaret Gayfer first undertook her research on women and adult education.

The idea of "feminism" had been raised earliest in North America and Europe, but the protection of patriarchal practices important in the "South" raised new questions. Debates about the primacy of a "South" vs. "North" ideological framework, stumbled over the issue of transformative adult education, where issues of balance and alliances are critical. How do we understand the relationships of issues of class, patriarchy, regional autonomy, decentralization, or community focus? The experience of oppression varies greatly, depending on one's race, class, physical ability, and so forth, and all of these issues can be found in the life of the ICAE. The giving of primacy to the issue of women's oppression over the issue of oppression of the South by the North, has been seen by some, mostly but not exclusively men, as splitting the ranks, thus weakening the organization of resistance and transformation in the South.

POPULAR EDUCATION MEETS THE WORLD: BUENOS AIRES, 1985

The Third World Assembly was held in Buenos Aires, Argentina, in December 1985, shortly after the country's return to democratic rule under President Alfonsin. The Assembly, orchestrated and designed by the then secretary-general of the Latin American Council for Adult Education (CEAAL), Francisco Vio Grossi, was the first world meeting in the field of adult education to be held in any part of Latin America and served to highlight the maturation and rapid dissemination of the concept of popular education. The Assembly brought together for a few days in one city the experiences of nearly six hundred educators from nearly one hundred countries. It combined them with a people who were excited by the realities of democracy after so many years of military rule. It made full and practical use of the extensive and articulate Latin American experiences of popular education to weave the group together. But for most, the deeper meaning of the week was symbolized by the Plaza de Mayo Mothers and Grandmothers, who had walked each day for years carrying photos of their missing children and husbands, eventually taking on the role of conscience of the nation and contributing to the downfall of the military. The World Assembly of Paris had linked adult educators with broader social movements; Buenos Aires allowed adult educators to experience themselves as a movement.

THE LAUNCH OF INTERNATIONAL LITERACY YEAR, 1990

The Fourth World Assembly of Adult Education was held in Bangkok, Thailand, January 8–18, 1990. The theme for the assembly was "Literacy, Popular Education and Democracy," and the event marked the launching of the United Nations International Year of Literacy (ILY). The Council, having proposed such a year at one of its meetings in 1982, went all out to provide the very best possible beginning. With the logistical support of the remarkable Thai Department of Nonformal Education and the planning mind of Rajesh Tandon of India, the Bangkok event marked the beginning of the ICAE's phase of "Adult Education and Democracy."

Building on the momentum of Buenos Aires, strengthened by the dramatic events in the former Soviet Union and by the deepened aspirations of the people of Africa for real democracy, the Council entered its next phase. It marked the end of the eight-year presidency of Dame Nita Barrow and the election of Francisco Vio Grossi of Chile, the architect of the Latin American Council for Adult Education, and founder of the Chilean popular education center, El Canelo de Nos.

EVALUATION OF COUNCIL WORK

There have been two major institutional evaluations. One in 1979–80, under the leadership of Alan Etherington, was a means of reviewing the work of the Kidd years and setting new agendas. The results were brought to the 1981 Executive Committee Meeting in Trinidad. Five years later, there was a second major evaluation, done this time by Ted Jackson, formerly of the participatory research group, who had set up an independent consulting firm in the early 1980s. In addition, the Council has encouraged its component programs to be self-reflective.

In 1985, the Council created a structure to strengthen its reflection and evaluation capacity. The Programme Advisory Committee (PAC) has historically been composed of a combination of some of the most creative and effective program leaders and some of the regional leadership. Every year, each of the programs would do a self-assessment of its accomplishments and determine plans for the next year. The Programme

Advisory Committee would go over all of that material and make practical recommendations.

COUNCIL CREATOR OR REFLECTOR OF TRENDS?

It is sometimes said that leadership is the art of finding out where people are going and helping them get there! Inevitably, the Council has been both a reflection of local or regional trends, as well as a means by which local or region educators make connections with broader trends and pick up new ideas. For example, Third World countries, particularly in Africa and India, which have a vast number of nonreaders just within their own borders, insisted that literacy should have a higher place on the world agenda. Their emphasis on literacy was directly related to the Council's recommending to UNESCO and the United Nations that there should be a Year for International Literacy. When this came about in 1990, the ICAE played a leadership role in the mobilizing of global public opinion, which in turn stimulated literally thousands of groups to take direct action on their own literacy programs.

The ICAE has undoubtedly been an instrument for influencing the field of adult education. However, it could not do that unless elements of those changes already existed in society. Participatory research was taken up with such enthusiasm because it struck a chord: it resonated with problems which many adult educators had with earlier more rigid notions of research. The fact that the Council gave visibility to ideas around participatory research made it possible for those ideas to move much more quickly. It created a trend which is still with us. The same is true for women's issues which went far beyond just "courses for women."

One of the priority programs of the Council has concerned peace and human rights, and this has helped validate this issue when, in fact, militarism seems to be yet too central. The Council can give visibility to such issues, but it does not have any power other than a strong voice in the international discourse of the movement.

New ideas and networks do not always work, however. The Council tried very hard to support a permanent international network in worker's education, but the international trade union bodies thought that the Council was not the appropriate vehicle for that network. Workers' own organizations were the vehicles for that. The ICAE met with a series of frustrations and political difficulties at the international trade union level and eventually was unable to find the economic support necessary to make such a network more permanent. Eventually, it had to let go of that network. There was no economic support for an autonomous Worker's Education Network, because the international scene is dominated by the workers' own organizations, and that may well be for the best.

The Council has been able to intervene over the years to help individuals come to justice or even survive. Carlos Gaspar is a brilliant popular educator working with the people in rural areas of The Philippines. During the Marcos years, Gaspar was a leader in the use of popular theater techniques in building the democracy movement. A Roman Catholic brother who was imprisoned for his adult education work by the Marcos regime, Gaspar was named by the ICAE as the recipient of its J. Roby Kidd Award, while still in prison. The Council wrote to the government officials asking for permission to present the award to Gaspar in prison, and asked its members to write calling for his release. Gaspar was ultimately released several days prior to the large ceremony that was being organized for him in his home town.

THE ROLE OF CONVERGENCE

Convergence has been the major publication of the Council since the earliest days. One of the things that the Council learned early on is the power of information: getting things out and into the hands of people. *Convergence*, which recently celebrated its twenty-fifth anniversary, has played a quite remarkable role in documenting innovation, giving particular emphasis to important developments in countries which are not covered by the European/North American journals. Under the very able editorship of Karen Yarmol-Franko, it has become a network of its own, linking theory and practice, and is widely used in Europe and North America as a rich source of teaching material. Paulo Freire was first published, for example, in 1971. Early Tanzanian developments were reported, as well as many other firsts in adult education, such as the articles on popular education, participatory research, the feminist challenge to adult education, reports on the literacy crusade in Nicaragua, special issues on prison education, the environment, the struggle of indigenous people, and many more. Even today, in the age of electronic networks, if you can get materials into print and into the hands of people so that they can see and read, it gives a sense of reality. The informational connective role the Council has played is probably its most important contribution to this day.

THE ICAE AT THE EARTH SUMMIT

In June 1992, the United Nations organized the International Conference on Environment and Development in Rio de Janeiro, Brazil. The environment had been an issue for the ICAE since its own World Assembly in 1976, so the Executive and membership of the Council were committed to making as significant contribution as possible at the Earth Summit itself. The key role which the ICAE played was the articulation through a broad consultative process of the International Treaty on Education for Sustainable Societies. This treaty was the highlight and final product of a week long "Journey for Environmental Education," itself a year-long process animated by Moema Viezzer and Darlene Clover of the Council.

DIFFICULTIES AND CHALLENGES

Any world-wide structure is difficult to finance. With changing conditions in the world, the decline of international aid, and increasing polarization leaving the poorest nations in even worse shape, the ICAE faces a serious challenge. Continuing to operate in a democratic manner with less money for necessary planning meetings means much more effort needs to go into making use of electronic conferences and networks. While the Council took an early lead in this field, in general, the adult educators do not use the electronic communications capacities nearly as much as more affluent NGOs, such as the international environmental NGOs.

As funds for international cooperation become more scarce, the choices of how best to support a diverse international movement become critical. Earlier innovations, such as the policies of decentralization of programs, were being called into question. Gleazer, ICAE Treasurer, has noted:

> By 1993, prior to the Executive's meeting in Madrid, the problems as well as the advantages of a decentralized approach were becoming apparent. ... As just one example, each had its own newsletter, conducted its conferences, disseminated information in various ways, sought funds for program support, and maintained its financial records. In offices with limited staff, the variety of expertise required was obviously limited for the span of activities conducted.[3]

Transitions in leadership in large and far-flung organizations are often more difficult than in smaller organizations. This is because relations of trust and knowledge of the personalities of others are often the basis for taking decisions or moving forward. When Hall stepped down in 1991, Kassam stepped down as well, leaving a new and quite unknown adult educator, Retta Alemahehu, the secretary-general designate of the Executive Committee, to move forward with a complex organizational agenda. Within a year, he found the challenges more than he had agreed to and moved on. That the Executive was able to find a solution and move through a second transition in such a short period is evidence of the commitment and creativity of both the Secretariat staff and the Executive members responsible.

STRENGTHS OF THE COUNCIL

One of the strengths of the Council is that it is genuinely an international organization where the decision-making process involves people from literally all over the world. Having studied a great many other international nongovernmental organizations in my years since leaving the Council, it is clear that the Council is one of the very few such international NGOs which has been able to create a structure where the decision making, and the issues taken up, are done in such a geographically democratic manner. A second strength is the sheer geographic scale of its network. It has a vast mailing list of thousands of names of key people in every country in the world. Third, within the field of adult education, it has been able to be a voice for the least powerful in our world, raising issues about prison reform, the struggles of the oppressed, the poor, those who do not read, indigenous peoples, peace and human rights, and working people. As the only worldwide body in the field of adult education, it is important that it be preserved and supported. It represents a unique source of thinking and talking about adult education in the world.

THE PATHS FORWARD

These are challenging times everywhere. The pressures of economic, political, and cultural globalization are transforming the nature of domestic and international work. In some cases, it is becoming impossible to distinguish between the two. In Canada, for example, the adult education of women in the Maquiladora Free Enterprise zones on the Mexican-U.S. border is very much a domestic issue, under the terms of the North American Free Trade Agreement. So the very nature of an organization, such as the ICAE, is changing. In 1992, the first woman secretary-general, Ana Maria Quiroz, who possesses dual Chilean-Canadian citizenship, took over responsibilities for the Secretariat of the Council. Peter Basel, a veteran of international adult education collaboration in Hungary and the countries of the former Eastern European bloc, joined the Council as the programme director. The leadership of Francisco Vio Grossi as president and the experienced members of the Executive will move the Council through the next phases in its history.

The Council is also playing a leadership role in an alliance of community-based networks, organizing to challenge and support the 1995 UN Social Summit, and continues its involvement in a variety of other efforts.

As from the very beginning of our adult education movement, our future is linked to concepts of deepening democracy and broadened rights and transformed lives. Vio Grossi, ICAE president, put it this way:

> Adult education for democracy ought to teach working and learning collectively, taking into account different contributions, diverse points of view, different abilities . . . it is about learning to contribute, to listen and discuss in order to describe the richness of 'the other,' to advance to a synthesis where differences remain visible even while searching for a broader sense of collectivity and community. It should draw from and return learnings of democracy to daily lives (Vio Grossi, 1993).

NOTES

1. With thanks to Dan Andreae, Darlene Clover, Francisco Vio Grossi, Margaret Gayfer, Gordon Selman, and Edmund Gleazer Jr.
2. I am grateful to Gordon Selman for his recollections of the first formal meeting to discuss the setting up of an international council.
3. From personal communication to the author, August 3, 1993.

BIBLIOGRAPHY

Gayfer, Margaret, and Anne Bernard (1983). *Women hold up more than half the sky: Research report on women and non-formal education.* Toronto: International Council for Adult Education.

222

210   ADULT EDUCATION THROUGH WORLD COLLABORATION

Hall, Budd L., and J. Roby Kidd (eds.) (1979). *Adult learning: A design for action.* Oxford: Pergamon Press.

ICAE (1974). Report of the Secretary-General to the Board of the International Council for Adult Education. Toronto: ICAE.

ICAE (1991). Report of the Secretary-General to the 19th Executive Committee Meeting, 4–7 April, in Gothenburg, Sweden. Toronto: International Council for Adult Education.

Vio Grossi, F. (1993). Adult education for democracy today. (draft paper for the International Council for Adult Education, May, Santiago, Chile).

CHAPTER 12

Adult Education for Peace

HELENA KEKKONEN

The inclusion of peace issues in the curricula of the various levels of education, and especially adult education, is a fairly recent development. Only since World War II have demands for education to prepare people to live in harmony with one another been expressed in earnest. The challenge was met primarily by a number of bold individuals, mostly working with children and youth, who believed that teaching the new generation was the fastest way of changing attitudes toward resolving conflicts by peaceful means.

Unfortunately, peace education did not produce any immediate impact on society, since the majority of adults approved of the use of violence, especially in conflicts between nations. Furthermore, compulsory military service was instituted in many countries, and the minds of young men were influenced in favor of violence and wars in the name of defense and heroism. Additionally, some peace education had the stigma of being one-sided leftist propaganda. All of these factors worked against the universal ethical content of peace education.

A significant advance in the prospects of peace education was made in 1974 with the UNESCO recommendation concerning education for international understanding, cooperation, and peace. Stressing that structural violence is connected to open violence and war, it charged the schools with helping children to understand the imperative of learning peace and incorporating it in their daily lives.

> Education . . . should bring every person to understand and assume his or her responsibility for the maintenance of peace. It should contribute to international understanding and strengthening of world peace and to the activities in the struggle against colonialism and neo-colonialism in all their forms and manifestations, and against all forms and varieties of racism, fascism and apartheid (UNESCO 1974: Chapter III, 6).

Although all of the member states of UNESCO approved the principles of the aforementioned recommendation, its practical implementation fell short of expectation. For one thing, peace education was sidetracked by those who misguidedly conceived it as only learning tolerance and mutual understanding, overlooking the deficiencies of society and how they might be resolved. For another thing, it became obvious that adults themselves needed help in understanding this distinction.

Toward this end, the founding of the International Council for Adult Education (ICAE) in 1973 represented a distinct turning point in world studies and peace education. The fruitfulness of the cooperation between UNESCO and the ICAE is reflected in the following excellent recommendation on the development of adult education ratified in 1976.

> Generally speaking, the aims of adult education should be to contribute to a) promoting work for peace, international understanding and cooperation; b) developing a critical understanding of major contemporary problems and social changes and the ability to play an active part in the progress of society with a view to achieving social justice (UNESCO, 1976: Chapter II, p. 2).

It is interesting to note that in the 1976 recommendation, peace education is placed ahead of international understanding and cooperation, and emphasis is placed on the significance of the active social role of adults in achieving social justice.

THE ICAE AND PEACE EDUCATION

By the end of the decade of the 70s, it became obvious that a global coordinating effort was needed to promote peace education. Previous efforts were often in isolated situations, and of considerable variation in contents in different countries and different cultures. In Western countries, emphasis was usually on opposition to the arms race and the development of new weapons, and support of disarmament. In some situations, peace education was construed to mean world studies. As important as these two aspects of peace education are, they do not cover the whole subject.

The ICAE stepped in to organize international seminars and meetings for people from different cultures to share ideas. Those from developing countries and socialist countries questioned the dominating role of western values, which they suggested should be reassessed and even re-formulated.

The next step for the ICAE was to put in place a Peace Network composed of adult educators from different countries, founded in conjunction with a meeting of Finnish adult educators in 1981. Then and there, sixty adult educators from nineteen countries joined the network. Their purpose was the development of peace education by disseminating information and by holding joint meetings. They agreed to make known the results of peace research in the context of adult education, to participate in the debate on the subject of developing nonviolent methods of defense, and to promote the overall cause of peace culture.

To aid the Peace Network, the Finnish Adult Education Organizations began publishing the journal *Peaceletter*, which was aimed at disseminating the goals and applications of peace education globally. In addition, the seminar, "Meeting in Finland," became the annual contact and forum for the Peace Network adult educators, which continues to this day. The Peace Network's membership, representing the adult educators of some eighty countries, rose to nearly 800 persons in the space of a couple of years.

In 1981, the work of the ICAE Peace Network was recognized by UNESCO, when it awarded the Prize for Peace Education of that year to Helena Kekkonen, the coordinator of the Network (and the author of this chapter) and jointly to the World Organization of the Boy Scout Movement. Peace education began to enjoy growing support the world over, and many of the suspicions as to its political biases or one-sidedness gradually gave way.

The decade of the 80s was the golden era for peace education. Lectures, seminars, and theme days became commonplace. Traditional peace movements placed increasing emphasis on education. The leadership and the economic support of the ICAE enhanced this work, especially in developing countries.

Peace education requires a methodology that is both affective and cognitive, designed to win the hearts and train the minds of individuals. Authoritative, fact-based teaching should be replaced by instruction which is problem-centered, one that focuses on the everyday life of individuals. It should lead to an understanding of the need for the positive promotion of peace in our time, not just the elimination of the arms race. In other words, peace educators have endorsed Paulo Freire's methodology of "conscientization" to help people wake up to the critical need for individual responsibility in the quest for peace.

Information on peace education appeared in many forms in various countries: reports, books, and articles on the pedagogics of peace education, and research results. The ICAE made materials available in French and Spanish, as well as English.

The 1980s saw a rapid development in the contents of peace education. Previously, adult educators in the developing countries criticized the industrialized nations for treating peace education as if its only purpose was to settle the Cold War. Now, peace education came to include much more. The question was asked as to how there could be peace without human rights and equality, without a reduction in the great inequality between North and South, without attention to the great cause of saving the environment, of dealing with hunger, of reducing unemployment, and doing away with oppression of any kind?

Thus, the subject of disarmament and the study of world cultures were seen as no longer enough. It was now deemed necessary to investigate and clarify the conditions in which peace would be possible. The role of structural violence in precipitating conflicts was defined. People began to realize that a lasting peace among nations requires the creation of the premises for peace.

It became obvious that a succinct definition of peace education was needed. The following was developed by the author of this chapter, based on her long practical experience, and was approved by the Peace Network.

> The goal of peace education is to help individuals to grow into citizens capable of critical thinking, empathy, solidarity toward the less privileged, of carrying responsibility, able to engage in active cooperation with others in the endeavour to create just and peaceful conditions for people the world over (Kekkonen, 1990, p. 73).

The purpose of the definition was to stress the following points:

(1) The necessity for independent, critical thinking. It has been possible to prove that many shortcomings in our world, and even the outbreak of wars, have been due to the fact that ordinary people are indifferent to social inadequacies. Peace education was intended to create bold citizens, citizens able to appreciate the causes of conflicts and injustices and to react in time to prevent conflicts from breaking out.

(2) Empathy. The preservation of a live sympathy was considered essential in a time of pronounced rationality and one-sided development of the mind. It was thought that without genuine sympathy, people would

not be able to act on behalf of the downtrodden and the weak, especially if these people were living in a foreign country.

All around development of the arts was found to be essential in the development of empathy. To take an example: Merely explaining to people the nature of weapon systems, their numbers, the relationships between countries, and what peace movements advocate, had turned out to be insufficient. Knowledge, as such, had not led people to take action on behalf of peace. In order that this knowledge might be internalized, it was found that, alongside efficient pedagogical methods, there was a need for versatile use of art, especially of films, music, theater, dance, literature, poetry, etc.

In addition to increasing people's knowledge of foreign cultures, artistic performances have the added benefit of appealing to emotions. People can identify with the fate of those suffering in situations of war, poverty, hunger, and deprivation of human rights, and are moved to take action.

While the curriculum of peace education will obviously be wide-ranging, five aspects should be given priority:

(1) Cultural education—working towards profound understanding of foreign cultures, their history and values, and everyday life; and preparedness for cooperation across borders.

(2) Environmental education—understanding the need to protect natural resources, their significance for different nations, and natural resources as causes of international conflicts.

(3) Human rights education—including political, civic, economic, and social rights, and rights to peaceful development.

(4) Development education—increasing knowledge about the relationship between developing and industrialized countries, and the structure of trade in the developing new world order.

(5) Moral education—accepting the global values of respect for human dignity, equality between people, nonexistence of an "enemy," and individual responsibility in the promotion of peace.

Two examples of peace education which were carried out by the author will be instructive. The first was a twelve-month course of study, "The Difficulty of Being Human," established for the inmates at the Helsinki Central Prison. Based on a pedagogy of mutual trust and open discussion, and without a teacher in charge, the inmates learned over time to trust in their own possibilities to change their way of life. Discussion began with the problems of the individual in the various structures of society, moved on to the correction of prison conditions, and then on to the world situation and issues of war and peace. Each inmate prepared a personal action plan to be implemented as far as possible within the prison and, especially, after release.

The second was a course in natural science at a Finnish vocational school. Along with technical aspects of the study, students took a close look at the history of chemistry, from its beginnings down to the splitting of the atom. This was followed by an analysis of reasons for the outbreak of World War II, and to an examination of the justifications given for the bombing of Hiroshima and Nagasaki. These discussions led to a recognition of the responsibility for peace of ordinary people as representatives of their professions and as members of society. Peace education came to have a permanent place in the curriculum of the school, and students individually joined peace organizations.

FUTURE PROSPECTS OF PEACE EDUCATION

Economic and political conditions in the 1980s—the economically prosperous years in the industrialized countries, and the continuance of the Cold War—contributed to the expanding development of peace education. However, the radical changes that have taken place recently—the end of the Cold War, the economic problems of the former socialist countries, the rise of nationalism, and, finally, the economic recession in industrialized countries—have had a negative impact on peace work and peace education. Now there seem to be negative or, at least, indifferent attitudes toward peace work.

Now that countries are suffering from recessions, subsidies to peace organizations have been cut both by state and private sponsors. Moreover, peace organizations themselves have also become somewhat confused. A reassessment of goals and action models is now essential. People who claim that the end of the Cold War did away with the need for peace work and education are thinking only in terms of questions of disarmament.

It is all too clear that peace education is not only still needed, but perhaps needed more than ever before. The Gulf War and the Yugoslavian conflict prove that pro-war and pro-violence attitudes continue to prevail. Ours is still a world of tough competition, inequality, and, in many places, little respect for human rights. It continues to be a world in which the weakest, such as the elderly, women, children, and the sick, become victims of war and social subjection. Peace education is ethical education in its purest form. Humankind must learn to be humane.

At the core of peace education are the values of a civilized society. What do we live for? What do we strive for? What are the consequences of what we do or fail to do? What are our personal rights and responsibilities now and in the future? What can we achieve through violence? Who are the victims? What are the nonviolent options open to us in critical situations? What have peace movements achieved? How should they be developed?

Many aspects of the world situation today give cause for deep concern. Damage to the environment is increasing with the capacity of nature to withstand the influence of mankind strained to the extreme. Human rights are violated even by so-called "civilized" countries, with capital punishment and torture in prisons commonplace. Nowhere is the equality of the sexes, or of ethnic groups, even close to being achieved. Developing countries are suffering from unjust trade practices with industrialized countries resulting in continued poverty and squalor. The destruction of native peoples continues. Illiteracy is actually increasing.

To date, inadequate attention and resources have been directed at remedying these problems. The earlier idea that we could train the next generation to deal with them has been exploded. The remedies must begin with the adults of today. In so far as most adults have not been trained to think of their individual responsibilities in these matters, they must have educational opportunities to develop this critical thinking. In its latest international report, *The First Global Revolution,* the Club of Rome points out that the human race now lives in a "value vacuum" (King and Schneider, 1991, p. 103). The loss of values is the outcome of general disappointment in politics, in which words and deeds have not matched each other; in religion, where fine goals have not been realized; and in the lack of mutual solidarity, where the less well-off are left to the welfare of the state or are just forgotten. The report asserts that the human race needs a revolution in critical thinking and attitudinal development.

The Peace Network of the International Council for Adult Education has been established for this very reason—to promote the urgency, status and practice of peace education. No one expects dramatic and immediate results. However, we must be prepared to look far into the future, into the world of our children and grandchildren, and to act in their best interest. The significance of education, at all levels, is far greater than anyone has dared to believe.

BIBLIOGRAPHY

Kekkonen, Helena (1990). *Rauhankirja* (Peace book). Helsinki: Peace Education Institute.

King, Alexander, and Bertrand Schneider (1991). *The first global revolution: Report by the Council of the Club of Rome.* London: Simon & Schuster, Ltd.

UNESCO General Conference (1974). *Recommendation concerning education for international understanding, co-operation and peace; and education relating to human rights and fundamental freedoms.* 19 November. Paris: UNESCO.

UNESCO General Conference (1976). *Recommendation on the development of adult education.* 26 November. Nairobi, Kenya.

CHAPTER 13

Learning for Environmental Action: Building International Consensus

DARLENE E. CLOVER

"Helping people to become environmentally literate requires that we stimulate knowledge, understanding, awareness, commitment, skills and then action."

—Victor Johnson

The above quotation by the late Victor Johnson, first coordinator of the Environmental Education Network of the African Association for Literacy and Adult Education (AALAE), describes environmental popular education as understood by the International Council for Adult Education (ICAE). It encapsulates the role which environmental education needs to play in providing knowledge, creating understanding and awareness, building skills and a sense of commitment, and, most importantly, stimulating action. Dr. Victor Johnson, originally from Sierra Leone, was formerly head of environmental education for the United Nation's Environmental Programme (UNEP) in Nairobi and a professor of biology at Makerere University in Uganda. He was the motivating force behind both AALAE's and the ICAE's move to launch an adult education effort on the global scale by taking part in the 1993 Earth Summit in Rio de Janeiro. Victor Johnson died suddenly in early 1990. This chapter is dedicated to the strength, power, vision, and humor of this very gentle man.

The need to preserve and protect the natural and human environment has become an essential part of the lives of thousands of groups and individuals around the world. Publication in 1987 of "The Bruntland Report," or *Our Common Future*, as it is formally titled, brought world attention to uncontrolled global economic development which has created severe environmental problems which are fast becoming irreversible. It makes clear the need to protect the natural world against degradation and contamination of its air, water, and soil, for the very survival of humanity and the planet. The report outlines the link between environmental degradation and poverty, stating that environmental deterioration has had its most dramatic and drastic effect on people of the popular classes.

The Bruntland Report emphasizes the important role which education can play in providing comprehensive knowledge on environmental issues, to foster a sense of responsibility for the state of the environment. Such education is essential if those who are not currently part of the dialogue are to act on behalf of their own demands for improved living conditions, democracy and citizenship (Bruntland, 1987). Every day, humans around the globe are fighting for the right to breathe pure air, drink pure water, and eat wholesome food. Tragically, few if any national constitutions include the right to a clean and healthy environment.

In 1988, in response to the growing global environmental crisis and in the spirit of its earlier exploratory work begun in 1976 at the First World Assembly of Adult Education in Tanzania, the ICAE began a process to create a worldwide environmental popular education program. The goals were to promote environmental education in the work of popular-oriented social movements, strengthen and support the work of those already engaged in such education, and encourage the integration of this dimension in the work of nongovernmental organizations (NGOs), solidarity and policy groups, and institutions.

HISTORY

In November 1988 the ICAE disseminated a questionnaire to all of its national and regional member associations in 102 countries, in an effort to identify particular interests in environmental education and to locate those who had the knowledge and skills to help create a global environmental education network. Three organizations responded with enthusiasm and energy: the African Association for Literacy & Adult Education (AALAE), the Latin American Council for Adult Education (CEAAL), and Samnemda of Norway. Key members of these three organizations met in November 1989 in Toronto, Canada, in conjunction with the Faculty of Environment Studies at York University, which had also showed a deep interest in the subject and offered to host the meeting. The planning workshop brought together adult environmental educators from several parts of the world: Victor Johnson from Kenya, Moema Viezzer from Brazil, Kavaljit Singh from India, Astrid Thoner from Norway, and Budd L. Hall, Carroll Blair and Dian Marino from Canada. During the opening session, much of the discussion centered on whether the final product should be an informal information network or an action-oriented program.

The idea began simply as the Environmental Education Programme but, after careful deliberations, it was decided that a key element in the struggle for a healthy planet was far more than information sharing, it was the need to act. Therefore, it was agreed unanimously that the ICAE should establish an action-oriented global program and that it should be titled "Learning for Environmental Action," because it would link the principle notion of ongoing learning, vis-a-vis the relationship between nature, society and individuals, with an activist concept. The meeting ended with a decision that the participants of this workshop would form the core coordinating group of the environmental education program.

In January 1990, during ICAE's Fourth World Assembly of Adult Education in Bangkok, Thailand, this core coordinating group came together with others, to determine the future directions of the program. The needs identified included:

— information about environmental issues, examples of activities, political actions, case studies, alternative production, and economic consequences;
— stimulation and consciousness-raising;
— incorporation of information about popular education methods, the development of an instrument to lobby and pressure governments at the local, national and international levels.

The group outlined their main target groups as the general public, schools, media, trade unions, women's groups, and farmers, and made various recommendations to the World Assembly participants which they hoped would stimulate increased consciousness and creative actions by all toward a sustainable global future. These included:

— that the Fourth World Assembly of Adult Education strongly endorse and support the formation of an Environmental Learning Action Network;

— that the Fourth World Assembly strongly support the current effort to draft a UN Charter on Environmental Rights;
— that all participants take committed action to recycle unneeded paper or books on leaving the Open University conference location;
— that all ICAE member organizations take immediate steps to cut back on paper consumption and to use recycled, unbleached paper whenever possible (ICAE, 1990, pp. 123–25).

Equipped with a rationale for the creation of a global environmental education program, objectives, target groups, a needs assessment and recommendations, the ICAE secretary-general, Dr. Budd L. Hall, proposed the new network at the next meeting of the Programme Advisory Committee (PAC) in April 1990. PAC not only agreed to the proposal, but recommended that environmental popular education become one of the four priority programs of the ICAE, along with literacy, women and education, and peace and human rights. Moema Viezzer, internationally known as a leader in the women's and environmental movements, was appointed as coordinator of the program. An international environmental education liaison group was established to begin the task of research and area/group specific needs assessments, information sharing, and outreach environmental education work in their specific regions.

During the 1991 Executive Committee meeting of the ICAE in Gothenburg, Sweden, Moema Viezzer articulated the premise of the program:

> The new Learning for Environmental Action Programme of the International Council for Adult Education will offer a holistic approach which links environmental concerns to other social issues. The Programme will play an important role in strengthening the popular movements involved in environmental issues placing special emphasis on the 1992 UN Conference on Environmental and Development (UNCED). The Programme will operate in five languages, English, Spanish, French, Portuguese and Arabic in all seven regions where the ICAE works.[1]

She explained that the program would be divided into five subprograms: Management of the Program; Participatory Action Research; Information Service; Media Relations; Mobilization and Action.

The new program office was set up in Sao Paulo, Brazil, and staff members were hired. Research began with a participatory process, to collect information on the experiences of groups and institutions working in environmental popular education, to be shared in the tri-monthly newsletter, *Pachamama*. The Earth Summit was selected as the obvious place to launch this global adult environmental education effort. Therefore, the mobilization component of the program was begun, leading the ICAE on an exhilarating, exhausting, challenging and often overwhelming journey to the Earth Summit in June 1992 in Rio de Janeiro.

"THE ROAD TO RIO"[2]

ICAE's journey into the world of environmental education began at the final Preparatory Conference of the United Nations Conference on Environment and Development (UNCED PrepComm IV) in New York, where a group of people from within the ICAE networks merged with a globally representative NGO Working Group on Education, to review the chapter of *Agenda 21* entitled "Education, Public Awareness and Training."[3] Although put forward as an "action plan," the UN document was judged to be weak, passive, and generally unresponsive to real global environmental education needs. The ad hoc group recommended many changes but a few of the most important include:

— the strengthening of equity in education for women;
— acknowledgement of the responsibility of the North, or industrialized countries, in environmental degradation;
— an increase in attention to the important role of nonformal, informal, and popular education;
— a research which is people-centered;
— sustainable development, which includes justice/equity and the concept of "education for sustainable societies"
— understanding of the global dimension of local issues.

With this new more forceful and dynamic document in hand, the NGO Working Group on Education lobbied governments for their consideration of the changes. As a result, a number of government delegations promoted different aspects of the NGO recommendations in formal negotiations and revised the *Agenda 21* chapter on education to include a significant number of those recommendations. An action-oriented approach to the environmental crisis was begun. The PrepComm opened a window of opportunity for hundreds of NGOs, women's groups, social activists, church and other religious groups, voluntary organizations, popular educators, indigenous peoples, environmentalists, and concerned individuals from around the world, to come together to share their views, deliberate on contemporary global environmental issues, and present a united voice which could influence global environmental policy.

THE INTERNATIONAL JOURNEY
FOR ENVIRONMENTAL EDUCATION

From June 1–4, 1992, under a big tent nestled in the Flamenco Park in the heart of Rio de Janeiro, Brazil, the ICAE played host to the International Journey for Environmental Education, under the auspices of the NGO Global Forum. The setting and dynamic is described by Edmund Gleazer of the United States:

> Rio de Janeiro is a city of physical and social contrast, with a population of nine million, in a spectacular setting of mountains and beaches. Overlooking it all is the Christ the Redeemer statue on Mount Corcovado. Broad boulevards and walkways separate white sand beaches from densely stacked buildings, and traffic is incessant and aggressive. . . . Social and environmental problems, poor housing, lack of health care, economic inequalities, rising inflation, massive foreign debt have all contributed to make Rio the ideal setting for the conferences; the issues discussed at the Summit are visible in Rio (ICAE, 1992).

The title, "journey" was chosen for the four-day seminar/workshop, because that word best described the undertaking: an adventurous voyage into the as yet still fully unexplored world of environmental popular education. There were two distinct parts to the International Journey: the seminar itself, which included panels and audience participation, and a series of workshops on an environmental education treaty, entitled "Education for Sustainable Societies and Global Responsibility." The various panels were organized around the theme of "learning" in keeping with the idea of the program itself, that in this complex world, we are all learners, in relation to ourselves, to other human beings, and all other species which make up this living planet.

On the first panel, "Learning Anew," Vandana Shiva, a leading ecofeminist and grass-roots environmental activist from India, discussed the two tensions around knowledge in the world today. She described this polarization as arrogant or scientific knowledge, and knowledge which recognizes ancient and different forms/types of knowing. She precisely noted that the so-called age of enlightenment had "forced all other learning and knowledge into darkness;" that men in European societies were the only people who knew; that women and others in different parts of the world needed to be taught and "civilized;" and that they had rendered invisible other ways of knowing, such as native or traditional knowledge, peoples' spirituality, and especially women's knowledge. She concluded by stating that "Learning anew must be linked to learning from tradition."

Echoing words in her earlier book, *Staying Alive* (1989, p. 224), Vandana Shiva stated:

> The two central shifts in thinking that are being induced by women's ecological struggles relate to economic and intellectual worth. The first relates to our understanding of what constitutes knowledge, and who the knowers and producers of intellectual knowledge are.[4]

By using environmental popular education techniques, the knowledge of others can become a basis on which to create a new vision of the world. Popular education is a process of learning, which begins with the experiences of the learner and knowledge of the learner. It involves participation and works towards democracy and social justice. Incorporating the knowledge of other groups such as the women who work the land, and indigenous respect for the natural world into all training projects and curricula will provide a wealth of learning which could lead to a transformation in thinking and acting.

On the second panel of the International Journey, "Learning from Yesterday and for Tomorrow," Lillian Holt, an indigenous woman from Australia, and member of the ICAE Executive, echoed the need to learn anew, and the value of emotion and passionate commitment to bring about concrete change. She spoke of the way she had been schooled around the old "stiff upper lip" tradition, constantly being told that women were too emotional and that their emotions were unhealthy and a hindrance to progress. She believes that women's passion and anger should be used to challenge those in positions of power and to begin to make fundamental environmental and societal changes, as we move forward into the twenty-first century.

Patricia Mische, a leading environmental educator from the United States, took part on a panel, "Learning for Life." She spoke of the need to learn to reinhabit the earth and understand that we are only part of a whole. She believes that there needs to be "a new life-long learning linked with spirituality, an understanding of our cosmic story, and a deeper appreciation of the earth's creativity," if environmental degradation is to be halted. On the same panel, Chief Bisi Ogunleye, an environmental activist working with grassroots women's organizations in her native Nigeria, talked about what she called a "bottom-up learning approach." She believes that the environmental crisis will be solved through community-based groups taking charge of their own lives and environments. She was very quick to point out some of the flaws of western scientific education which have contributed to the global crisis with which we are now faced.

Few participants missed the opportunity to criticize the North for creating an unsustainable model of development, one based on wasteful use of resources and excessive consumerism, as well as the staggering impact of environmental degradation on the women and children of the South. High on the agenda was the human tragedy and fundamental economic and environmental error of Structural Adjustment Policies, which force governments to cut internal spending on social programs to support and sustain a healthy lifestyle, in order to repay the external debt.

"ENVIRONMENTAL EDUCATION FOR SUSTAINABLE SOCIETIES AND GLOBAL RESPONSIBILITY"[5]

The Education Treaty was one of twenty-nine different citizens' treaties, which were collectively entitled *The Earth Charter* (NGO Global Forum, 1992). This was disseminated by the Global NGO Forum at the end of the Earth Summit. The Education Treaty has been translated into English, French, Portuguese, and Spanish. The final text of this document was the result of a year-long global participatory consultation. The first draft had been sent out to about 8,000 educational institutions and organizations, students, and community and grass-roots educators around the world. Their suggestions and remarks were then incorporated into the text, which was taken to the fourth PrepComm in New York in March, where it was further developed by the ad hoc NGO education working group which had worked on *Agenda 21*. It was then taken to the International Journey participants in Rio, where it was finalized.

The Treaty, a normative document with international impact, was the first such global statement produced by nongovernmental organizations. Women's groups, which had played an important role every step of the way, endorsed the term "sustainable societies," instead of "sustainable development," which has come to carry connotations of destruction and individuality. It was finally agreed that the term "societies" reflected a more harmonious pattern of growth and the idea of change through collective participation. The Treaty begins with the statement:

> We signatories, people from all parts of the globe, are devoted to protecting life on earth and recognize the central role of education in shaping values and social action. We commit ourselves to a process of education transformation aimed at involving ourselves, our communities and nations in creating equitable and sustainable societies. In so doing we seek to bring new hope to our small, troubled, but still beautiful planet (Ibid., p. 1).

The key elements of the Treaty include:

- The fundamental need for an environmental education which affirms values and actions which contribute to human and social transformation and ecological preservation;
- Education as the right of all; all are learners and educators;
- Environmental education is not neutral but is value-based. It is an act for social transformation;
- Environmental education must stimulate solidarity, equality, and respect for human rights, involving democratic strategies and an open climate of cultural interchange;
- Environmental education should treat critical global issues, their causes and interrelationships in a systemic approach and within their social and historical contexts. Fundamental issues in relation to development and the environment, such as population, health, peace, human rights, democracy, hunger, degradation of flora and fauna, should be perceived in this manner;
- Environmental education values all different forms of knowledge. Knowledge is diverse, cumulative, and socially produced, and should not be patented or monopolized;
- Environmental education must stimulate dialogue and cooperation among individuals and institutions in order to create new lifestyles which are based on meeting everyone's basic needs regardless of ethnic, gender, age, religion, class, physical or mental differences.

The Treaty also contains a plan of action calling for the promotion of partnerships between NGOS, social movements, and UN agencies; the circulation of information about people's wisdom and traditional methods of farming, living, and working; support for appropriate technologies; the promotion of training for environmental conservation; establishing criteria for education projects, assuring that ecological organizations and movements popularize their activities and that communities incorporate ecological issues in everyday life (Ibid., pp. 1–2).

228 ADULT EDUCATION THROUGH WORLD COLLABORATION

LESSONS LEARNED IN RIO: CHALLENGES TO
ENVIRONMENTAL ADULT EDUCATION

Three key lessons were learned at the Earth Summit: (1) that people living in the North/West will need to learn to live a simpler lifestyle, if all the world's peoples are to enjoy basic, fundamental, human rights and to survive; (2) that modern "scientific" forms of knowledge have cut the world off from ancient knowledge and ways of knowing, such as indigenous and women's knowledge, which are critical to the survival of the planet and the human race; and (3) that the role of women as educators and key social and environmental activists must be recognized.

As stated in the Treaty, environmental education must work closely with the media, to ensure that constructive and creative programs get their share of coverage. Public relations and publicity should be a component in all programs. This is a vital part of the work in raising the consciousness of the public, which otherwise often hears only the doomsday themes.

Headlines which screamed out such things as "Earth Summit Sputters" and "Talks on Collision Course" were a misunderstanding and misrepresentation of the complexities of the processes which were involved in the many meetings, workshops, and seminars which contributed to the process. Media, at least in North America, often focus on governments and their decisions and reactions to the environmental crisis, and this usually amounts to a focus on personalities instead of issues. Education can play a key role in helping people to sift through the media hype, in order to understand fully the true nature of environmental problems and what they, as global citizens, can do to bring about fundamental change.

Environmental educators will also need to understand and work with the vast array of attitudes which people are developing towards the environmental crisis. In a Canadian poll taken in May 1991 by Angus Reed, various attitudes surfaced vis-a-vis the environment. The report began by stating that 76% of Canadians consulted agreed that environmental pollution is a priority and then profiled different groups and attitudes. The poll encountered *activists*, who were usually young and well-educated, but pessimistic; *enthusiasts*, who are concerned but believe behavior can be changed; the *anxious*, who are older, low income individuals, who are fearful and want tough measures to be taken; *privileged optimists*, who are well-off, powerful, conservative, (most often) males, who believe technology and science will solve the problem in due course; the *apathetic*, who are older, have little income and are, therefore, too busy making ends meet; *fatalists*, who believe it is beyond repair, so why be bothered to try; and, finally, the *hostile*, who are educated, affluent, and believe that the environmental crisis is over-played. This last attitude is most interesting, because of its direct link to education.

A critical message which needs to be articulated over and over is that all human actions impact on the environment, either negatively or positively. It is very simple to fall into the trap of believing that, since companies pollute on such a large scale, the small efforts which individuals make to not use fertilizer on gardens, to recycle waste newspaper, and to use less water, to name a few actions, will not make any difference in the larger scheme of things. People often become paralyzed by the catastrophic environmental disasters which often seem to take place daily; they are too overwhelmed and confused to know what to do. True environmental transformation means an attitude change and an action focus. Future-oriented teaching and learning, which recognizes everyone as a key player who can make a difference, is critical.

The Earth Summit in Rio was an educative process and one which had a great impact on all those who participated. They came to the realization that, in order to bring about a fundamental change, all social movements must begin to share their knowledge and skills and work more closely together. The environmental movement must continue to learn strategic and popular ways of teaching, and the education movement must work with environmentalists, in order to clearly understand the issues and needs of the global community and its ecosystem. Rio put education on the environmental map, and education and learning have become key elements in the environmental process. To be in Rio was to see the range and strength of NGOs, and the growing momentum of an international environmental movement determined to change the direction in which we are headed, because, according to the lesson of an old Chinese proverb, "unless we change our direction, we are likely to end up where we are headed."

NOTES

1. Proposal, "Learning for Environmental Action: A Popular Education Programme of the International Council for Adult Education."

2. A term used by the media to reflect the year-long preparatory process.

3. *Agenda 21* is the United Nations blueprint for action, which will establish an agreed environmental and sustainable development work program of gov-

ernments and the international community for the period beyond 1992 and into the twenty-first century.

4. From notes taken during Vandana Shiva's panel presentation, June 2, 1993.

5. Treaty approved and accepted by the International NGO Forum and Social Movements in the Rio '92 Global Forum.

BIBLIOGRAPHY

Bruntland, Gro Harlem (1987). *Our common future*. Report of the World Commission on Environment and Development. Oxford: Oxford University Press.

Developing an environmental education curriculum (1989). *Connect* 14 (3).

Diezmos, Lilia M. (1985). Curriculum development in environmental education in the Philippines, *International Educator* 3: 20–28.

Education on environmental values (1986). *Connect* 11 (3): 1–4.

German Adult Education Association (1991). *Adult education and development*, 37. Bonn, Germany: DVV/German Adult Education Association.

Harmony Foundation of Canada (1991). *Community workshops for the environment*. Ottawa.

ICAE (1990). Learning from and for environmental action, in *Literacy, popular education and democracy, building the movement*. Toronto: International Council for Adult Education.

ICAE (1992). A message from Rio, *ICAE News* 4.

Ideas for a world environmental education charter (1992). Environmental Education Programme: International Journey for Environmental Education. Toronto: International Council for Adult Education.

NGO Global Forum (1992). *The Earth charter*, 11 June. Rio de Janeiro, Brazil.

Pflug, Bernd et al. (1985). The project-method in environment education, in *International Educator* 3 (2 & 3): 9–16.

Rugumayo, Edward B. et al. (1987). *Environmental education through adult education: A manual for adult educators, instructors, teachers and social extension workers*. Nairobi, Kenya: African Association for Literacy and Adult Education.

Shiva, Vandana (1989). *Staying alive*. New Delhi: Zed Brooks.

CHAPTER 14

History and Development of the ICAE Literacy Program

PATRICIA RODNEY

Research has shown that global illiteracy is a symptom of a much deeper problem. The majority of people who are illiterate are poor, marginalized, nonwhite and live in Third World Countries or "Third World-like" conditions in industrialized countries. They experience poor health, substandard housing, and are either unemployed or underemployed. The social factors associated with illiteracy generally affect more women than men, accounting for the gender differences in global illiteracy rates. Of the 963 million illiterates in the world in 1990, 63 percent were women and 37 percent men, a 34.9 percent and 20.5 percent increase, respectively, from 1985. Unfortunately, the situation continues to deteriorate, accelerated by the serious world economic crisis and resultant reductions in government spending on already poorly funded programs (UNESCO, 1989, p. 1).

The realization that specific actions were needed to address global illiteracy prompted the United Nations in 1990 to focus world attention on the crisis; the creation of an International Literacy Year (ILY) was one strategy used to deal with the phenomenon. Initial work done by the UN and other agencies revealed that illiteracy was merely a symptom of deeper socioeconomic problems and that simultaneous attention to other sources which maintain inequality was needed to eradicate the problem.

The UN's recognition that illiteracy was a global problem helped to change the perception that it was confined to Third World Countries. This resulting shift in thinking was expressed in the UNESCO Plan of Action to assist Member States worldwide to eradicate illiteracy by the year 2000. UNESCO hoped that the "Year" would contribute to a greater understanding of illiteracy by world public opinion and intensify efforts to spread literacy and education. It was envisaged that the interest and support of major international organizations, such as UNESCO and the UN, would now give literacy the necessary visibility and financial support it deserved. However, after ILY, literacy lost its prominence and was removed from the international agenda, making room for another topical issue.

This short evaluation focuses on the contributions and successes of the International Task Force on Literacy (ITFL), and highlights its limitations; for despite its creativity at promoting learners as leaders of illiteracy internationally, this was not enough. The International Council for Adult Education (ICAE) realized that it needed to do more than just create awareness of the problem and that provision of direct support to grassroots organization was necessary. Accordingly, the International Literacy Support Service (ILSS) was developed as a mechanism to strengthen the literacy work of ICAE and coordinate the efforts of its regional networks. It was one attempt to ensure that work started during the ILY (1990) would be sustained through the decade.

ICAE

Nongovernmental organizations such as the International Council for Adult Education, based in Toronto, were forced to become proactive, as a result of governments' inability to provide even basic literacy and adult education programs. ICAE provided an international structure to collectivize the concerns and struggles of adult education movements of nongovernmental organizations working at the grassroots, national and regional levels.

To facilitate its role, the ICAE found it beneficial to attain status with UNESCO and to continue working closely with the UN and its other agencies in a variety of activities. The multidimensional ways of working and learning through programs, publications, research, seminars, workshops and international exchanges, fostered and built the work and expertise of the organization.

THE EARLY DAYS

ICAE's interest and work in literacy preceded the UN adoption of the 1987 resolution proclaiming 1990 as International Literacy Year. Although literacy was not a central focus of the ICAE before 1979, it was addressed within the priority program areas of primary health care, education of older adults, women's perspectives, peace and productive work. During the mid 1980s, ICAE joined in major literacy activities, in collaboration with organizations such as the German Foundation for International Development (DSE) and UNESCO. In 1983, new interest in literacy was stimulated through a major seminar in Berlin, cosponsored by the DSE and the ICAE. Then, in 1987, through joint consultations, the two organizations established a five-year strategy for the development, implementation, and delivery of ICAE's literacy programs. These were based on the "People's Right to Learn" and consisted of an advocacy component that focussed on the role of NGOs in literacy exchange visits, networking, documentation, and information exchange (Fordham, 1983, p. 9).

The establishment of ICAE as of a focal point was a critical step in efforts to unite the literacy movement around the world and to strengthen and improve the practice of adult education. However, the literacy contributions made by the ICAE and other partners up to this point were minuscule in comparison to global needs; and the Evaluation Report (Jackson et al., 1987) criticized ICAE's handling of its literacy programs. Specific recommendations were made to the Council, in the hope of improving service delivery and program effectiveness. The Report suggested that (1) additional resources be allocated to peace, literacy, and older adults; (2) a Literacy Committee be established for program planning and monitoring; and (3) strong consideration be given to appointing an international coordinator from the South where operations would have a greater impact at the grassroots level. ICAE, however, did not immediately implement these recommendations, but, instead, began investigative research on how to do so most effectively. In the meantime, the Council concentrated on the need for increased global awareness and stronger NGO advocacy for literacy and became involved in the establishment of an international coalition.

FORMATION OF THE COALITION (ITFL, 1987–1991)

More than fourteen years of work in the field on a world-wide scale, put the ICAE in a position to play a critical role in the international literacy movement. Having built a wide and experienced network, the organization possessed the confidence to establish a task force to coordinate the literacy work of NGOs internationally. In order to determine what should be done for ILY, in 1988 the ICAE carried out a needs assessment survey of its member associations; the main findings revealed a lack of funding for literacy programs, diversity of approaches, and limited access to documentation and expertise (Marshall, 1988). To address these deficiencies in a democratic manner, the ICAE promoted the idea of a coalition, and, thus, the International Task Force on Literacy (ITFL) was born.

Key organizations working in the area of literacy were encouraged to mobilize and provide an umbrella coalition for International Literacy Year (ILY). The intention was to (1) ensure active cooperation in all ILY developmental phases and activities by nongovernmental and voluntary organizations; and (2) foster international cooperation between developing countries, and between developing and industrialized countries. It seemed a natural progression when the ICAE was entrusted with the responsibility for housing and coordinating the ITFL Secretariat. The coalition started with sixteen members in 1987, and by 1991 had increased its membership to forty organizations.

International meetings were used by the ITFL as the major decision-making and accountability mechanism. Planning for joint activities, information sharing, and feedback were carried out in six separate meetings held over a period of five years in Toronto, Canada; Bonn, Germany; Chantilly, France; Mombasa, Kenya; New Delhi, India; and Paris, France. Members of the Task Force participated in several international gatherings, including the World Education Conference for All (1990) in Jomtien, Thailand. The ITFL also organized several important events, such as the pre-launch of ILY, the International Media Colloquium and the innovative Book Voyage project. These were described as "good ideas, . . . simple, powerful and effective" (Ryan, 1991, pp. 16–20).

DIFFICULTIES ENCOUNTERED

"Perhaps the most valuable lesson of ILY concerns the power and promise of partnerships" (Ibid.).

The formation of the ITFL, in response to the major global problem of illiteracy, was itself significant, since, internationally, few attempts had been made by NGOs to work collectively in contractual relationships on common issues. The ITFL was built on the premise of partnership: a sharing of risks and profits by member organizations. This idea of a partnership was promoted as an entity with the ability to bring together an impressive combination of resources, to access increasingly limited resources, and to influence major policy decisions.

While the overall vision of the ITFL may have been two-fold, building the partnership and accomplishing the tasks, in reality the short life span of the coalition and funding restrictions forced it to become more task oriented. On reflection, the lack of attention devoted to the relationship building process was a major shortcoming and resulted in the breakdown of the lines of communication. The lack of homogeneity in the members should have forewarned initiators that nurturing the coalition was necessary and that more time should have been devoted to consultation and maintenance. This would have avoided the friction, irritation, and lack of trust and support that the ITFL endured.

Despite the myriad of problems, the achievements of the ITFL were impressive and creditable. As John Ryan (*Ibid.*) wrote:

> UNESCO had greatly appreciated the efforts of NGOs, rendered both through the ITFL and individually. The NGOs were among the earliest proponents of ILY and it was the advocacy of NGOs which helped to transform ILY from a formal celebration to a lively movement aimed at broader educational, social and economic goal.

DEVELOPMENT OF THE ILSS

> "The ILSS was conceived as a decentralized grassroots-focused service, whose primary mission was the empowerment of facilitators and learners" (Browne, 1992).

The recommendations made in the Evaluation Report in 1987 were finally ready for implementation. In 1991, the International Literacy Support Service (ILSS) was developed simultaneously with the culmination of the ITFL. The decision to discontinue working in a broad-based international coalition was not premature or unplanned, but was the result of a series of consultations involving researchers, practitioners, and learners over a four-year period. Initially, the ICAE had planned to establish an International Literacy Centre to fill the vacuum created after the termination of the international services provided by the International Institute for Adult Literacy Methods (IIALM) in Teheran. However, the recommendations growing out of the consultations supported the establishment of a support service that would respond to the needs of grassroots practitioners and learners and continue the work of the ITFL after it dissolved.

The ideas developed in these processes were incorporated into a draft proposal, presented to the members at the final ITFL meeting in Bonn, Germany (February 1991), and later further developed to reflect their concerns. This participatory approach in information gathering and decision making utilized by the ICAE, encouraged support and gained the endorsement of the members. The final decision to invest ICAE resources in building up the expertise and resources in the South and decentralizing all programs through the establishment of the ILSS was made by the ICAE Executive in 1990.

The organization proposed to meet the needs of the literacy practitioners and learners by strengthening the flow of relevant and reliable information and building on the work started by the ITFL during ILY. In order to do this effectively, a steering committee comprised of regional literacy coordinators was established as an advisory, supportive and monitoring mechanism. The Steering Committee's first task was to select a site and interregional coordinator; this was accomplished in Toronto (October 1991) using defined selection criteria set by the Programme Advisory Committee (PAC) of the ICAE. After lengthy and intensive deliberations, it was agreed that the ILSS should be based in the Caribbean region for a period of three years and that Didacus Jules, who resides in St. Lucia, be appointed as the interregional coordinator. Asia and the South Pacific were earmarked as the next site for the ILSS. These recommendations were approved by the secretary-general and ratified by PAC in December 1991.

THE MOVE

The move to St. Lucia took just over four months and involved a number of stages and changes, and the development of a new and defined working relationship between the ICAE, the new interregional coordinator, the Folk Research Centre (host agency), and various ministries of the St. Lucian government. The ILSS was the ICAE'S first program to be granted international status by a government—a privilege that entitles them to purchase equipment and transact business duty-free and tax-free.

CONSOLIDATION

The first planning meeting of the Steering Committee was held in July 1992 in St. Lucia, to develop a mutually agreed upon two-year Plan of Action. Discussions covered key areas of the ILSS "identity": philosophical character; structural configuration; administrative aspects and programmatic content. The coordinators agreed that the ILSS should embody—and reflect—a humanistic and integrated conception of literacy. They argued that "this conception of literacy must deal with the totality of the human person which is not simply functional but takes into account the contribution of literacy to self-fulfilment, social purpose, and the civilizing impulse." During its first year, the ILSS worked to strengthen and consolidate its work. It maintained an effective communication network through the dissemination of a newsletter to literacy practitioners and an internal news brief for coordinators.

CONCLUSION

This account has traced the development of an interest in literacy within the ICAE, from the early growth stages through its progression into a priority program. The ITFL was a timely experiment which managed to achieve a durable and constructive "partnership." The coordination and management of the ITFL no doubt contributed to the expertise and knowledge base of the ICAE. The ICAE was fortunate to have had this experience on which to build the foundation of the ILSS. In particular, the organization's knowledge of the relationship-building process, and its requirements for ongoing consultation, management, and maintenance, proved invaluable. The ILSS started out in a favorable position, and, while it is still in its infancy, it must be given the flexibility and autonomy it needs to be innovative. The service must be able to respond quickly to changing needs of learners and practitioners, in order to advance grassroots interests and gender equity in all its programs. Decentralization is a process and not merely a mechanical solution of shifting a program from North to South. It must be seen as a channel and strategy for developing stronger links, participation, and decision making. It is only through this dynamic process that a new model of literacy partnership will evolve. A major task for the ILSS is to ensure that a sense of ownership is present in all regions and in particular among practitioners and learners.

BIBLIOGRAPHY

Browne, Michael (1992). ILSS report. May. St. Lucia: International Literacy Support Service.

Dave, Ravindra (1993). *From awareness to action: Evaluation of the ITFL experience for future development.* Toronto: International Council for Adult Education.

Fordham, Paul (ed.) (1983). *One billion illiterates, one billion reasons for action.* Report on the international seminar, "Co-operation for literacy," October. Berlin (West), Germany.

From awareness to action: Building the literacy decade (1991). Report of the first meeting of the International Task Force on Literacy (ITFL), February. Bonn, Germany.

Jackson, E. T., G. Beaulieu, and I. Pascal (1987). *Expanding the partnership.* Report of the evaluation of the International Council for Adult Education, prepared by ICAE and CIDA, February. Toronto: International Council for Adult Education.

Jules, Didacus (1992). ILSS report, presented to the Steering Committee of the Regional Literacy Coordinators, May. St. Lucia: International Literacy Support Service.

Marshall, Judith (1988). Needs assessment survey of member associations for international literacy. Toronto: International Council for Adult Education.

Ryan, John (1991). *From Awareness to action: Building the literacy decade 1990-2000.* Report of the Seventh Meeting of the International Task Force on Literacy, 4-8 Feb. 1991, Bonn, Germany. Toronto: International Task Force On Literacy.

UNESCO (1989). *International literacy year: UNESCO information document.* Paris: UNESCO

CHAPTER 15

Women's Education: Challenges to the Adult Education Movement

PATRICIA ELLIS

Over the last few decades, the realization has emerged that people are crucial to the process of development, whether of community or nation. As a result, we see more people-centered, or participatory, approaches to development. While there has been a general belief that education is a necessary and important tool facilitating the process of development, it is evident that formal education systems in many instances have not had the capacity to equip people fully to live and function effectively in their societies.

Even though more emphasis is being placed on the role of adult education in facilitating personal, community, and national development, analysis of traditional adult education programs has revealed that, like formal education, these programs are often failing to equip the poor, oppressed, powerless or marginalized groups in society with the critical skills they need to improve their lives and bring about social change. Thus, new concepts and practices have emerged. These include "conscientization," emphasis on experimental learning, "popular education," and participatory methodologies. Thus, the adult education movement has become more dynamic, as it has attempted to meet these social demands with a different kind of education: one that empowers, liberates, and enables the disadvantaged in society to take control over their own lives, to contribute to and to benefit from development.

Women represent one of the underserved groups. Activities during the UN Decade of Women (1975–85) increased awareness about women's contributions to development, and led to a greater understanding of how failure to pay attention to women's needs, problems, and concerns affects both the process and the outcomes of development. The women's movement also has generated a great deal of concern about women's education and has pointed out the ways in which traditional education has reinforced their subordination in society.

Research shows that a majority of the world's women have had little or no access to formal or nonformal education. Because of sex-stereotyping by teachers, those who have been exposed to such education have often followed inappropriate and irrelevant curricula. Consequently, girls and women suffer many disadvantages, such as low self-esteem, lack of self-confidence, and inability to compete in the labor market on equal terms with men.

Adult education has the responsibility to aid women in their own development, so that they may play a critical role in social and economic development. It can do this by (1) raising the consciousness of women about their role and status in society; (2) giving women the opportunity to define their own learning needs, to decide what they want and need to learn; (3) creating psychological space and physical spaces for women to meet; (4) helping women to reflect on, and analyze, their experiences, and to explore solutions to their problems; (5) helping women organize groups to act on issues of importance to them.

The United Nations document, *Nairobi Forward-Looking Strategies*, at the end of the Decade for Women, draws attention to these issues and stresses the importance of education as a tool for the advancement of women, and the need to improve women's access to all forms and levels of education (United Nations, 1986). This was the challenge presented to women's organizations, schools, and adult education.

RESPONDING TO THE CHALLENGE

Individual women, women's groups, and educational institutions and organizations have shown a new willingness to experiment and use more innovative and participatory approaches to facilitate learning and change.

The International Council for Adult Education (ICAE), the international organization at the forefront of the adult education movement, responded by conducting a research project on women and nonformal education. This initiative led to the creation of the ICAE's Women's Network, and the development of the Women's Program of the Council.

ICAE'S WOMEN'S PROGRAM: THE EARLY YEARS

Research studies were carried out by the Women's Program, which showed that many of the programs in which women participated did not meet their needs. As a result, women from many parts of the world—Africa, Asia, the Caribbean, Latin America, the South Pacific, and the industrialized countries—came together to discuss the findings and form a network. These women then participated in ICAE's World Assembly in Paris in 1982. During this event they took part in special workshops on women's education and organized several caucuses. However, they objected to the fact that the preponderant number of speakers at plenary sessions organized by ICAE were men.

Shortly after the Assembly, they established "The Women's Network," through which women from all over the world could share concerns and suggest action. The network had three main purposes: (1) to emphasize the educational problems that are of concern to women as educators and learners; (2) to address the role and status of women in the movement, within the ICAE itself and its member associations; (3) to work for the development of a structured "Women's Program" within the ICAE.

Between 1983 and 1986, the Network grew rapidly, gaining recognition as an integral part of the ICAE and serving as a useful mechanism for encouraging and facilitating dialogue, discussion, and debate on women's issues in adult education. Through its *Newsletter*, it shared information about the experiences of women in many parts of the world. At the same time, members of the Network began to agitate for greater visibility, a larger voice in the various activities of the Council, and office space to carry out their work. By 1986, the energy and dynamism of the Network had created a momentum which resulted in the establishment of "The Women's Program," the largest program of the Council.

THE DEVELOPING AGENDA OF "THE WOMEN'S PROGRAM"

In 1987, the *Newsletter* was replaced by a bulletin, *Voices Rising*, which in addition to news items about persons and events, produced more analytical and reflective writing, adding a new dimension to the program. An international conference on "Women, Education and Development: The Feminist Challenge to Adult Education" brought together over a hundred women educators to explore the theoretical and practical aspects of their work and experience. In this way, gender issues became recognized as a permanent part of the international adult education agenda. The conference served to consolidate and strengthen the Network, identifying leaders from the various regions.

The process of expansion and consolidation was continued in an international seminar in Quito, Ecuador, in 1988, entitled "Building the Movement," and in the Toronto meeting, in 1989, on "Women, Leadership and Decision Making in International Adult Education."

PROGRAM STRATEGY

Concurrently with the meetings mentioned above, efforts were made to strengthen relationships with women's groups and member organizations of the ICAE in all the regions, in order to create a world-wide base at the grass roots level. It was necessary to create a critical consciousness of feminist theory and link it to adult education practice at the community level. The result was a feminist critique of mainstream adult education, a critical questioning of the oppressive gender relations. Feminist analysis also helped women educators and learners to understand how global crises and events affect their lives and work.

The Women's Program of ICAE, with its headquarters in Toronto, serves the Network through the publication of the bulletin, *Voices Rising*. It also organizes various conferences and other activities to help women from diverse contexts to realize the importance of solidarity.

Two activities which were organized in 1990 illustrate this. With a commitment to build an international program rooted in the regions, community women from several countries, who work in the areas of health and literacy, made a visit to Mali and Tanzania to observe programs and share information. This program was undertaken in collaboration with the Women's Network of the African Association of Literacy and Adult Education. With the Women's Resource Centre in Manila, a regional workshop was held, aimed at strengthening local women's organizations in Asia.

The main strategy of the Women's Program of the ICAE is networking. As well as through *Voices Rising*, published three times a year in three languages, networking includes a constant flow of correspondence with ideas, information, questions, and suggestions among women around the world, stimulating discussion and debate on women's education and gender issues in adult education.

The Women's Program also established an International Resource Centre and Data Base. Its research activities have highlighted the many constraints under which women work. Among the documents published by the Centre are *Two Reports on Women and the Micro-Chip Industry* (ICAE, 1987), and *The Moon Also Has Her Own Light* (ICAE, 1989). The latter is an account of the struggle to develop women's consciousness among Nicaraguan farm workers.

The Resource Centre collection includes a wide variety of research reports, books, newsletters, learning kits and pamphlets, which are available for the use of all adult educators.

As is suggested above, one distinct purpose of the Women's Program is advocacy for equal representation of women in the structures of the ICAE, at all levels—international, national, regional, and local. Women in the Program and the Network have worked tirelessly to improve the status and role of women.

In 1989, on recommendation of the Women's Program, the Council of ICAE appointed a task force on the participation of women in the organization. It examined the existing situation and devised a plan for improving it. In addition, the Women's Program took steps to ensure that many more women were given the opportunity to participate in the world assemblies, that leadership opportunities for women would be promoted, and that women's and gender issues would be prominent in all assembly events.

In spite of the rapid expansion and success of the Women's Program in many of its efforts, women are still frustrated. Their numbers in positions have increased somewhat, but in spite of the fact that most of those who participate in adult education programs are women, men are still firmly in control of the movement. Most of the positions of power are held by men. The heads of the regions, and most members of the international and regional committees, are men.

PROBLEMS AND CONSTRAINTS

As an international program attempting to build and maintain a relationship with a large and diverse constituency, the Women's Program

ADULT EDUCATION THROUGH WORLD COLLABORATION

is facing many challenges. With limited human and financial resources, it has to develop and implement programs to serve the myriad differences among the regions. It must provide opportunities for women from the various cultures to meet, to share experiences, and learn from each other.

Managing the coordination of the various aspects of such a world-wide program is a notable challenge. It is important to work with regional structures in a way that respects their priorities, which may be different in every case.

Several steps have been taken to meet some of these problems, including the establishment of a Women's Advisory Committee comprised of members from regional organizations and other individuals representing geographic areas and working groups. This committee is responsible for monitoring the Women's Program, to ensure that it reflects the concerns of women in the regions.

Exchange visits between women in the North and the South have intensified dialogue, and have helped to create opportunities for more women to meet at international events.

The management problem was addressed by setting up an organizational review of the program in 1989 by two outside consultants. Their review made a number of concrete recommendations for strengthening the Program and for improving its coordination and management.

And, finally, a decision was made to relocate the Secretariat of the Program from Toronto to a country in the South (Senegal), in order to decentralize, and in an attempt to involve more women from the South. This has proved to be problematic and very complex, in that the support and the services of the Toronto office are very far distant, while the women in the South are endeavoring to meet the organizational challenge of the Program.

IMPACT

In spite of the problems cited above, the Women's Program is flourishing. There can be no doubt that it has had a significant impact on the practice of female and male adult educators, and on the lives of women learners throughout the world. It has made a valuable contribution to the literature on women and adult education, and has enhanced the role and status of women in the adult education movement.

BIBLIOGRAPHY

ICAE (1989). *The moon also has her own light: The struggle to build a women's consciousness among Nicaraguan farmworkers.* Toronto: International Council for Adult Education.

ICAE (1987). *Two reports on women and the micro-chip industry.* Toronto: International Council for Adult Education.

ICAE (from 1987). *Voices rising.* Newsletter of the ICAE Women's Program. Toronto: International Council for Adult Education.

ICAE (1987). *The women's kit.* The Participatory Research Group/ICAE Women's Programme. Toronto: International Council for Adult Education.

United Nations (1986). *The Nairobi forward-looking strategies for the advancement of women.* New York: The United Nations.

CHAPTER 16

Coming of Age

ANA MARIA QUIROZ

In its first twenty-one years the ICAE has achieved much. This is clear from the previous chapters in this section. A great idea was born and has been nourished into an effective organization at work for adult education throughout the world. While attempting always to focus on the needs of societies at the local level, the Council has faced a great challenge organizationally. The problem of involving the regions, networks, and national organizations in the decision making of the Council is still to be solved. It behooves the organization to look with a more critical eye at areas in which improvement is needed.

In a special issue of *Convergence* published in 1992, to commemorate 25 volumes of publication, pioneers of the adult education movement expressed their vision as to what the major challenges for adult education are in the future. The present author will comment particularly on ideas expressed by three authors who have had a long history of involvement with the International Council.

Dame Nita Barrow, who was president of the Council from 1982–1990, in an interview conducted by Karen Yarmol-Franko, editor of *Convergence*, described how she became president. Only then did she realize that women were underrepresented in the leadership of the organization. "When the executive election was completed, I found myself looking at a table of 24 men. Not knowing that the microphone was open. I commented, 'This has to change.' " Eleven years have gone by since that statement, and there is certainly improvement in this area. We have more women (seven) in the Executive participating at the policy-making level. Dame Nita continued, "At the same time within the territories, I still seem to see male presidents most of the time with the women doing the hard work within the organization."

247

The major challenge for adult education is to achieve genuine, not token participation. "You don't want just to push people into positions, you want to recognize the work they have done and accept their ideas for change. . . . This applies particularly to the participation of women especially in leadership positions in our national and local associations" (Yarmol-Franko, pp. 50–52).

The Council is now preparing for the Fifth World Assembly, with the theme "Women, Literacy and Development: Challenges for the 21st Century." An obvious first step is to ensure women's participation. There was 24% participation of women at the Second World Assembly in Paris when Dame Nita Barrow was elected in 1982, 40% participation in the Third World Assembly in Buenos Aires in 1985, and 30% in the Fourth World Assembly in Thailand in 1990.

In 1990 the UN Commission on the Status of Women undertook a five-year review and appraisal of the implementation of the "Nairobi Forward-looking Strategies" adopted in 1985. The results were discouraging. It found that the situation of women had deteriorated in many parts of the world, especially in developing countries where economic stagnation or negative growth, continued population increases, the growing burden of debt, and the reduction of public expenditure for social programs, had further constrained opportunities for women to improve their situation. There was also evidence of an alarming regression in the status of women in the spheres of education, employment, and health.

Achieving literacy continues to be one of the urgent challenges in the process of enabling women to take control of their own lives, to participate on a more equal basis in society, and eventually to free themselves from economic exploitation and patriarchal oppression. Any emphasis given to literacy must take into account other issues, such as general health and reproductive health, agricultural extension, post-primary skill training, community development, and women's organizations. Such services not only complement literacy but widen the choices women make about self-employment and self-development.

The theme of the World Assembly was chosen in concert with the host country to try to make a difference in this area for women at every level.

Chris Duke is the second author selected from the special issue of *Convergence*. His article on the history of ICAE was entitled "Illusions of Progress." He wrote, "Rapid and dramatic growth piled success upon success . . . until the end of the 1980s. Suddenly not one but three key officers left within months of one another; and the scale and staffing of the Secretariat has dropped to a small part of what it was. . . . It may be here, that crisis and traumatic thinning were needed before ICAE can reshape itself to a new form and structure more suited to its maturity, and to the maturity, confidence and aspirations of its members" (Duke, p. 60).

In times of such rapid change, it is difficult for an organization like the ICAE to take time to evaluate and consolidate gains because of the need to use scarce resources to meet the new demands constantly arising. However, at this point in the development of the organization, it is important to do just that and adjust organizational structures accordingly. There are more than one hundred members from about eighty-two countries, and seven regional organizations at different stages of development. The regional organizations have grown in membership, extent of their programs, areas of development, and financial base, all of them at a different pace and rhythm.

The Council's decentralized structure of autonomous, collaborating national and regional member organizations provides a new model for building up internationalism for other NGOs and the international community at large. There is still much to learn in this unique process, and many challenges remain. As a recognized NGO at the United Nations, the ICAE has demonstrated leadership responsibilities which it must not fail.

Alexander Charters is the third adult education pioneer selected. His article, "Impressions of Adult Education 1968–1992," highlights the crucial problem of accountability. "Accountability to either students or sponsors is certainly not built into the adult education endeavour in a systematic way" (Charters, p. 87). The same applies to ICAE as well. It needs to develop ways in which to achieve its program objectives. It is not easy to measure whether it has done so in particular cases. Evaluation and monitoring have to be an integral part of the learning process.

With the emergence of the so-called "new world order" in the 1990s, the international NGO community has called for a new paradigm of institutional development toward more equitable and sustainable impacts. Recognizing the importance of coalition building, the ICAE is proposing a reflection process that will encompass the whole international NGO community, to enable it to contribute more actively to policy formulations and analysis in both North and South. This important process will culminate in the Fifth World Assembly in Cairo in 1994.

Another area that needs attention is ICAE's Information and Networking Service, which is an important part of the organization's work. The demands for its help are increasing dramatically, requiring careful management, as the efficiency and effectiveness of the organizations's work depends largely on the quality of the information it provides and the speed at which it reaches those who need it.

The ICAE is a knowledge-based organization with important information to share, based on its two decades of experience—information to help eliminate illiteracy and to foster democratic principles in development, the awareness of human rights, and the empowerment of women, to name a few areas of concern. If the Council is to contribute to a better world, it must learn from the experiences of the past twenty years, and take into account the advice of those mentioned above. Then it will be ready to face the ever new challenges of the twenty-first century.

BIBLIOGRAPHY

The articles mentioned in this chapter appeared in *Convergence* 25 (4) (1992):

Charters, Alexander N. Impressions of adult education 1968–1992.
Duke, Chris. Illusions of progress: Confessions of an unreformed optimist.
Yarmol-Franko, Karen. The coming of age of adult education: An interview with Dame Nita Barrow.

INDEX

251

Rahnema, Majid, 189
Reed, Angus, 228–29
Rights of the Child, Convention on (UNICEF), 16
"Right to Learn," declaration on (UNESCO), 6, 10, 233
Robinson, Brandon, 167
Rogers, Alan, 168
Ruggles, Robin H., 87
Rural workers, ILO recommendation on, 12
Rusimbi, Mary, 142
Ruyter, Theo, 168
Ryan, John, 234, 235
Rydström, Gunnar, 79, 84

Samnemda of Norway, and environmental education, 220
Schneider, Bertrand, 217
Secondary education, 36
Selman, Gordon, 188, 209
SEVA MANDIR, India, DVV cooperation with, 102
SHAPLA NEER ("white lotus flower"), Japan, 123–24
Shaw, Saundria Kay, 171
Shiva, Vandana, 224–25
SIDA. See Swedish International Development Authority
Sierra Leone, DVV cooperation with, 106–9
Singh, Kavaljit, 221
Smagghe, Bernard, 200
Society for Participatory Research in Asia (PRIA), 102
Society for the Promotion of Resource Centres (SPARC), India, 102
Soriano, L. B., 157–58
Sotoshu Volunteer Association (SVA), Japan, 124
Southern African AIDS Training Programme, 43
Spinoza, Baruch, 187

Staudt, Kathleen, 173
Stock, Arthur, 188
Strong, Maurice, 75
Structural Adjustment Program (World Bank & International Monetary Fund), 14, 19
Study Circle (Sweden), 128
Sullivan, Jackie, 194
Sundén, Rolf, 127
Swedish Central Organization of Salaried Employees (TCO), 133
Swedish Cooperative Center (SCC), 134
Swedish International Development Authority (SIDA), 130 and passim
Swedish Mission Council, 134
Swedish Trade Union Confederation (LO), 133

Tandon, Rajesh, 54–55, 204
Tanzania, SIDA cooperation with, 132, 140–41
Technical assistance (ILO), 16
Technical education, 36
Third World, debts, 61, 62; development plans, 64; and the International Monetary Fund, 64, 65, 66; and transnational corporations, 66; and the World Bank, 64, 65, 66
Thoner, Astrid, 221
Thybergin, T., 156
Tinker, Irene, 173
Todorov, T., xxiv
Tototo Home Industries Project of Kenya, 48
Training, 36
Trudeau, Prime Minister Pierre Elliott, 75
Truman, President Harry S., 171

Uganda, DVV cooperation with, 101–2